WHO'S THAT WITH CHARLIE?

*Lessons Learned and Friends
I've Made along the Way*

CLERISY PRESS

Who's That with Charlie?

Copyright © 2013 Charles S. Mechem, Jr.

For further information, contact the publisher at:
Clerisy Press
306 Greenup Street
Covington, KY 41011
clerisypress.com
a division of Keen Communications

Distributed by Publishers Group West
Printed in the United States of America
First edition, first printing

Editor: Donna Poehner
Text design: Annie Long
Photos courtesy of the author

Library of Congress Cataloging-in-Publication Data

Mechem, Charles S., Jr., 1930-
    Who's That with Charlie? Lessons Learned and Friends I've Made Along the Way /
by Charles S. Mechem, Jr. -- First edition.
        pages. cm
    ISBN-13: 978-1-57860-532-3
    ISBN-10: 1-57860-532-6
    ISBN-13: 978-1-57860-533-0 (eISBN)
    1. Mechem, Charles S., Jr., 1930- 2. Businessmen--Ohio--Biography. 3. Lawyers--
Ohio--Biography. 4. Ladies Professional Golf Association--Employees--Biography.
I. Title.

    HC102.5.M358A3 2013
    340.092--dc23
    [B]

A Dedication

THE ENTIRE WORLD was shocked and saddened by the passing of Neil Armstrong on August 25, 2012. Several months before he died Neil graciously wrote the Foreword to this book. This Foreword was very special to me and is even more so in light of his death.

Neil was a true American hero, yet one of the most modest men I ever knew. That modesty is beautifully reflected in his Foreword.

It seems fitting and appropriate then that I dedicate this book to Neil—a truly wonderful man.

I was deeply honored to be asked to deliver a eulogy at his memorial service in Cincinnati on August 31, 2012. With his wife Carol's permission, I am including a copy of my eulogy in the Appendix of this book.

—CSM, Jr.

Pack up your troubles in your old kit bag
And smile, smile, smile.

—World War I marching song written in 1915 by George Powell

When you're smiling,
When you're smiling,
The whole world smiles with you.

—Song written by Larry Shay/Mark Fisher/Joe Goodwin

TABLE of CONTENTS

FOREWORD

FOLLOWING IS THE Foreword that Neil Armstrong wrote several months before his death. The Foreword came to me in an e-mail that read as follows:

> Hi Charlie,
> I perused the Internet trying to determine the proper differences between a foreword, an introduction, and a preface. I left still mystified.
> So this might not properly be a preface. But you probably already have an excellent foreword (and a "beginnings").
> So this may not fit the bill for you. But it is yours to use or discard as you see fit.
> If you choose the former, a bit of editing will certainly be appropriate. You may excise as appropriate.
> Good luck!!
>
> *Neil*

MIDWAY BETWEEN WORLD WARS I AND II, two boys were born only one month apart. Both were raised in small Ohio towns in families of modest circumstances during the hardships of the Great Depression and the tragic times of World War II. The surrounding homes had small flags in the windows, some with a blue star indicating a family member was serving in the armed forces, some with a gold star indicating a family member who would never return. It was a frightening time, but one which strengthened the backbone of all who endured it.

The boys enjoyed the process of learning and nearly always had part-time and summer jobs with very modest wages which primarily were "saved for college," and secondarily provided the satisfaction of having "a little spending money." Working gave them the opportunity to learn the importance of responsibility and the consequences of errors and bad judgment. The value of that experience can hardly be overestimated.

They both enjoyed many athletic activities and mastered none. They were fortunate to have benefited highly from their collegiate and military experience. Neither could predict, nor even imagine, the unexpected turns their careers would take, the people they would meet, or the surprising achievements that would accrue to them.

The author of *Who's That with Charlie?*, Charles Mechem, was one of those boys. His interests and his background prepared him well for an unusually broad career in law, business, professional sports, and acting as a consultant and advisor to a number of individuals and businesses. As CEO of the Taft Broadcasting Company, Charlie often held the annual meeting of shareholders at an auditorium inside Taft's Kings Island theme park near Cincinnati, Ohio. Shareholders, along with their invitation to the meeting that arrived in the mail, would receive a ticket to enter the theme park with its many thrill rides and other entertaining attractions. A few people bought one share of the company, listed on the New York Stock Exchange, just to get the free ticket to the park.

Taft was an entertainment company, and the meeting of shareholders was an opportunity to showcase their talents. Charlie's dynamic speeches together with music, video, and the help of Yogi Bear and Fred Flintstone dazzled the shareholder audience like Luciano Pavarotti at a Tupperware party.

Charlie is a speaker with a touch of genius. At one unusual meeting of senior management and the board of directors, due to a combination of corporate setbacks and uncertainty, the mood was somber and the faces long. Charlie gave the opening address, spoke candidly and humorously about the challenges faced, turned up the tempo, congratulated all on their great work and the bright future ahead. By the time he finished, the entire gathering was standing and cheering like their team had just won the World Series.

In *Who's That with Charlie?* you will find much of the magical character of Charlie Mechem through his recollections of a wide variety of individuals and many of the life lessons which he learned from them. These people and these experiences became a significant part of Charlie's life and have become etched indelibly into his memory.

I have enjoyed revisiting those years and am confident that the reader will discover interesting insights into twentieth-century American history, a lot of great "Lessons Learned," and a great deal of humor well written about Charlie's life, times, and friends.

Neil Armstrong
The other boy

A Word from Arnold Palmer

OVER THE YEARS, I have been able to benefit from the advice of quite a few wise people as I made my way through the challenging business career that sprouted from the early success I enjoyed on the pro golf tour. Right at the top of that list is my close friend Charlie Mechem, whose counseling I have relied on for going on twenty years.

One of the best decisions I ever made was to bring Charlie on board as a personal consultant shortly after he completed his five-year term as LPGA Commissioner in the mid-1990s. As Charlie points out later on in this unique and entertaining book, much of the valuable advice that I got from him was literally face to face for ten years as he sat in an office next to mine with the door always open at my Bay Hill Club & Lodge in Orlando, Florida. I always looked forward to the steaming paper cups of coffee he would bring to the office for the two of us to start the new business day. I think one of the reasons that Charlie and I get on so well is that our backgrounds are very similar. We were both small-town boys who grew up during the Great Depression and World War II and were raised by parents with solid, basic American values. Not a bad heritage!

Although Charlie and his lovely wife, Marilyn, moved west in 2005 to be closer to their children year-round, our association has since continued, mostly on the telephone, except for the time we get together during the few weeks I spend at Tradition Golf Club in La Quinta, California, in the dead of winter.

It's no wonder that Charlie has been so successful in the various executive positions he has held during his business career. He is a meticulous person. He thoroughly investigates the matters at hand. He prefers to know the bottom line before there is a bottom line. He likes to participate in creative activities and inspires people to do their best no matter what they are pursuing.

I first got to really know him during his years with the LPGA and, like everybody else in the world of golf, could see that he was certainly the person who could stabilize and advance the LPGA at a critical stage of its existence. He was clearly the right person at the right time. That was proven during his term as Commissioner and since then. He brought a sense of purpose to the organization beyond its public face in competitive sports.

Besides the business side of things, Charlie has been a great companion and sincere friend. I am pleased to be counted among the many who dot the pages that follow.

One final note. One of my favorite things about Charlie is his sense of humor. We both love to joke and laugh—as the pictures in this book clearly show. In that spirit let me note that I'm not going to say anything about Charlie's golf game except that it was not a major contributor to his success! Happily, he didn't need it.

Arnold Palmer

Introduction

CHARLIE MECHEM STILL loves roller coasters.

It's a remarkable statement to make about any eighty-two-year-old, let alone one who spent several decades in the staid upper reaches of the business world, but somehow not at all surprising upon meeting the man. All you have to do is take in the amiable smile and warm handshake, feel the youthful enthusiasm with which he tells a story, or be amused by the playful banter between him and his wife of more than sixty years, Marilyn. Very quickly, Charlie becomes the octogenarian you can see hurtling down the scariest drop, his face full of wonder and his hair blown back.

Although growing up in the Great Depression left him with an unceasing sense of diligence and duty, Charlie Mechem knows fun, and the thrill ride is his personal metaphor. As a kid in Nelsonville, Ohio, he couldn't wait for the carnival to come to town. Forty years later, as the CEO of Taft Broadcasting, Charlie not only oversaw the building of "The Beast"—at the time the world's longest, fastest, and steepest roller coaster—at the Kings Island theme park near Cincinnati, but led the company's executives in test runs. The man revels in the ups, sees opportunity in the downs, stays steady in the turns, and is always looking forward to the excitement of a new go-round.

Whatever that turned out to be—from toiling on a road crew as a teenager to his current posts as personal advisor to longtime friends Arnold Palmer, Jack Nicklaus, Nancy Lopez, and Annika Sorenstam—Charlie's favorite part of any enterprise has been the human interaction. As you will see in the following pages, Charlie likes people—all kinds. His natural empathy makes him wise, observant, and trustworthy, a good listener, a masterful persuader who is understood because, better than most men, he understands.

That whole package was never more evident than when Charlie accepted the position of Commissioner of the Ladies Professional Golf Association in 1990. The association was coming off one of the most difficult periods in its history. Tournament sponsors were pulling out, players were becoming discouraged, media coverage intimated impending doom. Charlie instead saw an intriguing opportunity, at age sixty, to apply his know-how and solid associations from three decades at the highest levels of commerce to help a group in need in a sport he loved.

Among his many tools, Charlie brought an enlightened sensitivity—learned from his strong relationships with the women in his life—toward the cultural gender issues that have always made promoting women's professional sports difficult. That insight helped him identify the LPGA's central problem—"a massive institutional inferiority complex"—that once articulated gave the players a renewed spirit and purpose. Charlie then followed through by attending, often with Marilyn, every single LPGA event—nearly two hundred in total—from 1991 through 1995.

It was at the tournaments that he stabilized the LPGA's foundation by tirelessly going one on one with sponsors and media in spreading the gospel of what he earnestly believed was an underappreciated product. His example, along with gentle but well-timed prods, inspired his leading players to be more engaged in promoting their sport. His reign was remarkably free of dissension or controversy, chiefly because he followed a mantra by achieving consensus among the players before making important decisions. By the time he completed the job on December 31, 1995—the date he had publicly pre-set five years before—the LPGA was in better shape than it had ever been, and Charlie had established himself not only as the best Commissioner the LPGA ever had, but also as one of the best sports Commissioners ever. Every person who has held the post since, including current the Commissioner, Michael Whan, has faithfully sought Charlie's counsel on issues large and small.

What follows is the selective but remarkably diverse history of rich experiences, strong friendships, fascinating encounters, and enduring lessons. It's the summing up of a solid, happy, fulfilled life—in many ways a classic portrait of the fleeting American Dream.

Charlie would hasten to add that he's been more lucky than good, but that's a bit misleading. Sure, he's been fortunate to share some amazing times, rub shoulders with the great in the worlds of sports, entertainment, politics, and commerce, and achieve much individual success. But there's also no doubt that right from Nelsonville, he was possessed of an attitude that turns every experience—triumphant or difficult—into some manner of good fortune. It takes a special quality to continue loving the roller coaster, to steadfastly regard the ride not as a beast, but as a beauty. That quality permeates every day of Charlie Mechem's life, and every page of this book.

Jaime Diaz
Editor, *Golf World*

Part One

WHO IS THIS GUY?

CHAPTER 1

Why I Wrote This Book

NOT LONG AGO, having just entered my ninth decade on this earth, I was sitting in an airplane looking out over the wonder of our vast country. The immense landforms put me in a contemplative mood. Not for the first time, it occurred to me that as miniscule as we are in the grand scheme—and especially from thirty thousand feet—the best part of life is sharing it with other people.

It's why my own life has only gotten richer with each passing year, which became very clear to me as I sat in that plane. I became increasingly excited when I thought about all the sports, entertainment, business, and political figures that my life had given me a chance to meet. I still think of myself as a small-town boy from Ohio, and I still wonder if I'm really in a dream. I was feeling especially so while cruising above the clouds, and as I allowed those special relationships—and others—to roll around in my head, I was suddenly compelled more than I had ever been to get it all down on paper. I have been fortunate to live several quite different lives—lawyer, business executive, sports Commissioner, consultant, and mentor. The stories and people that you will read about in this book are the happy result of this life.

Always a list maker, I took out a legal pad and started jotting down—at first slowly and then in rapid succession—stories about the amazing individuals with whom I have been associated. Many have been famous, some haven't, but all have left their mark on me. That list was the genesis of this book. Writing it has allowed me to vividly relive a lot of wonderful moments. Even better, it's allowed me to share them. I have gone into some detail on my own life on the premise that it will put the "people stories" and other stories in some context and make it easier to understand how they were part of my ongoing life. But, this is by no means an autobiography. Rather, a "stage-setter," a backdrop for the people and stories that have meant so much to me.

Inevitably, some readers will feel that I'm engaging in excessive name-dropping. A fair comment, but I plead "not guilty." Name-dropping, at least to me, means dropping the names of famous people to make the "dropper" seem more important. My intent, however, is precisely the opposite. What I have tried to do is to show a side of the various people I speak of that underscores the kind of people they truly are and has nothing to do with me—except that I was there!

A brief word about the title of this book. There is an old, old joke about the guy named Joe who went to Rome and, quite by accident, had his picture taken with the Pope. When he got home he proudly showed the picture to friends who were suitably impressed. One of his friends, however, had a most unexpected response. He looked at the photo and said, "Who's that with you, Joe?" I was reminded of this story as I reflected on the personalities that I profile in this book. With few, if any, exceptions they are far better known than I. Hence, the title *Who's That with Charlie?* The final section of the book is titled "Lessons Learned" As the name suggests, in this book I want not only to share the stories about the wonderful people I met along the way, but also to share with the reader the lessons that I have learned from these associations.

I hope you enjoy!

CHAPTER 11

Growing Up

As I REFLECT on my life, I've come to realize that folks of my vintage have had the great good fortune to live during the most wonderful, exciting, and fulfilling years that I can imagine. I was born in 1930—September 12 to be exact—in the master bedroom of my parents' home in the small town of Nelsonville, Ohio, a community of about five thousand people located in the extreme southeastern corner of the state. I joined the Mechem family a little late. My parents already had two children, my brother, Bill, and my sister, Alice. Bill was twelve years older than I and Alice ten. Whether or not I was a mistake or simply an afterthought is irrelevant. Whatever I was, no child could ever have been more loved. I always regarded myself as an "almost" only child. By that I mean that I had all the advantages of being an only child without any of the disadvantages.

My parents were wonderful—bright, hardworking, and with classic Midwestern, small-town values. Mother was the daughter of a coal miner and taught seven grades in a one-room schoolhouse before they married. Dad was the son of the owner of a dry-goods and shoe store, and a veteran of World War I. Mother was devoted to her church, loved music, and laughed easily. Everyone loved her. Dad could be stern and remote but was a great role model because of his work ethic and strong sense of right and wrong. When he was fifty, he was elected to the Ohio State Senate and rose to become President Pro Tem, the second-most powerful position in the state government after the governor. He had a great sense of humor, and his speeches were homespun classics. One of my favorite memories is when I asked Dad at his ninetieth birthday party what had been the most important invention of the ninety years of his life. I was expecting the automobile, electric light, or the telephone. Instead, with a twinkle in his eye he said, "That's an easy one—indoor plumbing!" I could write another book about my brother and my sister—and perhaps someday I will—but I'll simply say that they were two of the finest people I have ever known. My brother was a kind, gentle man, who spent much of his life helping others. In later years, he became a lay minister and had his own church in the tiny town of Carbon Hill, Ohio, not far from Nelsonville. When people would ask Bill what he did for a living, he would smile and say, "I marry and bury." It is unbelievable the number of people I still run into who were either married, baptized, or sent to their eternal reward by my brother, Bill. (Okay, so I don't actually run into the latter group!) When Bill died we celebrated a very uplifting funeral service, which he had written in its entirety, including scripture readings and songs. So, we did it "his way." We all miss him very much. My sister, Alice, is still living and still a source of great pride and joy for me. She lost her beloved husband, George, a few years ago, but continues to be healthy and happy living in the same town (Athens, Ohio) and the same house that she and George built shortly after they were married. Alice has a level of intellect and perceptivity that has always amazed me. I really hope that someday I can write that book about Bill and Alice.

Speaking of Bill and Alice brings back a funny memory. Frequently people are asked what is the first thing in their life of which they have any memory. In my case, although the memory is not vivid, it is clearly the first. My parents took my brother, sister, and me to the 1933–1934 Chicago World's Fair. While I have some general memories of the fairgrounds, my most vivid memory is the image of the "rooming house" in which we stayed. In those days people rented out rooms in their own homes to tourists, and we rented several rooms in such a house. Though I know it is strange, I can see the house in my mind's eye and recall it as being a very pleasant place to stay.

My brother and sister, however, have much more vivid memories of the World's Fair—two of which they teased me about for much of my young life. First, I apparently was a "wind bag" even at that early age. They said that, as we walked around the fairgrounds, I would jump up on a bench and, to their great embarrassment, begin making some sort of speech, which I'm sure made little, if any, sense.

The second thing they teased me about was a time when I apparently got very upset by something when we were out in a rowboat on one of the lakes. They took a picture of me standing up in the rowboat crying loudly but holding my fingers to my ears—presumably in the hope that I would not hear myself cry! Bill and Alice always said that, from that moment on, they were worried that I might not be the "brightest bulb in the chandelier."

Now don't get me wrong: 1930 was anything but an idyllic year. Indeed, I am not sure that there was anything very idyllic about the decade of the 1930s. The depression lingered on, probably, as historians look in retrospect, until the outbreak of WWII when massive industrial mobilization gave the economy its needed jolt. But I didn't know very much about this for at least ten years. My dad was a retail merchant and we always had food and clothing and a nice home. It wasn't until later that I realized how hard Dad and Mother worked to provide these comforts (not, by any means, luxuries). Indeed, they sent my brother and sister to college in 1937 at nearby Ohio University, and everybody (except, of course, me) worked hard to make that happen. As I look back now, my first hint that there might be some gloom in my otherwise cheery environment was when my mother would say, "Charles, when you come home from school, if the big blind on the front living-room window is pulled down, that means your dad has a sick headache . . . and is resting. So, be especially quiet and let him rest." I strongly suspect now that those "sick headaches" were migraines brought about by the pressures of running a shoe store when so many people couldn't afford to buy shoes!

Like most kids, I suspect, I don't remember a lot about my first five years, except that nothing unpleasant happened and there was a comfortable home and lots of love. That's about all I need to remember!

MY ELEMENTARY SCHOOL was literally a four- or five-minute walk from our front door. It was called the West School. There was also a Central School and an East School in town. There was no North School or South School—I guess they just didn't need two more schools! My teachers from the first to the fourth grade were all lovely women (all grade-school teachers in those days were women) and progressively more disciplinarian. My first- and second-grade teachers, I remember so well, seemed always to be hugging us and smiling at us—or with us. As we reached the fourth grade, my teacher, Miss Cook (who was also the principal), was kind, but very stern and strict. Then it was on to the Central School for grades five and six. This, too, was a happy time. My most memorable teacher was also the principal, Mr. Tomlinson. He was an energetic, strong man, much respected by all of us. In a quirk, which I have always remembered fondly, he was also a housepainter. School-teachers' salaries in those days were presumably no better than they are today. Periodically, my mother would hire him to paint our house, either inside or out, and I always helped him. I should probably put help in quotes. He would probably have been quite content to have me watch and not dabble, but that's not the way of twelve- or thirteen-year-olds!

Then on to junior high school—grades seven and eight. I've always thought of junior high school (now referred to as "middle school"—ah! our Anglican heritage!) as an interregnum—in between—yes, a "middle." One is a bit too old to be young and a bit too young to be old. For me it was a time of discovery, most notably sports and girls. Speaking of girls, I had only one girlfriend during my high school years—a beautiful girl named Rosemarie. We had a lot of fun together, but one activity was far more fun for her than for me. She loved to roller skate and was very good at it. I didn't like it and therefore wasn't much good. But, I wanted to be with her as much as possible and tried to learn to roller skate. One night at the skating rink she was taking a rest just outside the iron bar that separated the seating area from the rink, and I was flailing around trying to look graceful. I decided to skate over to where she was sitting and take a rest. Then, tragedy struck. As I got about three or four feet from her and tried to stop, my legs flew up in the air and I fell flat on my back and proceeded to slide under the bar right past Rosemarie and into the wall behind the rink. I decided at that point that if our relationship depended on my prowess as a roller skater, we didn't have much of a future.

As I've mentioned, Nelsonville was a small town. If you wanted to participate in a particular sport, you were welcome—you just did it! So, I played baseball, basketball, football, and ran track. I was not particularly good at any of these, but I was on every team. I was—and am—a great believer in team sports for every young boy and girl. The lessons learned last a lifetime. Three brief stories will tell you all you'll ever want to know about my "illustrious" sporting career.

First, I almost drowned on the football field during a game. I repeat: I almost drowned on the football field. It happened this way. In the middle of the game there was a virtual cloudburst, a torrential rain that lasted for a half hour or so. Of course, football games don't get cancelled for bad weather, so the game went on. Our quarterback called an end-around play in which I was the lead blocker. Ironically, the trouble started when

I made a really good block. I hit this big, tall left end below the knees, and he fell like a tree. Unfortunately, most of him fell on my head and shoulders, pushing my nose into one of the many huge puddles of water that had formed on the field. I remember thinking, "What a stupid way to go—drowning on a football field!" I held my breath but it seemed that the big guy would never get up. He finally did. I came up sputtering and rubbing mud out of my eyes but otherwise intact.

The second of my great sports moments also came in a football game. Our regular quarterback got banged up a little and the coach took him out for a few plays. I was the substitute quarterback and not a very good one. The first play I called was a run-around end with me carrying the ball. As I made my turn to go around the end, I saw four huge guys from the other team waiting to annihilate me. So I kept running towards the sideline and must have also run backwards because in the next day's newspaper was the following quote describing this play: "Substitute quarterback Mechem was tackled for a ten-yard loss while he was fading to pass." I really didn't realize how far and wide (and back!) I must have retreated that it looked like I was "fading" to pass. Thank God our regular quarterback re-entered the game soon.

The final story occurred in a basketball game. We had a pretty good team in my senior year, and we advanced to post-season play where we were scheduled to play one of the top teams in the state. The game was played on the Ohio University basketball court, a large facility quite unlike the one on which we played our home games in Nelsonville. We had a very small gym that actually doubled as the stage for the high school auditorium. Just imagine—the back part of the foul circle was only a few feet from the centerline! I was very nervous as the game began because we had never played a team this good. We kept up for a while but then began to fall back. Our coach told us in a timeout that anytime our center or forwards got a rebound, I was to "fast break" towards our basket, and they were to throw the ball to me. We had done this scores of times, and the timing for it was pretty well burnt into my brain. Well, the moment came, our center took the ball off the backboard, I broke for the basket, and he threw the ball to me. I caught the ball, took the two or three steps that I was used to taking in the Nelsonville gym, and then went up for what I thought would be an easy layup. There was only one problem. The court was dramatically longer than the one I was used to so that when I went up in the air for the easy layup I was about thirty feet from the basket. Obviously, a layup was not in the cards, but I was already in the air, and as I recall I simply threw the ball at the basket. It was really all I could do. I completely missed the basket, and I came down thoroughly embarrassed. One of my more humbling moments, especially because it was in front of a large crowd.

I could write yet another book (probably more than one) about the rest of my high school years. But, again, this is not my autobiography. Suffice it to say, my high school years were happy. At that time, the world (well, at least the United States) was a very happy place. The war was over, the depression had been wiped out in the tsunami of the war's industrial might, reconstruction of much of the world had begun, and "terrorism" was a word and a practice that did not exist yet.

BEFORE MOVING ON to the next chapter in my life, let me mention two pieces of my early life that had significant impact many years later.

When I was a little boy growing up in Nelsonville, one of my most eagerly anticipated events was the yearly visit of Gooding's Traveling Carnival. This was a carnival of the 1930–1940s era complete with rides (none of which would have passed OSHA muster), games (very few of which one could ever win), sideshows, and food of every kind. Because the carnival used land directly behind my dad's shoe store and he only charged a small amount of rent, Dad always got a lot of free tickets, which he passed on to me. I went every night with my pals and loved it.

This deep-seated love of the carnival reasserted itself in a most unexpected way many years later. While I was CEO of Taft Broadcasting Company, one of our areas of expansion was the themed-amusement park business. We moved in that direction after acquiring the Hanna-Barbera Productions company in 1966. In thinking about ways to enhance the Hanna-Barbera image, it wasn't much of a stretch to see what Disney had done in their parks to merchandise the popularity of their cartoon characters. Therefore, we decided to build a large theme park just north of Cincinnati, named Kings Island. As an aside, I might note that the park was a success from the beginning and is an even greater success today—some forty years after it was opened.

While I firmly believed in the soundness of the business venture, I have to admit that I was overjoyed at my opportunity to reassert my "carney love." Marilyn, the kids, and I visited the construction site several times every week for two years and literally watched it emerge from the ground. As the park was nearing completion and the thrill rides were being tested, I made a point to ride on all of them as soon as the builders of the rides would let me. It is probably a bit of a stretch to say that I was a test pilot, but I certainly tried out the rides long before they were open to the public.

Not long after the park opened, the *Wall Street Journal* did a front-page story about the park and made numerous references to my enthusiasm for the project. It was a very favorable article, but there was one phrase that made me the butt of many jokes. The author, knowing of my love for the thrill rides, described me as a "roller-coaster nut." I suppose one could wish for a more distinguished description when appearing on the front page of the *Wall Street Journal,* but I loved it, and I certainly couldn't argue with its accuracy.

So, I guess the moral of the story is "once a carney boy, always a carney boy."

SINCE WE WERE growing up in the depression, my brother, sister, and I were all expected to have a job when we were not in school. When I was old enough to have a "real" job, my dad talked to the County Engineer and got me a summer job with the County Highway Department. Athens County, where Nelsonville is located, was a rural county with many dirt roads that the county was obligated to maintain. The work crew was a group of fellows of all ages and backgrounds. Some of them had worked for the Highway Department for many years; others were guys who were probably just trying to make a living while looking for a better job.

This was hot, tiring work, but at my age, it took a lot to wear me out. I dug ditches, repaired guardrails, cut brush, cleaned culverts, and did whatever else I was told to do. The older guys were really nice to me, and I honestly enjoyed the work. However, as I think back, I probably enjoyed it largely because I knew it would end in late August, and I would go back to school! By the way, the pay was extravagant—65 cents an hour! But to me at that age and time, it was a fortune.

I learned two very important lessons during the four summers that I was with the "Highway Boys." First, as I just mentioned, my work was temporary, and I was young and looking to the future. But most of the guys I worked with were in a very different category. This *was* their life. This is how they supported themselves and their families. For most of them this *was* their future. It gave me a new and different perspective on the lives and dreams of what, I suspect, was the vast majority of people at that time.

The other lesson I learned came from an old guy who was very friendly to me from the very beginning. His name was Emmett, and he had been part of the highway gang for many years. He was an intelligent, pleasant man and very popular with all of us. He and I were working together one day to dig a trench for some pipe. He watched me stabbing furiously at the ground with my shovel and stopped me to give me some advice. He showed me how to shovel slowly and carefully and taught me all the tricks of the trade. He was obviously proud of the fact that he could do something well and that he could pass this knowledge on to someone else. This may seem a trivial incident, but it had a real effect on me both then and now. No matter how menial a task may seem, it can be done well or it can be done badly; it can be done with pride or with resentment; it can be done with total effort or with disdain. I think that lesson applies— or should apply—to any task that anyone ever undertakes. It's funny how and where you learn important lessons!

I can't leave my highway gang experiences without noting my hopelessly unsuccessful attempt to learn to chew tobacco. Most of the guys chewed tobacco partly, I'm sure, for the nicotine fix but also because it kept their mouths moist during the hot, dry, and dusty days that followed one after the other, especially in July and August. I thought it would be "cool" to chew, and I planned to brag about it to my pals. Regrettably, it never happened. Let me tell you that there is an art to chewing tobacco, as surprising as that may seem. The trick is to do it without swallowing any of the tobacco juice that is generated by chewing. This is obviously foul stuff and spoils all the fun! Try as I might I could never master it. I guess this just proves that there is skill required in this ancient habit, and it was a skill that I simply did not possess!*

I graduated from Nelsonville High School in 1948. There were fifty-two of us in the graduating class. It was truly a wonderful group of kids. We got along wonderfully well together, and I still count many of them among the closest friends I have ever had.

---

*An interesting note: Chewing tobacco was undoubtedly far more common in southeastern Ohio than in most places because of the number of underground coal mines that existed there in the first half of the twentieth century. The mines were often filled with gas, which would explode if a match was struck. Thus, cigarette and cigar smoking was very dangerous to one's health—and not just because of the cancer risk!

My mother and dad on their honeymoon at Niagara Falls in 1916.

Yes, that's me!

My dad, grandfather, and uncle in front of the family shoe store.

My mother and her one-room schoolhouse class. Note the number of bare feet!

Dad, as President Pro Tem of the Ohio Senate, with Governor Jim Rhodes.

In spite of a weak link (me), we had a pretty good basketball team. I'm in the first row, second from the right.

My brother, Bill, my dad, me, my sister, Alice, and her husband, George, on the occasion of my receiving an Honorary Doctorate at Ohio University in 1984.

The four horsemen we ain't! I'm number 13—seems fitting.

CHAPTER III

Miami University

MY CHOICE OF a college was not complicated. For financial reasons, I needed to go to a state-supported Ohio college. I really only thought about two—Ohio University and Miami University. I rejected Ohio University, even though it was and is a fine school, because I wanted to get farther away from home (it was only thirteen miles from Nelsonville), but not too far. I had never been to Miami (forty miles north of Cincinnati), but I liked everything I knew about it and the few people I knew who went there as well. So, off I went to Miami in the fall of 1948, and I have never regretted the decision. It marked a major turning point in my life, in more ways than one.

I knew very few people when I arrived at Miami, and so I was looking forward to meeting my roommate and becoming pals. I just knew that would make it easier for me to adjust and be less homesick. (I knew I was going to be homesick!) So, after unpacking and bidding my folks goodbye, I waited anxiously in my room for my new pal.

They arrived! Yes, I said they for I was to have not one roommate but two! Not just any two guys. Oh no! These guys were high school buddies from nearby Dayton. They were nice guys and we got along, but they didn't need me to be a friend. Moreover, they went home to Dayton almost every weekend, and I was by myself. The result was that I studied a lot—far more than I would have if my roommate situation had turned out as I had expected. This in turn got me into study habits that led to better grades than I had ever imagined and made it possible for me to seriously think about attending Yale Law School. And thereby hangs another tale of good luck.

In those days, Miami had a system of faculty counselors. I was assigned to a political science professor named Straetz. When I first met him he looked me right in the eye and asked where I wanted to go to law school. I said that I didn't know. He said, "Don't you think you should try to go to the best law school in the country?" I acknowledged that seemed the right thing to do. He then said that as far as he was concerned the best school was Yale, and that's what I should strive for. He made it very clear, however, that I had no chance unless my grades were very good.

So, I had an advisor who set me on a tough, but wise, course and an environment in which I had plenty of time to study! I call that good luck! In spite of all this, my first semester was not a happy one. I was lonely and missed my home and family. When I went home for Christmas, I told my brother that I wanted to leave Miami and enroll at Ohio University—close to home. Instead of lecturing me, he said he understood, but suggested that I finish out the year, and if I still wanted to transfer he would help me convince my father that it was the right thing to do—not a task I wanted to handle by myself!

By the end of my freshman year nothing could have persuaded me to leave. And, again, good luck was on my side. I went on to build an academic record that allowed me to get into Yale. I was elected president of the student council and developed a wonderful group of friends, particularly my fraternity brothers.

HOWEVER, THE GREATEST stroke of good fortune came in my junior year—when I met the lady who became my wife and who remains so today. I am sure everyone remembers how and where he or she first met his or her spouse. I surely do! Again, my good luck!

One of my duties during my term as president of the student council at Miami was to meet the candidates for freshman council and explain to them the rules of election—such as no signs on trees. We assembled in a classroom late in the afternoon on a rainy day. Shortly after I had begun to speak, a late arrival came into the back of the room and quietly sat down in the last row (it was, by the way, the first and last time in her life that Marilyn Brown was late for anything).

In any case, I was instantly smitten. She was the prettiest thing I had ever seen. When I finished my remarks, I handed out a printed copy of the election rules. But, I slyly made sure to walk to the back of the room and hand-deliver copies to those in the last couple of rows, including, of course, Miss Brown. I might add that she was even prettier up close.

All the candidates signed the sheet with their names and addresses. I noted that Miss Brown lived in a dormitory called Swing Hall. After the meeting, I went back to my room at my fraternity house and located one of my fraternity brothers, Sam Badger, who worked as a waiter at Swing Hall. I asked Sam if he knew Marilyn Brown who lived at Swing. He said he did, and I asked him if he could arrange a date for me. He did and—as they say—the rest is history.

Another one of my duties as president of the Student Faculty Council at Miami University was to head up the so-called Artists Series, which was a program of music and drama that lasted throughout the year and featured six or seven different performances. The most memorable one by far, indeed the only one I recollect, was when a quartet of the world's most distinguished actors came to Miami to perform George Bernard Shaw's great play *Don Juan in Hell*. This group—Charles Boyer, Charles Laughton, Sir Cedric Hardwick, and Agnes Morehead—were certainly four of the world's great performers, and they were taking *Don Juan in Hell* on the road after a dazzling success in New York City. The nearest airport to Miami University is Cincinnati/Northern Kentucky

International Airport, and that is where the group was arriving. I managed to borrow a clean but fairly old car (since Miami did not permit students to have cars) and drove to the airport to meet the group. In retrospect, I simply cannot imagine that I did this. Why I didn't have the presence of mind—or why someone didn't tell me—to hire a limousine and escort the actors in the manner to which I'm sure they were accustomed, I simply can't imagine.

But, in any event, I met them and we drove from the airport to the Miami University campus with Mr. Laughton (a large man) in the front seat with me and the remaining luminaries crammed into the back seat. Nevertheless, we made it, and they performed brilliantly, just as they had on Broadway. Perhaps, however, more memorable to me than their performances was what happened after the show. I was to take them back to Cincinnati, where they were spending the night. After I got the same "trusty" automobile ready, I walked into the dressing room to see how nearly ready they were for the trip. The first thing I saw was Charles Boyer, the handsome Frenchman who had played numerous dramatic roles and who was perhaps one of the most famous performers in history, taking off his stage makeup in front of a large mirror. However, Mr. Boyer's hair was on a dummy's head! I had not known that Mr. Boyer wore a toupee—why would I know such a thing?—and I was completely flummoxed when I saw the bald Boyer and the hairpiece on the dummy's head. I don't think I made a fool of myself, but it was a little while before I was able to calmly assemble the group to head back to Cincinnati.

I continue to marvel on this evening and why one or more of the four didn't let me have it for not treating them with the dignity they certainly deserved. Perhaps, however, they found it a relief from the usual hoopla and adoration to which they were normally accustomed.

THE REMAINING YEARS at Miami were happy ones. Marilyn and I got engaged (I bought a ring for three hundred dollars, which exhausted most of what I had accumulated from that summer's highway work) and planned our wedding for August 31, 1952, just before heading to New Haven, Connecticut, to attend Yale Law School (yes, I got in!).

Three final Miami memories. It's funny the things you remember—that stick in your mind—after a lot of years have gone by. I had—and have—scores of happy memories of my days at Miami University. But a quirky story is one of my very favorites. One of my fraternity brothers was getting a degree in education, and in his senior year was doing student teaching at a local school. One day when I walked into the fraternity house where I was living, I saw my friend sitting at the top of a flight of stairs that went from the first to the second floor. As I walked in, he threw a sheaf of papers up in the air and they landed on several different steps. I couldn't imagine what he was doing, so I asked him. He said, "Charlie, I have got all these papers to grade, and I don't have the time or energy to do it. So, I am throwing them up in the air and the steps on which they land will each have a grade. Those that land on one step will get an 'A,' on the next step a 'B,' and so forth." I said, "You can't be serious." He assured me that he was. I don't recommend this to any aspiring teacher, and I certainly hope that no "A" students had their papers land on the "D" or "F" steps, but I suspect that in the big picture it didn't really make a whole lot of difference.

My roommate during my junior and senior years at Miami became one of my dearest friends and remains so today. Dan Brower and his beautiful wife, Phyllis, were constant companions for Marilyn and me, and we had many, many happy times together.

But, there was a "dark" side to Dan Brower. I have one phobia—I really hate spiders, and the bigger they are the more I hate them. Somehow Dan learned this and here's what he did. He bought one of those giant rubber spiders that is about five or six inches across with horrible colors and so forth, and he put it under some papers next to my type-writer, obviously knowing that at some point when I was going through the papers I would uncover it. His plan worked even better than he dreamed because I accidently knocked the papers onto the floor, which made the spider virtually jump out at me, and I went screaming out the door. Dan and my buddies had so much fun with this that they concocted an even more diabolical scheme. All of us in our fraternity house slept in a large dormitory-like area in double-decker bunks. My bed was one of the lower bunks. One of the guys got in the upper bunk and dangled a big spider on a thread and lowered it down inches from my sleeping face. They then spotlighted it with a flashlight and woke me up. I don't think I need to describe any further the trauma that ensued. Thank God I've always had a good heart because if I didn't, I would have long since been gone. Finally, a memory that always makes me smile but certainly wasn't funny at the time. Before being accepted as a full member of a fraternity in those days, one had to serve something of an apprenticeship—called pledging. As a pledge one had to perform a number of duties around the fraternity house to make the lives of the active members more pleasant. One such duty was called "wake boy." As the name implies, this consisted of waking the older members of the fraternity based on a list that was posted each night with names, times, and any other instructions. This was normally a fairly simple matter but there was one important and ongoing warning. One of the active members was a fellow named Mike Saborse. Mike was a veteran of World War II and had been engaged in quite a bit of combat. His memories were still fresh, and, if he was awakened too abruptly, he might come up swinging. So, we all took special care to wake him up slowly and tenderly! One morning I went to the fraternity house as "wake boy." It had snowed during the night, and as I came to Mike's bunk I found that he had left the window open and was covered with about an inch of snow. Unconsciously, he had buried under the covers, and the snow had covered the blanket over his entire body. When I saw this I was absolutely terrified because I had no idea what might happen if I awoke him in a way that caused him to have snow descend on his warm and cozy frame. So, what I did was to pull up one edge of the covers very quietly and whisper, "Mike, it's Charlie Mechem, don't move. You are covered with snow and you must get up slowly and let me brush the snow off as you sit up." Happily, this worked, and I brushed the snow off as he slowly awakened. A disaster was averted. A singular incident indeed and nothing remotely like it has happened to me since!

I need to reiterate that these years were amazing in retrospect—not just for us but for the United States itself. World War II was over, the Great Depression was over, and the Cold War had not escalated to a point where it was of great concern. General Dwight Eisenhower was elected president in 1952. He was the ultimate war hero and was immensely respected and popular, and this simply added to the healthy and robust mood of the nation. Those years now seem light-years away!

The mood of the 1950s is beautifully described in a wonderful book, *Rules of Civility* by Amor Towles. He puts it this way:

> In the 1950s, America had picked up the globe by the heels and shaken the change from its pockets. Europe had become a poor cousin—all crests and no table settings. And the indistinguishable countries of Africa, Asia, and South America had just begun skittering across our schoolroom walls like salamanders in the sun. True, the Communists were out there, somewhere, but with Joe McCarthy in the grave and no one on the Moon, for the time being the Russians just skulked across the pages of spy novels.

Our wedding, at the First Methodist Church in Marilyn's hometown of Newark, Ohio, was wonderful. Not fancy, not huge, just the kind of ceremony that I am sure thousands of Midwest boys and girls celebrated during those years—friends and family, smiles and tears. Marilyn was beautiful in her wedding gown on her dad's arm. I knew this was a tough day for Brownie (that is what everyone called Marilyn's dad), because they were very close, and I knew how much he would miss her. We were told later that the day was oppressively hot—hardly uncommon for an August day in Ohio! But we were oblivious to it. For us, everything about the day was wonderful.

Immediately after the reception we set off for New Haven in an old Nash* that I had bought for four hundred dollars. That old car served us well for several years, but we finally had to get rid of it when it began to use more oil than gas and put a smoke screen out the exhaust pipe that in today's world would contribute significantly to global warming.

---

*If you are under sixty you probably never heard of a Nash. It was one of the many respected brands of automobiles that is lost to history.

CHAPTER IV

New Haven, Here We Come!

As I mentioned earlier, we took off for New Haven as newlyweds and we obviously had more stars in our eyes than sense in our brains because we arrived there with no place to live and with no job for Marilyn. However, again my good-luck charm worked. We found a little spot north of New Haven that was literally a lean-to on a garage. The owner ran a beautiful tourist home next door (named Moose Manor!) and had built two lean-tos on his garage. There was only one room with a pullout bed, a little kitchenette, and a bathroom. That was our first home and it worked just fine.

There were a few adjustments that needed to be made. For example, I studied till quite late every night, and Marilyn would go to bed. In order for me to get from my desk when I was finished studying to hit the bathroom before going to bed, I had to literally walk over the bed where she was sleeping. However, we were both young in those days— she didn't stir and I didn't trip!

Another humorous story from these days concerns Marilyn's experience with a gas stove. At her parents' home they had always used an electric stove, so Marilyn had no experience with a gas stove until we moved here. Just as her family had done at home, Marilyn stored items such as cereal and bread in the lower drawer of the stove. Of course, this turned out also to be the broiler! So, the first time Marilyn turned on the broiler, not really understanding where or what it was, everything in it burned up. No harm done and a good lesson learned!

This was a disarmingly idyllic little place, close to the ocean and in a very rural area. We lived there through a glorious New England fall. Then we both began to focus on the fact that fall would turn into winter, and we had to drive into the city each day. So we decided it was time to move. So our next stop was the spot where we lived the rest of our time in New Haven, 320 Edgewood Avenue. I'll have more to say about that later.

Our other major challenge was also successfully met when Marilyn found a terrific job as an assistant to the Dean of the School of Fine Arts. Marilyn was a great secretary (that's what they called executive assistants in those days) and, as everyone who knows her knows, was (and is) great with people. So, this job worked out wonderfully for her and also exposed her to many top people in the School of Art, Music, and Architecture. She always laughingly said that her specialty was uncorking wine bottles for the seemingly endless stream of cocktail parties and receptions that took place at the school. This was only one of her skills, and as with everything else, she did it with great aplomb!

Our home at 320 Edgewood Avenue had three rooms—a living room, bedroom, and kitchen, but they were separate rooms connected by a central hallway. So, to go from the bedroom to the kitchen, for example, meant going out in the hall. This was really no big deal, however, because there was only one other couple living in the building in addition to the landlord and his wife. We loved this place and, as I said before, lived there for all three years in New Haven. Our landlady and landlord were delightful people and were wonderful to us, making our lives both richer and much simpler.

CHAPTER V

Yale Law School

MY THREE YEARS at Yale Law School changed my life. I know that is a strong statement, but it is true. First of all, Marilyn and I were newly married, looking for our first "home," meeting scores of new people, and beginning our married life in a part of the country that neither one of us had ever even visited.

Beyond that, I was about to become part of the first-year class that included the smartest people I had ever known. They had all been top students at their undergraduate schools, and I quickly realized that the competition would be strong. Indeed, in my very first class, I learned that the fellow on my left had been first in his class at Yale College, and the fellow on my right had been tops in his class at Notre Dame. When I got home that night, I told Marilyn this and then said, "Don't unpack our stuff yet! I'm not sure how long we'll be here!" I was also exposed to a covey of professors who were national and international scholars of superb reputations and records.

Our political views also were about to be challenged. Both of us had come from small Midwestern towns and conservative families. Now we became part of a community of liberal thinkers from big-city backgrounds. At first this was a little unsettling, but it probably did more to mold our thinking and teach us respect for other people's views than we had ever imagined. However, I never lost the fundamental ideas and influences of my upbringing. Indeed, one of the most exciting things

I was involved in was the formation of the Conservative Society of the Yale Law School. We wanted to remind our classmates that there was a philosophy different from theirs and that the Yale Law School needed to understand and entertain some of these thoughts and ideas. The experience was great fun, partly because it infuriated many of our liberal friends. We were thrilled to attract five or six well-known conservative figures to the law school to make speeches. Our kick-off speaker was William F. Buckley, Jr., who had just stirred things up in the Yale community for publishing his controversial book *God and Man at Yale*. I had the great privilege and fun of having dinner with Buckley after his speech and being absolutely astonished at his ability to communicate his views. I hope that the Conservative Society, in some form, continues at the law school to this day. If it doesn't, it should.

Meanwhile, Marilyn and I were settling in, making friends (primarily with the other married couples), and enjoying immensely living in New Haven. For example, many of the plays and musicals that were headed for Broadway tried out in the Schubert Theater in New Haven. We bought third-balcony seats for practically nothing (binoculars were a must) and saw an incredible array of shows while we were in New Haven. Some of them went on to be great Broadway hits and others were never heard from again.

I HAD MANY memorable experiences during my academic career at Yale—such as the time I was running late for a final exam in property law and forgot to bring the course textbook with me. This may seem trivial, except that it was an open-book exam! I managed to survive by borrowing a book from a student who had taken the exam the day before.

But if I had to pick one episode as the most memorable of my law school years, it would probably be my involvement in the Moot Court finals. Moot Court was a program in which every student argued cases in an elimination process that ultimately led to four students surviving and arguing before a very distinguished panel of judges in the "finals." I was fortunate to be in that group of four, and we argued before three judges—a U.S. Supreme Court Justice (Tom Clark), the Chief Judge of the New York Court of Appeals, and Bruce Bromley, an outstanding trial lawyer from one of the large New York City law firms.

My colleagues were extraordinary. My partner was a fellow named Gordon Spivack, one of the most intelligent human beings I have ever known. He went on to be a significant figure in the Anti-Trust Division of the Department of Justice. Our opponents were two equally impressive classmates—Charlie Haight, who went on to become a U.S. Circuit Court Judge and Bill Dempsey, a standout speaker and debater who had led his class at Notre Dame, later clerked for Earl Warren, the Chief Justice of the U.S. Supreme Court, and had a very distinguished legal career. I was excited but extremely nervous. My mother and dad came from Ohio to watch the argument, and I worked extremely hard to prepare. Although I was intellectually ready, physically I was struggling. I had done a lot of public speaking, but I had never done anything quite like this, and I must confess that I was intimidated by the quality of the three-judge panel and by my opponents. Though I have never admitted it publicly, I spent a half hour or more before we left home soaking in a tub of hot water to attempt to calm my frazzled nerves. Marilyn of course was supportive and helpful and continued to reassure me that I would not make an idiot of myself.

To make a long story short, everything went very well. Once into the arguments, the nerves went away, and the "thrill of the game" made it a very memorable evening. In the final judging, Bill Dempsey was recognized as the best, and I came in second. Although I have never been thrilled when coming in second, in this case I had no qualms or reservations. Bill Dempsey was a fantastic speaker and debater and deserved the honor. I felt privileged to snuggle up to him in second place. Bill remains a dear friend, and I admire him as much today as I did then.

As my third year began to wind down, all of my thoughts turned to getting a job. Representatives of firms from all over the country came to the law school, and we students signed up for interviews with those firms in which we had an interest. Although I interviewed with several big-city firms, I knew that I really wanted to return to Ohio. Both my parents and Marilyn's were living, and we had many, many friends in the area. This turned out to be easier for me than I thought it might be because I got a job offer from the highly respected Cincinnati firm Taft Stettinius & Hollister, and, upon graduation, we headed back to Ohio.

In the Yale Law School library.

CHAPTER VI

Back in Ohio

THE FIRST ORDER of business when we got back home to Ohio was to study for, take, and hopefully pass the Ohio State Bar Examination. This was a three-day ordeal upon which, literally, your entire future rested. Technically, in those days, if you failed in your first effort, you could take the exam again. But, obviously, a failure on your record was not calculated to enhance your career opportunities! I frankly admit that I was traumatized by the enormity of the Bar Exam. I found it very hard to focus, and, as the day approached, my nerves were increasingly frayed. I even contemplated postponing taking the exam until another time, but my father put me straight on this in a hurry. He insisted that I stop being a "wuss" and go forward with the exam. He was right. It was a very good lesson for me at a relatively early age. Postponing dealing with major decisions or challenges only makes them more difficult to deal with and undermines your confidence in your own abilities.

To make a long story short, I took the exam, passed it, and officially joined the law firm of Taft Stettinius & Hollister. Though it is hard to imagine now, I was only the twentieth lawyer on the firm's letterhead. Today there are more than 250. There are only two of us left of that original twenty.

Robert Taft, Jr., later to become a United States Senator in the footsteps of his distinguished father, was a good friend of our family and took me under his wing from day one. I remember him showing me into my small, spare office, and giving me my first assignment. I have often laughed to myself that that was the last time my desk has ever been totally free of papers!

My time at the firm was limited because I knew that I would be drafted into the Army within a year. Indeed, I entered the service in the late winter of 1956. However, my seven months at the law firm before entering the Army were challenging, exciting, and extremely intense. I was assigned to the senior partner in charge of the corporate department, a man named John Bullock. He was a brilliant and demanding boss from whom I learned a tremendous amount, not only about the law, but also how to deal with and relate to clients.

My experiences over the months before I went into the Army were quite varied. In a small firm, you are required to do a variety of things. However, there was one especially memorable episode. There was a case that had been around the office for years. It involved an attempt by the U.S. government to collect a significant sum of money from one of our clients, arguing that this was money owed by our client to a German company, Maschinenfabrik Augsberg-Nürnberg,* and could be appropriated by the U.S. government because of Germany's status as an "enemy nation" during World War II. Although every young lawyer who came into the firm was given the case, nothing really happened for some years. But, as fate would have it, shortly after I was assigned to the case, the government became aggressive. This had nothing to do with me but rather with the government's need to accelerate the case so as not to be precluded by the statute of limitations. My boss called me into his office one day and said, "Charlie, I need you to go to Germany and review all the files of the German company to see if there is any way we can defend against the government's claim." Needless to say, I

---

*The German company was a huge multi-national organization with the very German name Maschinenfabrik Augsberg-Nürnberg (MAN). They were the world's largest manufacturer of diesel engines and, indeed, Rudolf Diesel reputedly invented his engine in the MAN factory in Augsberg. My client was Baldwin-Lima-Hamilton which manufactured, among other things, railroad locomotives. They bought their engines from MAN.

was overwhelmed. First of all, neither Marilyn nor I had ever been out of the country, and, further, I had been handed a big and challenging assignment.

I could write a chapter on this case alone, but suffice it to say, Marilyn and I went to Germany, and I had the great good fortune to find some documents in the files of the German company that became a complete defense to the government's claim, and the case was dismissed. Again, luck played a significant part in my success. I was given full access to the files at MAN, but was warned that most of the records had been destroyed in the bombings of World War II. However, some documents that were in a safe had survived. In going through these documents (which, of course, were all in German) I found a ledger page which appeared to show that the amount of money owed by my client to MAN had been written off. I excitedly asked my German interpreter to ask the financial people whether the document indeed reflected a write-off. The answer was yes, and the reason was fascinating. It is hard to imagine that any company would bother, in the midst of the destruction of Nazi Germany, to do the actual bookkeeping needed to void the debt. But, it was explained to me that the financial people had concluded that, because of the war, there was no hope of ever collecting the debt and with classic German precision, they simply wrote it off! Therefore, they were able to give me a sworn affidavit that their records showed no money owed them by Baldwin-Lima-Hamilton!

After finishing my work in Germany, Marilyn and I went to Paris, where we spent several incredible days. Since we had very little money, we scrimped and saved but still had a wonderful time. Ironically, when we got home, my client was so pleased with the result of the trip that it paid all our expenses in France! If we had only known!

In February of 1956, the time came for me to enter the service, and I did so without qualms. Of course, I hated leaving my family and my law practice, which I had enjoyed immensely, but in those days you expected to serve in the armed forces and you simply regarded it as part of your obligation as a citizen.

I had no idea how much I would actually enjoy my time in the service or how rewarding it would be. That's the next chapter. But let me first tell you about one of my most humbling moments as a young lawyer.

WHEN I JOINED Taft Stettinius & Hollister in July 1955, everyone knew that I would only be there for a few months before I entered the service. There was certainly no point in hiring a secretary for me for that short period of time. The solution that the firm came up with was logical and reasonable but, for me, very unsettling! The senior partner and a founder of the firm, John Hollister, had been named to President Eisenhower's Cabinet and had, of course, moved to Washington. Thus, his secretary (in today's world she would be called executive assistant, a much more accurate phrase in my view), a delightful Auntie Mame–type personality named Doris Voorhees, had no boss. So the firm assigned her to me so that we would both be satisfied. I was certainly satisfied—and terrified! I don't know how Doris felt about it.

The first time I had reason to dictate a letter (which I had never in my life done before), I asked Doris to come into my office. She arrived with steno pad in hand and I commenced. When I finished I felt rather proud of my effort. Doris had other thoughts. She sat back in her chair, looked at the notes that she had taken, and said, "Well, that was a little gem, wasn't it!" It was neither the first nor the last time that I realized that I was not nearly as good as I thought I was. There is a delightful postscript to this story. Many years later when I was CEO of Taft Broadcasting Company and, incidentally, had probably dictated five thousand letters over the years, I was asked to speak to a women's club in a northern suburb of Cincinnati. When I arrived I was thrilled to see that Doris Voorhees was a member and she was sitting in the first row. So, I obviously had to tell the story and I did it with great relish. Everyone laughed, including Doris, but she did so with a very red face! Doris Voorhees was an extraordinary person—bright, funny, and irreverent. I could not have had a better secretary to launch me on my way.

Next stop—the United States Army!

CHAPTER VII

The Army

MY THREE YEARS in the Army turned out, to my considerable surprise, to be three of the most interesting and rewarding years of my life. My obligation under the draft was only for two years, but I learned that if I enlisted for three years I could choose my assignment after basic training.* I decided to do this and chose the Counter Intelligence Corps. It meant another year in the service, but it turned out to be the right decision.

It all started with a train ride from Cincinnati to my basic training location at Fort Leonard Wood, in the Ozark Mountains of Missouri. On our way the train stopped in Detroit and several more recruits got on board. They were young, sixteen- and seventeen-year-old boys from the streets of Detroit. In those days it was not unusual for a young man who got in minor trouble to be given a choice of going to jail or going into the Army. These boys had chosen the Army. One of the boys was a tall, engaging kid named Bobby, and we struck up a friendship on our way to Fort Leonard Wood. He and his pals simply could not believe that I was a lawyer. Their logic was compelling: If you're intelligent enough to be a lawyer, you should be smart enough to not be on a train taking you to Army basic training! Hard to argue with, but I convinced them by showing them my Ohio Bar Association membership card.

---

*I had applied for a commission in the Judge Advocate General's Corps but they had enough lawyers at that point and had frozen the granting of any new applications. However, they kept my application on file with very surprising consequences, which I shall detail later.

They were persuaded and were much more impressed than they should have been! I go into this much detail about the train ride because my new friendship became very important to my well-being in a very short period of time.

We reached Fort Leonard Wood and were directed to our barracks, where we began to get our gear organized and began visiting with people around us. Later that night, after our first dinner, we came back to the barracks and Bobby and his friends were telling everyone that I was a lawyer and therefore, in their eyes, unlike anyone else in the whole place! You have to understand that most of these kids had never finished high school, and having a lawyer in their midst was a unique experience.

It turns out that one of our barracks mates was not so impressed. He was an older guy who obviously resented the attention I was getting. He walked to where we were all sitting and began to say some not-so-kind things about me. Then he stepped forward, and I firmly believed he was preparing to beat me up. As I stood there, not knowing quite what to do, my new friend Bobby stood up, walked over to the older guy, pulled a switchblade knife from his pocket, flipped it open under the older guy's chin, and said quietly but forcefully, "Don't f_ _ _ with Charlie." That ended the confrontation and cemented our friendship forever!

BASIC TRAINING LASTED twelve weeks, and I can't begin to go into detail about all of my experiences. Rather, I'll quickly note several high points—and low points!

Surprisingly, I gave up cigarettes during basic. I knew that at age twenty-five I would have a hard enough time getting through basic training even if I was in the best of shape and certainly would have a real problem if I continued to smoke. So, I gave it up and, as a result, was the only guy in my company that gained weight during basic training!

When the commanding officer learned that I was in the group, he called me into the orderly room one day and told me that he wanted me to help him with a project. Obviously, I could not decline. He explained that he was about to retire after twenty years in the service and wanted to go to college. He wanted me to help him put together applications to get him into a good school. I was happy to do this and had fun getting to know him and spending some time with the other officers, even though I was a lowly enlisted man.

One of my favorite memories involves the deputy company commander, a first lieutenant who had recently graduated from Princeton. I was an oddity as an enlisted man because of my educational background, and he had a lot of fun kidding me—in a good-natured way. The incident I remember best happened at the end of a drill where we were marching with our rifles (the legendary M-1) on our shoulders and then came to a halt. We had done this scores of times, and at the moment we came to a halt the lieutenant *always* called out the next command (known in the manual of arms as "order arms"), which was bringing your rifle from your shoulder to the ground. This time he decided to have some fun with me, so when we came to a halt he did not automatically give the next command. I anticipated the command and brought my rifle to the ground. None of the other guys moved a muscle. The lieutenant came over to me, looked me straight in the face with a smile, and said, "Mechem, you're thinking again!" The lesson was clear: in the military you never anticipate a command. It was a lesson well learned.

Another wonderful lesson in how the world works came one day when we were on the rifle range. One of the duties that fell to our group was to go to the area (called "the pits") where the targets were placed and be responsible for pulling the targets up and down depending on how the shooter had scored. In other words, if a shooter got a bull's-eye, you ran up a particular flag. If, on the other hand, he missed the target entirely, you ran up what looked like a pair of red underwear that was affectionately called "Maggie's Drawers." This particular day, when I was tending one of the targets, the sergeant in charge of our group came down and said, "Mechem, the commanding general of the post is firing at your target. No matter where his shots go, put up the bull's-eye flag." I did as I was told even though some of the shots merited a Maggie's Drawers. This is when I grasped the full meaning of the phrase "rank has its privileges."

Finally, an experience that I still can't believe really happened. It was spring in the Ozark Mountains. This meant that it was freezing cold in the mornings and frequently quite warm mid-day. The result was that, by afternoon, you were overdressed and perspiring. This led to more and more cases of pneumonia, bronchitis, and strep throat. This was bad enough, but the real problem was that if you had to go to the hospital and stay for several days, you were "cycled back" and had to start basic training all over again. The result was that guys put off going to the hospital as long as possible and inevitably their conditions were even worse when they did go. I seemed to be getting along okay until my throat began to hurt. It got worse and worse and finally became so bad I could eat nothing except ice cream or something of similar consistency—which was not easy to come by. I was determined not to go to the hospital and risk having to start basic training all over again. Finally, in desperation, I bought a jar of Vicks VapoRub and literally ate large chunks of it. This was not great for my digestion, but unbelievably my throat got better, and I didn't have to go to the hospital! I could have given Vicks a great testimonial, though I am certainly not suggesting this form of treatment.

I FINALLY FINISHED basic training and was sent to the Counter-Intelligence School at Fort Holabird, Maryland, where I entered an intense four-month program on how to become a "spy." I'm kidding when I characterize it in this way. In fact, we were trained to be counter-intelligence agents and were drilled in subjects like interrogation techniques, profiling, surveillance, clandestine entry, and the like. It was a terrific program and I learned a lot. Much of it served me well as a lawyer in future years.

When I finished the school, they decided to keep me at Fort Holabird as part of the faculty of the school. Although I would have preferred to be sent to some exotic location, staying put was fine. We had a nice little apartment in the suburbs of Baltimore and were enjoying being close to Washington and New York City.

By this time, I had literally forgotten about my Judge Advocate General's Corps application. But a big surprise was in store for me. Every Saturday morning the battalion commander, a lieutenant colonel, inspected the troops by walking up and down the lines and checking dress and overall military bearing. I never had any trouble in these inspections, but on this particular Saturday morning I was singled out by the battalion commander for several problems, including my uniform, my shoes, the shine on my belt buckle, and so on. I was puzzled by this and even more puzzled when he called me to the front of the formation and said, as I best recall, essentially the following: "Mechem, you are a sloppy soldier. You are an embarrassment to the enlisted ranks. I think the only thing for you is to become an officer!" He then produced from his pocket a set of first lieutenant's silver bars and pinned them on my shoulders. He explained to the troops, who were as stunned as I was, that my Judge Advocate General's Corps commission had come through, and he wanted to have a little fun awarding it to me. I was greatly relieved and pleased, and all of the guys in our company were excited and noisy. I spent another few weeks at Fort Holabird before being transferred to the Judge Advocate General's school, which was operated in collaboration with the University of Virginia Law School in Charlottesville, Virginia. The few weeks that I remained at Fort Holabird—now as a first lieutenant—were amusing. Suddenly I outranked virtually everybody in the company, many of whom had been tough on me, along with all the other enlisted men, during our time there. They suddenly became my best friends!

So, the next move was to a very different environment—the law school at the University of Virginia. And that's the next chapter. But I first must tell you about one of the most unforgettable characters I ever met.

ALL OF US, I think, meet a few people in our lives who are truly unforgettable. I'm not referring to relatives or close friends, though some of them are indeed unforgettable!

One of the most unforgettable characters I ever met was a fellow that I knew for only a few months when I was going through the Counter Intelligence Corps School. I have not seen him since the day we parted in 1957. Nonetheless, I have never forgotten him. His name was Tom O'Hara. Tom, if you're still living, I hope these stories don't embarrass you. You were a terrific guy and took all the bad breaks with good humor.

Tom was a very pleasant Irish fellow who was part of the platoon to which I was assigned while I was at the Counter Intelligence Corps School. Purely by happenstance, our platoon was designated as the honor guard for the months that we were at the school. Once every week there was a review of troops by the commanding general, and it involved a parade and military bands. Our honor guard platoon marched at the head of the rest of the troops, resplendent in chrome helmets and bayonets, purple neck scarves, and white shoelaces in our boots. It sounds ridiculous, but we actually looked pretty darn good!

The famous cartoonist Al Capp created a wonderful character named Joe Btfsplk, who occasionally appeared in Capp's *Li'l Abner* comic strip. Joe always had a little dark rain cloud over his head and was constantly beset with bad luck. O'Hara was the living, breathing Joe Btfsplk. Three incidents stand out in my mind, though there were many. The first happened when we were marching in the review parade one day. The boots we wore (called combat boots) had very thick heels on them—well over an inch. As we were marching in review to the stirring music of the military band, the guy directly behind O'Hara stepped on the heel of his boot and ripped it completely off the shoe. Now, just imagine Tom's gait from that point on. He lurched from side to side in a very "non-honor guard" way. Even the stirring Sousa march couldn't disguise this disaster!

The second incident would have been sad if it hadn't been so hilarious. During one of the troop reviews, our honor guard was standing at rigid attention as the band began to play "The Star-Spangled Banner." Then O'Hara's little black cloud started to rain on him. Those of us in the line behind him saw a mosquito land on the back of his neck. He, of course, could not do anything to swat it—he couldn't move, certainly not during the playing of the National Anthem. He did everything physically possible to move the muscles in the back of his neck without moving any other part of his body. Regretfully, it was not enough and the mosquito, who must have thought he was in mosquito heaven, made his strike! Tom told us later that it was one of the worst things that ever happened to him—and that covered a lot of territory!

The third is my favorite. O'Hara, like many of us who were married at the time, lived in private housing off the post. This meant that he needed to get up earlier and travel farther to make the early formation, which, as I recall, was at 8:00 a.m. He was constantly late, and the company commander became increasingly irritated. Finally, one day he told O'Hara that if he was ever late again he would be severely disciplined. That could mean a lot of things—none of them good! He said that he expected him to be on time the next day.

O'Hara was terrified and decided that the only way he could be sure of being on time the next day was to sleep in the barracks on the post where the unmarried guys lived. However, he wasn't sure that even this

Early Army days.
The warrior and his lady!

The Mechem ladies reviewing the "troops."

Baby Melissa in 1958. Can't believe I was ever this thin.

Our family in 1978. Me, Marilyn, Allison, Melissa, and Dan. Still together after all these years!

would save him because, if he overslept at all, he would not have time to put on his uniform and still make the formation. So, he decided to sleep with his uniform on except for his shoes.

The next morning he managed to make it on time, though it was clear that he had only been up a few minutes. The company commander came up to Tom and said, "Well, well, how nice to see you here on time. But, you look terrible. Your uniform is a disgrace! You look like you slept in it." O'Hara sheepishly responded, "I *did,* Sir." In what I am sure was a severe breach of military discipline, we all broke down and laughed uproariously. Happily, so did the company commander!

I WAS A brand-new first lieutenant, and Marilyn and I were ready to leave for Charlottesville, Virginia, and the Judge Advocate General's School.

CHAPTER VIII

Judge Advocate General's School

THE JUDGE ADVOCATE General's School shared not only some physical facilities with the University of Virginia Law School but also some academic and teaching resources. There was an amusing contradiction in my status as we moved to Charlottesville. On the one hand, as a part of the faculty at the JAG School, I was accorded many of the privileges of any other faculty member at the University of Virginia, including access to the fine university hospital where our first child was born. (I'll have more to say on this later.) On the other hand, under the mysterious Army regulations, the JAG School was considered a "hardship post" because it had no Army facilities like a post exchange or a commissary. Some hardship post! A fine university located in one of the most beautiful spots in all of America. What made this all the more ironic is that, because it was a "hardship post," I received an extra $180 a month to help me deal with all of these hardships! Marilyn and I have often laughed that we probably had more free cash in those days than at any other time before or since.

My first assignment at the JAG School was unusual. Although I would be attending the school itself, inasmuch as I had already been in the service for well over a year and had been through basic training and Counter Intelligence training, it was decided that I would "double" as a student and a faculty member. My main responsibility as a "faculty member" was to help "militarize" the other fellows coming into the Army at the school. That is to say, virtually all of the students coming into the school were coming directly from civilian life and had absolutely no military training. My job was to help close the gap. Sometimes this was amusing and sometimes a little scary. For example, it was funny to see a brand-new, young officer knot his tie in a Windsor knot that looked about a foot wide instead of the narrow, clean, and neat four-in-hand knot that was necessary in the Army. An example of the "scary" part was when we would do exercises in the field involving weapons. Some of the new officers had never held a gun and sometimes waved their carbines around in a manner that caused the rest of us to hit the ground fast!

Once again, I was in an environment where I met a lot of very interesting people and made some good friends. One fellow that I remember very well was Derek Bok. Derek went on to teach law at Harvard, became the Dean of the Harvard Law School, and then the President of Harvard University for twenty years. While it was obvious even then that he was a brilliant young man destined for great things, what I remember best is that he was a dynamite softball pitcher who made the JAG Law School team a major force on the local softball scene.

After finishing the JAG School I was kept in Charlottesville because I only had a little more than a year left in my Army commitment, and it obviously made no sense for me to be sent into the field. While I would have enjoyed actually practicing military law, it was hard to argue with the wonderful opportunity to live in Charlottesville for an extended period.

My work at the JAG School was fairly routine and lackluster, but one of the most important things in my life—and quite obviously Marilyn's—was the birth of our first child, Melissa, at the University of Virginia Hospital on November 21, 1957. This was a blessed event in every way, but there was one especially amusing aspect. As I mentioned, we had full access to and the privileges of the University of Virginia Hospital where Marilyn and Melissa were wonderfully cared for. The funny part is that we had the benefits of this great hospital at an Army "rate" of twenty-five dollars. When we left the hospital I kept the receipt and, at Melissa's wedding rehearsal dinner many years later, I gave the receipt to her husband-to-be and said he should use it if she ever began to brag about how valuable she was!

Thus began our newest adventure—being parents!

CHAPTER IX

The Kids

EVEN THOUGH IT means jumping ahead a little bit, I think this is a good time to talk about all three of our children.

As I just noted, Melissa was born in 1957. Dan joined us May 24, 1960, and Allison came along ten years later in 1970, which has led me frequently to refer to her as our "caboose." Allison has insisted over the years (jokingly I think!) that she must have been a "mistake," but I think we have finally convinced her that nothing could be further from the truth. These are three wonderful kids who are truly different one from the other, which seems often to be the case with families. But they have several important things in common. They are bright, witty, and loving. We love being together and we have great fun when we are.

Melissa, a pediatrician, is involved in medical consulting in fibromyalgia and chronic fatigue. She and her husband, Ted, live in Mill Valley, California, where Ted is involved in the executive search business with Jackowitz & Co. Their son, Sam, is at Hampshire College in Massachusetts, and the family's only redhead, May, attends The Urban School in San Francisco and is a rabid San Francisco Giants fan.

Dan and his lovely Bolivian wife, Eliana, now live in La Quinta, California, with Eliana's daughter and Dan's stepdaughter, Almita. Happily, this is just five minutes away from where Marilyn and I live in the wintertime, and we are delighted to have them close by. Dan and Eliana both work with Mechem Media, a company that Dan and I founded a few years ago to develop entertainment product in the spirit of Hanna Barbera, once a part of Taft Broadcasting Company.

Allison and her husband, Ted, live in Niwot, Colorado, a suburb of Boulder. They have two children: ten-year-old Will and seven-year-old Ellie. Allison is a fourth-grade teacher at Boulder Country Day School, and Ted is a senior executive at Micro Motion, a division of Emerson. Everyone in the family is a skier, and they are blessed to be near the great Colorado ski resorts.

I well remember my dad saying that, as you grow older, your children mean more and more to you. Indeed, it is impossible for me to imagine old age without kids and grandchildren. Marilyn and I are blessed.

CHAPTER X

Years at Taft Stettinius & Hollister

AFTER MY DISCHARGE from the Army in February of 1959, I rejoined Taft Stettinius & Hollister in Cincinnati. We bought our first house for eighteen thousand dollars in a modest but very nice neighborhood and settled into "civilian life." I became a partner in the firm in 1965 and remained there until the winter of 1967. During those eight-plus years I had a fascinating and interesting career with clients such as Taft Broadcasting Company, the Cincinnati Reds, the Cincinnati Bengals, and Play-Doh, to mention only a few.

There had been a very significant change in the law firm since I went into the Army. A major upheaval had occurred in the Cincinnati legal world when the senior partner of another prominent firm had a disagreement with his partners and left his firm to join Taft Stettinius & Hollister. He brought with him a number of large clients, and the firm had almost doubled in size when I returned.

There was a humorous aspect to this. When I went into the service in 1956, I was the first person to enter the military from the firm since World War II. The custom in World War II when somebody joined the service was to put an asterisk by his name on the letterhead with a note indicating "In Military Service." The firm, quite understandably, decided to do the same thing with me. The amusing part was the unintended consequence of getting my name on the letterhead and then the

Taft Stettinius & Hollister letterhead when I joined the firm in 1955. I was number twenty! There are now more than three hundred lawyers in the firm.

sharp increase in the number of attorneys in the firm. In short, I was moving up on the letterhead rapidly without even being there! Some of my colleagues-to-be must have wondered about this absent figure who was making such rapid progress.

I remained at the firm until late 1967. These were busy years, to say the least. There was a strong work ethic, not to mention strong demands, and all of us worked very hard. It was common to work several nights a week until 9:00 or 10:00 p.m. and most of the day on Saturday. I have often reminisced about the dress code in those days, particularly in light of today's casual dress. In the "old days" a suit and tie were expected on weekdays, but things were "dramatically" relaxed on Saturdays, when only a sport coat and tie were required. Sunday morning work was also not uncommon, especially by those of us working in the Corporate Department, since the head of the department worked every Sunday morning. One of my most amusing memories is of a Sunday morning when I was at home and the phone rang. Marilyn answered and it was my boss who said, "Is Charlie there? It's awfully lonely down here." Marilyn handed me the phone and, covering the receiver, told me who it was and what he had said. Then she said, "If you go down to the office this morning it will become very lonely around *here*—permanently!" Naturally, I stayed home!

AFTER A FEW years, three of my colleagues and I were made partners in the firm, and our responsibilities correspondingly increased.
The friendships I made and the professional development that I experienced have been extremely important parts of my life.

These were busy and exciting years. My work with the Reds, including a highly publicized and controversial transfer of ownership from the
longtime owners (the Crosley family) to baseball executive Bill DeWitt
was exciting, especially to a baseball fan like me. Anyone from Cincinnati will be interested (and amazed) to know that the price Bill paid for
the Reds in 1962 was $4.625 million. The most recent sale of the club to a
group headed by Bob Castinelli was $270 million. Talk about an increase
in value! Even at the price DeWitt paid, the sale was challenged in court.
There were claims that higher offers had been made and rejected by the
Crosley Foundation, the charitable foundation that held 90 percent of
the stock in the ball club. The litigation was settled with DeWitt confirmed as owner after making some concessions, particularly agreeing
to keep the club in Cincinnati for an extended time.

Bill was a life-long baseball man, and his son Bill Jr. has continued
the tradition and is now the principal owner and the managing partner
of the St. Louis Cardinals. Bill Sr. was very good to me, and I very much
enjoyed working with him. One of the things that I enjoyed the most
was the couple of occasions that I went with him to the meeting of the
National League owners. These meetings were almost always held in
New York City, and all of the owners attended. While I don't remember
much about the business that was discussed at the meetings, I remember vividly some of the participants. Most particularly I remember Walter O'Malley, Horace Stoneham, Gussie Busch, and Judge Hofheinz.
O'Malley, of course, was the man who moved the Brooklyn Dodgers to
Los Angeles in an unprecedented act that shook the baseball world. He
was smart, shrewd, and dominated the National League. He was clearly

the most powerful force at the league meetings that I attended. Horace Stoneham was well known for following O'Malley's lead by moving the New York Giants from the Polo Grounds in New York City to San Francisco. Gussie Busch was the patriarch of the Busch family and owned the St. Louis Cardinals. He was a small man but very impressive. He was obviously used to control and leadership. I also remember two odd things about him. One was that, probably to help him stop smoking, he carried a plastic replica of a cigarette, complete with filter and ash, that he would hold in his hand and occasionally "smoke." I also remember that he always had near his seat a pail of ice that contained some cold beer, undoubtedly Budweiser. And, finally, Judge Hofheinz, who was the great showman from Houston who built the Astrodome and put the Astros in it. He was one of the greatest promoters in the history of the sport and was a huge character in every way. These were giants in the baseball world, but they were also colorful and fascinating characters and made a lasting impression on this young lawyer.

EQUALLY EXCITING WAS the opportunity to represent the group of Ohioans who persuaded the legendary Paul Brown to come back to Cincinnati and start the new National Football League franchise, the Cincinnati Bengals.

My relationship with Paul began when, as a young lawyer, I was asked by a group of Cincinnati and Columbus businessmen to represent them in their attempt to get the next professional football franchise to be awarded by the National Football League to go to Cincinnati. The then Commissioner, Pete Rozelle, had made it clear that his respect for Paul Brown was such that if Paul wanted to come back into professional football, the franchise was his. I say "come back" into professional football because a few years before, Paul had been unceremoniously fired by Art Modell, owner of the Cleveland Browns. It is a controversial story with both Brown and

Two of my dearest friends together—Paul Brown and Neil Armstrong.

Modell having their point of view and their supporters, but one fact was crystal clear—Paul Brown was angry and very anxious to return to professional football and prove that Modell had made a mistake.

I went with a couple of representatives of the ownership group to La Jolla, California, where Paul was then living with his wife, Katie. He was being compensated by the Browns in a separation agreement that required him only to file a few scouting reports each year to guarantee the payment of the agreed-upon amount. (I used to kid Paul that his forced isolation in La Jolla reminded me of that of a deposed banana republic dictator.) But this wasn't what Paul Brown wanted. He wanted back into football!

After three days of intense negotiations, we finally arrived at an agreement by which Paul would come back to Cincinnati and form a professional team. That team was the Cincinnati Bengals, and the similarities to the Cleveland Browns were eerie. Perhaps Paul didn't even realize some of the similarities. For example, the initials "CB." The colors of the Bengals were orange and black—the Cleveland Browns' colors were orange and dark brown. But, what mattered was that Paul built, more quickly than anyone dreamed, a very successful team, and his first victory over the Cleveland Browns must have been the biggest victory of his life.

The incredible story of Paul Brown is one that many people don't know. Oh, yes, he is certainly regarded as one of the greatest coaches in the history of professional football, but many people don't know that before he formed and coached the Cleveland Browns, he had coached national championship teams at the high school level (Massillon, Ohio) and at the college level (Ohio State University). Moreover, during the Second World War he coached at the Great Lakes Naval Training Center and during that time signed to prospective contracts a number of the players who went on to be greats with the Cleveland Browns.

Beyond his extraordinary record as a coach, Paul accomplished many things that are not as well known as they should be. For example, he pioneered the early version of the modern playbook that all teams use routinely today; he started the practice of sending signals in to the huddle by substituting guards virtually every play. Perhaps what might surprise most people is that he invented the early version of the modern face mask and got a patent on it. He once told me, with a wry smile, that he had made more money from royalties on that patent than he had ever made in coaching.

I HAVE SO many stories to tell about Paul that I could fill the rest of this book, but I'll try to choose a few to illustrate a side of this extraordinary man that most people never saw. The first story took place during our negotiations to bring Paul back to Cincinnati. As I indicated earlier, the negotiations were tough. Paul wanted very much to return to the game, but he made it clear that he would not do so if there was any chance that, as he put it, "what happened to me in Cleveland could ever happen to me again." We wrestled with this and a number of other problems for several days, but finally worked out an arrangement where all of the other owners would agree to put their stock into a voting trust with Paul as the voting trustee. This was the price that needed to be paid to get Paul. It was a price I recommended to my clients, and it was a price they were quite willing to pay. When the negotiations had concluded on a successful note, Paul invited us to his home for drinks and dinner. He and Katie had a beautiful home overlooking the Pacific Ocean from up high on a hill. During cocktails he and I ended up sitting alone on a couch staring out at the sun dipping into the Pacific Ocean, an absolutely breathtaking sight. I turned to Paul and very seriously said, "Paul, I know you think you've been pretty clever in these negotiations, but you should know—and I feel obliged to tell you—that we can dismiss you anytime we wish." He looked at me dumbstruck, those strong piercing eyes boring right through my head, and said, "What are you talking about?" I said, "Paul, there is a provision in our agreement with you, which is standard in virtually every employment agreement I have ever seen, that says we can dismiss you at any time if it can be proven that you are physically or mentally incompetent." "Well, of course," he said, "I understand that, but what does that have to do with what you said?" I said, "Paul, look out the window." He said, "Why?" I said, "Anyone who would leave this scene to come back to Cincinnati, Ohio, and start a brand-new football team is demonstrably mentally incompetent!" We both had a good laugh and another drink.

Paul's most intense passion, after football, was clearly golf. He loved the game and everything about it. Not long after we made our deal to bring Paul to Cincinnati, he invited me to play golf at La Costa, a great course near San Diego. I had never played golf with Paul before, and it turned out that he and I viewed the game somewhat differently. He was a total stickler for the rules, and I have always felt the players should have fun and enjoy themselves and not worry about some of the arcane, inexplicable rules. Of course, my view only applies in friendly games and not in formal competition, where USGA Rules are in effect. But I regarded my game with him that day as a casual one between friends. Was I ever wrong!

On the first tee, I hit my drive out of bounds to the left. Paul was standing seven or eight yards behind me, and I heard him say in a stage-whisper voice* that reached my ears, "You're hitting three." I turned around, thinking that he might be joking—everyone I ever played with gave a mulligan on the first tee—but it was clear that he wasn't. I hit my second drive fairly well down the middle of the fairway, and together we walked toward our balls. When I reached my ball, it was squarely in the middle of a divot. Normally, my buddies and I would roll the ball out of the divot and never give it another thought, but having been called by Paul on the first tee for my out-of-bounds shot, I thought I should at least ask his permission to roll the ball free. He was standing about fifteen or twenty yards away from me, about to address his own ball, and I called over and said, "Paul, can I roll this ball out of this divot mark?" The answer almost broke me up, but he was dead serious. He said, "Is there water in it?" I said, "What are you talking about?" And he said, "If there's water, it's casual water; otherwise, play it as it lies!" I played a lot of golf with PB over the ensuing years, and he never changed his approach to the game. I embraced it completely (if not enthusiastically) when he and I were playing together.

---

*Paul had a deceptively quiet voice for such a strong personality. Moreover, sometimes he didn't speak at all. I once asked Otto Graham, the Browns' Hall of Fame quarterback, how Paul acted when Otto came off the field after an unsuccessful effort. "Did he really yell and scream at you?" I asked. Otto smiled and said, "Oh no, that wasn't Paul. He would simply glare at you and then turn and walk away as though you were beneath contempt. That was far worse than yelling and screaming!"

For a number of years, Marilyn and I hosted an outing around the Fourth of July at Muirfield Village Golf Club in Dublin, Ohio. Our guests every year were Paul and his wife, Neil Armstrong and his wife, and George Rieveschl (the inventor of Benadryl) and his wife. This outing, I genuinely believe, was one of the high points of Paul's year—at least off the football field. We drove up from Cincinnati early in the morning, played golf, had dinner, and drove back. Paul had a vintage Cadillac, a big, roomy, powerful car. He always drove to Columbus but insisted that I drive home. This might seem, at first blush, like an equal trade, but it was far from it. Driving up was fairly simple. It was broad daylight, usually around 8:00 a.m., and everyone was rested. The drive back was something else again. We had played a round of golf on that magnificent and difficult golf course; it was usually hot and humid; and we finished the day with drinks and dinner in the clubhouse. By the time the drive back began, it was usually about 10:00 p.m., and my eyelids were about to close before we even got in the car. To his credit, Paul always sat up front in the passenger seat, and, though his eyes may have closed from time to time, he made sure that mine did not!

Of the many funny things that happened during our golf rounds, perhaps the most memorable (which Neil Armstrong and I have laughed about over and over again) came on a day when, before we had teed off, there was a light rain that left the golf course slick, but not by any stretch unplayable. We teed off and everyone was in reasonably good shape after his drive. Now, you must understand this central fact: Paul was a very good golfer. He was consistently in the fairway and almost always on the green in regulation (or close) without great difficulty. By that time in his life, he wasn't particularly long, but he was very accurate. In any event, his second shot slid off a little bit to the right (almost certainly because of the wetness of the ground and the ball) and skidded into a bunker to the right of the first green. My guess is that Paul Brown had not been in a bunker for many years, but he walked into this one and took his first shot. The ball hit the lip and came right back to where it started. Another shot produced the same result. Paul said, "Well, at least I don't have to move my feet." His next shot skidded across the green and rolled down into a bunker on precisely the other side of the green. By this time, he is lying about seven and by the time he finally got out and holed the putt, he had made a twelve. Now remember, this is on the *very first* hole of the match! That sets a rather dismal tone for the rest of the day.

We walked somberly to the next tee. No one said a word. We played number two, number three, and number four without a single word uttered by anyone. We didn't know what to say and we felt that we shouldn't say anything until Paul did. At long last, walking down the fifth fairway, Paul turned and said, "I think that was the most embarrassing thing that's ever happened to me in my entire life!" We all laughed, put our arms around him, and said, "Shake it off; you'll beat us anyway." And away we went.

AS THE YEARS went by I was becoming more and more involved with another of my clients, Taft Broadcasting Company. We took the company public in the summer of 1959 and followed that with the listing of the company shares on the New York Stock Exchange. I was named secretary of the company and later served on its board. I liked everything about this client. Little did I know that I would one day be part of it. Much more on this shortly.

AS I LOOK back after so many years, I truly believe that I learned more from my clients and the matters I handled for them than they ever learned from me. Let me give you a few examples.

The first story concerns a company called Rainbow Crafts and its founder Joe McVicker. Rainbow Crafts owned and manufactured Play-Doh, the incredibly successful children's molding compound. Joe McVicker was a very impressive fellow, and he and I became good friends. I once asked him how he had come up with Play-Doh, and the story he told absolutely amazed me. Joe's brother-in-law ran a company, Kutol Products, that made wallpaper cleaner; Joe was also involved in this business. Most of those under fifty reading this book probably don't know what wallpaper cleaner was; it was a spongy-type substance containing a cleaning agent that was used to brighten dirty or dusty wallpaper. Joe's sister ran a nursery school in the Washington, D. C., area, and she observed that if the wallpaper cleaner made by Kutol didn't have a cleaning agent in it, it would make a wonderful thing for the children in her nursery school to play with. Joe—and I assume his brother-in-law—figured out how to remove any harsh or toxic substances from the wallpaper cleaner and—it became Play-Doh! I'm sure it wasn't as simple as it sounds but many great ideas look simple in retrospect. As a kid I helped my mother and dad more than once clean the wallpaper using wallpaper cleaner. If I had only known the potential for the stuff I was holding in my hands! What I learned from Joe's story is that the essence of entrepreneurship—at least the American variety—is "think outside the box" (my friend W. R. Howell, former CEO of J. C. Penney, calls it "thinking the unthinkable") and always try to envision the greatest possible potential no matter how mundane the beginning may be.

Joe McVicker obviously was the classic example of American entrepreneurship at its best. Having said that, I want to say a word about the finest entrepreneur and business builder I think I have ever known—my good friend Dick Farmer of the Cintas Corporation. Dick's grandfather was actually a circus clown. In his off time he apparently was a "rag picker" who gathered up rags, cleaned them, and sold them. His son, Dick's father, took this humble beginning and started Cintas, a company that laundered and cleaned uniforms used by companies of all sorts. It was this company that Dick joined right out of Miami University. Through his personality, intelligence, and drive, he has built Cintas into a dominant force in the industry and one of the most respected corporations in the country. He also happens to be the greatest salesman I think I have ever met. I know it's an old joke to describe someone as a person who could "sell ice cubes to Eskimos," but I honestly think Dick could do it.

I am proud to say that Dick and I share the same alma mater—Miami University. Dick and his charming wife, Joyce, are among Miami University's major benefactors, and the business school, the Farmer School of Business, is named for Dick—as it should be.

THE SECOND STORY makes me smile every time I think of it—and I think you will see why. I represented a young man who was brilliant and hard driving, but he was one of the most unpleasant people I have ever known. He was constantly criticizing my work and berating me for not accomplishing more on his behalf. I always fought back and argued, and we had some pretty strong sessions. One day he called me and was particularly irate about something. I was suffering from some kind of bug that had settled in my throat and, during the ugly telephone conversation, I suddenly became unable to speak a single word or make any sound whatever! He would carry on and then pause waiting for a response, but I made none because I was unable to even utter a squawk. Finally, after several attempts to provoke me he finally said, "I guess you're just tired of arguing with me, aren't you?" Again I could say nothing. He said that he was sorry for the way he had dealt with me and hoped that I would continue to be his lawyer. Again no response. Finally, he said, "You must be really angry with me; we'll talk tomorrow." And he hung up. It is amazing, but I never had trouble with him again because he thought that I was so angry as to be speechless, and he decided to calm down. I never explained to him the reason for my complete silence, but, again, I learned something from the experience: When a situation becomes excessively unpleasant, it sometimes proves that the less said the better.

A YOUNG GERMAN immigrant named Ewald Pawsat came to the United States and settled first in Sheboygan, Wisconsin, and then in Maysville, Kentucky. He started a bicycle repair shop and called it Wald. Over the years, he built the company into the largest supplier of bicycle parts made in the United States, selling to all the big bicycle manufacturers. Our firm represented Mr. Pawsat, and I was asked to work on his estate plan. After many meetings, his will was finally ready for signature. I met him at his office in Maysville to take care of the signing. But before that, I told him that I wanted to be sure that he had disclosed all matters of significance regarding his holdings, because if he had not I could not be sure that the will was what it should be. Mr. Pawsat by this time was in his seventies and was a man of enormous integrity. He said to me, "Well, there is one thing that I have not told you about." When I asked what he meant, he explained that he was keeping some cash in the safe in his office that he had not mentioned to me. I assumed he was talking about a few thousand dollars. So I said, "Well, I don't see that as a problem—how much are we talking about?" He paused and said, "Around $300,000." This was in the mid-1960s! I swallowed hard and said, "Sir, I really think that's too much money to be keeping in your safe. You should have it working for you at a bank or whatever." At this point his voice got stronger and he said, "Let me explain something to you, young man. There was a time during the Great Depression that the banks closed and I was unable to raise enough cash to pay my employees, and that lasted for a whole two-week pay period. That was the most embarrassing thing that I had ever experienced, and I vowed that I would never let it happen again. That $300,000 is the amount I would need to meet a payday, and there is nothing that you or anybody else can say to make me take it out of that safe."

That comment has never really left my mind. Another lesson learned: Those who went through the Great Depression, including my own father, never really recovered from it in terms of their trust in the stability of our system. It led that generation to be watchful and careful and probably led to building more great businesses and organizations than anyone will ever know.

PERHAPS THE STRANGEST matter that I ever was involved in as a lawyer was being caught up in the great Northeastern blackout of 1965. Our firm represented the First National Bank of Cincinnati. One of its senior loan officers, Rolf Brooks, received a subpoena to appear before a grand jury at the District Attorney's office for the Southern District of New York at Foley Square in downtown Manhattan. I don't remember the purpose of the subpoena, but one never takes that sort of thing lightly. I do remember Rolf being concerned and anxious to appear and testify. We flew to New York on the night before we were to appear at the District Attorney's office. Midway into the flight the pilot came on the intercom and said that we had an emergency, namely that there was a massive blackout covering the whole New York City area and that, of course, all of the airports were closed. He said we would land in Philadelphia, and the airline would arrange bus transportation to the New York Port Authority Bus Terminal in Manhattan. We got off the plane and onto the bus and began the journey to Manhattan. But first I called the old Statler Hotel in New York City, where we had room reservations, and asked them to please hold our rooms, that we were on our way. Somewhat surprisingly they agreed to do so. We arrived at the bus terminal, and when we walked outside the building it was an eerie sight, to say the least. The only light came from automobile headlights and several peo-ple using newspaper torches to try and direct traffic. New Yorkers can always be expected to move into action quickly in times of emergency, and they were certainly doing so that night.

We struggled but succeeded in getting a cab. It was not cheap, prov-ing that the law of supply and demand was alive and well! I had called the Statler several more times, and they assured me that our rooms were available. When we finally got to the Statler, we found a chaotic scene. Candles were burning throughout the lobby, and hundreds of people were sleeping on couches, chairs, and anywhere they could lie down. We went to the desk and learned that one of our rooms was still available but that they had felt it necessary to sell the second room. This was not a problem for us—we were surprised and delighted to have any room at all. I'll never forget the clerk looking up and saying, "Gen-tlemen, you will, of course, need to walk up the stairs to your room because the elevators aren't working. So, here are two candles to help you find your way." I can't remember now what floor our room was on, but I think it was the eighth or ninth. In any case, as we started walk-ing up the stairs, we again found people sleeping everywhere, many of whom asked if they could please share our room. We declined, point-ing out that we were already sharing! We finally got to our room and fell into bed around 1:00 a.m. At around 4:00 or 5:00 a.m. all the lights came back on and wakened us even though we'd only had a few hours of sleep. We rested for another couple of hours and then got up, dressed, and went down to confront the day.

Things were still chaotic. There was little if any food for breakfast, and taxi cabs were nowhere to be found. The cab drivers had obviously made a fortune during the night and had gone home to bed. We finally man-aged to get a hard-boiled egg, toast, and coffee and began to make our way downtown to Foley Square. We took two or three different buses and finally arrived at the District Attorney's office at around 8:30 or 8:45 a.m.

1990

Golfing with Coach Paul Brown and Jim Brown, regarded by many as the greatest running back in the history of the National Football League.

The District Attorney, somewhat surprisingly, was in his office, and when we entered and introduced ourselves he was noticeably shocked. "How in the world did you two get here from Cincinnati, Ohio?" he asked. We explained and noted that we were in total compliance with the subpoena. He agreed but told us that he doubted if he would be able to get a quorum of the grand jury that morning because New York's communication and transportation systems were chaotic to say the least. He asked if we would be willing to postpone our appearance. I pointed out that we had gone beyond any reasonable effort to comply with the subpoena, and we were not disposed to postpone our appearance. I pointed out that Rolf was prepared to testify and expected to do so.

The District Attorney excused himself, conferred with a couple of his aides, rejoined us, and said that if Rolf would give a brief affidavit describing his knowledge of the matter the grand jury was investigating, he would consider us in compliance with the subpoena and dismiss Rolf from any further involvement in the case. We accepted his deal, provided a brief affidavit, and headed for home!

Funny how this momentous tragedy worked out to our distinct advantage.

WHEN I WAS a young lawyer I was assigned to an antitrust case that a small manufacturer of roofing materials in Meridian, Mississippi, brought against seven or eight of the largest roofing-material manufacturers in the country, charging an antitrust violation. We were legal counsel to one of these companies. The plaintiff argued that these companies were attempting to force him out of the business through conspiracy and predatory pricing practices. I spent a great amount of time in Meridian and in Jackson, Mississippi, working on the case. The deeper we got into it, the more troubling it became, and we began to take the case more seriously.

The case, as I recall, was filed in a federal court in Tennessee. We did some homework and came to the conclusion that we didn't want the case in that particular court. So we filed a motion for a change of venue, hoping to have the case removed to a friendlier tribunal. The motion was set for oral argument in the Tennessee federal court. Because of the importance of the matter, each of the defendants sent in its general counsel as well as its local counsel. When we walked into the courtroom there were fifteen or twenty defendants' lawyers lined up in the first couple of rows.

We had met previously and agreed that our case should be argued by a gentleman named Porter Chandler, who was with a large New York firm and was widely regarded as one of the finest trial lawyers in America. When our case was called, the judge said something like this: "I have reviewed this matter carefully, and I am convinced that the change of venue should not be granted. If, however, you wish to comment or make any statement, you may do so at this time." Porter Chandler, who was about six four and a very impressive gentleman, rose, walked to the front of the courtroom, and addressed the judge. "Your honor, we of course regret your decision, but we will not argue the matter further. I would, however, like to make a brief statement. I am compelled to observe, to paraphrase Winston Churchill, that never have so many come so far, been paid so much, and done so little."* We all (including the judge) had a good laugh, and we all went on our way.

ONE DAY I was called into the office of the firm's senior partner, Charles Sawyer, who was related to the Gamble family of Procter & Gamble fame. He told me that one of the granddaughters of James Gamble (one of the original founders of that great company along with William Procter) had passed away and that our firm was handling her estate. He wanted me to work with him on the estate, and the most immediate thing I needed to do was go to the bank and meet the tax official who would be making the customary visit to the deceased's safe deposit box, make an inventory, and then seal the box pending appropriate probate procedures.

I could not have been more "green" inasmuch as I had never done anything like this. However, I went bravely to the bank, met the tax

---

*The Churchill quote, made on August 20, 1940, was: "Never in the field of human conflict was so much owed by so many to so few."

official, and then proceeded to the safe depository area. I identified myself to the gentleman in charge of the depository and tried to sound poised and confident and said, "We are here to inventory Miss Elizabeth Gamble's safe deposit box." The gentleman pulled himself to his full height and with an unmistakable air of condescension said to me, "Young man, Miss Gamble did not have a safe deposit box; she had her own vault!" I honestly don't remember what my response was, but it couldn't have been very sophisticated because I was very embarrassed. In any case, we proceeded to the vault. We learned that a substantial portion of Miss Gamble's estate was in coupon bonds, each of which was bulky because of the unclipped coupons. As I recall, it took us a whole day to simply do the inventory of the bonds.

It was just one more learning experience, but I must confess that never again in any estate I was ever involved with was I exposed to a complete vault!

One last story of my days as a young lawyer—one that I will certainly never forget. I was asked to do some work for one of our major clients, a large insurance company. They were doing a deal with another large insurance company headquartered in Columbus, Ohio, whose CEO was a good friend of my dad's. His name was Fred Jones and he was a formidable presence—tough, smart, and very outspoken. When we first met, the first thing that he said to me went like this: "Charles, I'm glad to meet you. I intend to watch your work very closely because your dad is a good friend of mine and I simply want to see whether or not he 'bred up.'" I swallowed hard and then remembered that Mr. Jones owned a lot of horses and had been very successful in the horse business. So I understand his reference and, believe me, I worked even harder after that.

PHASE TWO OF my "three-phase life" was about to begin, and it would go on for more than twenty years. But, I want to say one final word about my days at Taft Stettinius & Hollister. In virtually every way, it formed the foundation for the rest of my life. I was associated with first-class people, and the friendships I made remain among the strongest in my life. Beyond that, my mind was constantly challenged by intelligent people and complex issues. Although the rest of my career was more visible and in some ways more "exciting," I wouldn't trade those nine years at Taft Stettinius & Hollister for anything! Happily, my Taft Stettinius & Hollister connection continues in a way. When I retired as board chairman of Convergys Corporation and was preparing to move out of my office there, the then managing partner of Taft Stettinius & Hollister, Tom Heekin, called and invited me to take an office at TS&H. I was delighted and use the office whenever I go back to Cincinnati. Not only is it a very comfortable office, but it is next door to my old and dear friend Charlie Lindberg, whom I have known since we were at Yale Law School together.

CHAPTER XI

Taft Broadcasting Company

MY INVOLVEMENT WITH Taft Broadcasting Company could be a book in itself, lasting as it did for over twenty years. However, I'll try simply to hit the high spots. Many of the "people stories" contained in this book would never have occurred had I not been involved with Taft.

My career with the company began in a strange and tragic way. I had been legal counsel to the company for several years and became secretary and a member of the board of directors. All of these came as a result of my friendship with Hulbert Taft, Jr., the founder of the company. Hub, as he was known, started the company in 1939 with the acquisition of WKRC radio in Cincinnati. He did this over the objection and advice of his father, who was the owner and publisher of the *Cincinnati Times-Star* newspaper. Hulbert Sr. like many newspaper barons of that day, was convinced that radio was a passing fad, and Hub Jr. would never see it prosper. He could hardly have been more wrong. The company grew rapidly in AM and FM radio, and over the years added television stations.

All of this changed tragically in November of 1967, when Hub was killed in the most bizarre accident I think I have ever known. He had built a bomb shelter on his estate in Indian Hill, a suburb of Cincinnati. A number of wealthy people living in the eastern United States did something similar in those days because they were greatly concerned that the Russians would fire missiles directed to the eastern part of the country from their bases in Cuba. This seems almost fantasy-like today but it was very real then. On a cold, rainy afternoon—November 10, 1967—Hub went into the bomb shelter and something (maybe a cigarette, maybe an electrical malfunction) caused a terrible explosion, most likely because there had been a propane gas leak. In any case, he was killed instantly at age fifty-nine. All of us who knew him were devastated. I felt the loss keenly because he had been so good to me and given me so many opportunities to learn and grow.

Hub's death, of course, was something that none of the shareholders (predominantly made up of members of the Taft and Ingalls families) had expected, and they had to reach a decision on his successor very quickly. I was totally surprised and not a little scared when I was asked to come into the company as chief executive officer. I had to make up my mind literally overnight. I decided to make the move after counseling with my wife, my father, and one of my law partners. Dad was mildly irritated that I even had to ask him what I should do. His answer was, "Of course you should do it. No one ever got anywhere by turning down a challenge." But it was not an easy decision because I was enjoying my law practice and thought the future was bright. However, I felt I might never have another chance like this and, therefore, moved forward with great excitement. My law firm was very supportive, so the transition was an easy one in that respect. However, I was overwhelmed with what I did *not* know about management and was determined to move slowly and with sensitivity until I gained the respect and support of the people in the company. The biggest problem I faced was that, since I was the company's lawyer, most of the senior executives concluded that I was put into the job to preside over and implement the sale of the company. Although I repeatedly told them that was not my mandate nor intention, I think it was at least a year before people were comfortable that I was there to grow and build the company.

By the way, one of my most amusing memories of my being named Chairman of Taft Broadcasting Company came to me from a good friend who called to congratulate me. He said, "Charlie, I think it's terrific, but have you considered the fact that the next move is out!"

The Growth and Development of the Company

LET ME TRY to give a brief overview of what happened over the next twenty-five years. When I joined Taft Broadcasting, we owned seven television stations, seven AM radio stations, and seven FM stations. We needed to expand outside of broadcasting because, in those days, the Federal Communications Commission limited the number of stations that one company could own. So, when you reached the legal limit you could not acquire any additional stations—even though the stations that you owned were generating a substantial amount of cash. Shortly before Hub died, we had made our first move outside of broadcasting with the acquisition of Hanna-Barbera Productions, the famous animation studio. In subsequent years, we bought another animation company (Ruby-Spears Productions) and built five major themed amusement parks utilizing Hanna-Barbera characters. All of the parks have been a great success except for the Australian park, which never really seemed to match the recreation needs and tastes of the Australian people. The other four parks, Kings Island, Kings Dominion, Carowinds, and Canada's Wonderland continue strong and successful to this day.

We also acquired Worldvision Enterprises, one of the largest distributors of television and film product in the world. We acquired other Hollywood production companies (such as the famous Quinn Martin Productions, creators of *The Fugitive, Barnaby Jones,* and many other great shows) not only for their own value but to add their product to the Worldvision distribution system. At the same time, we bought television and radio properties whenever the rules of the FCC allowed.

Interestingly, our broadcasting operations took us into still other nonbroadcasting directions, such as owning the controlling interest in the Philadelphia Phillies and having a small interest in the Cincinnati Reds. Amazingly the Phillies won the National League pennant in our first year of ownership. A funny thing happened in the World Series. The Phillies had acquired three of the great players from the Cincinnati Big Red Machine—Pete Rose, Joe Morgan, and Tony Perez. We had watched them play hundreds of times during the years we lived in Cincinnati. In the first game of the World Series, as I saw Tony on first base, Joe on second, and Pete in right field, I turned to Marilyn and said, "I think we've already been to this ball game!"

Winning baseball's National League Championship is not only a momentous occasion in itself, but a beautiful and very impressive ring is given to the players on a team that wins either the National League Championship or the American League Championship. What is less well known is that the owners and other officials of the teams usually receive such a ring as well. When the Phillies won in 1983, each of the owners (and, indeed, their spouses) received a magnificent ruby and diamond ring with all the appropriate inscriptions. It is a large ring, but it is very beautifully crafted. Over the years I have not worn the ring a great deal, partly because it is so large but more importantly because I didn't want to risk losing or damaging it. However, on a few occasions, for no particular reason, I have worn the ring for brief periods of time. Inevitably, when I have worn it, someone will spot it and ask me about it. As recently as March of this year, a flight attendant on a flight to Cincinnati spotted it and said, "Isn't that a baseball championship ring?" But, the funniest incident occurred when I was taking some of the family to Disney World and extended my right hand with money into the cashier's window. The young girl behind the counter said, "Oh my goodness, sir, that's a beautiful ring. What is it?" I explained that it was a National League Championship ring. She responded, "That is so impressive—what position did you play?" I couldn't resist, so I said something to this effect: "I was a short stop. I was not very well known but was proud to be part of a championship team." She said, "I am so impressed. I have never met a Major League Baseball player." I couldn't continue the charade any longer because I was laughing too hard, so I said, "Well, the truth is, young lady, you still haven't!" I then explained the whole story to her, and we both had a good laugh.

Further, among other enterprises, we embarked on a joint venture with the legendary John Malone's Tele-Communications Inc. by which we entered the cable television business. We also became a significant owner of Black Entertainment Television. When we entered into the joint venture with Tele-Communications Inc., John Malone had already helped a young man named Bob Johnson and his wife, Sheila, start Black Entertainment Television. Bob's vision was a cable channel that served a black audience with music and other programming that would appeal to that audience. Bob felt, correctly, that this was a very under-served market, and he also recognized that, even though cable channels in those days were frequently hard to come by, a channel of this sort would have a very good chance of being approved by the typical municipality, even cities that had put a freeze on new franchises. He and Sheila turned out to be right on both counts. They ended up building a highly successful and highly profitable enterprise, and our stock interest in BET multiplied many times in value. When we first became shareholders, Bob and Sheila were just starting out and had no infrastructure or "backroom." So, in the early days, Taft Broadcasting did all of their bookkeeping and accounting at our television station in Washington, D.C., WDCA. I have always kidded Bob by telling him that without us they might not have ever made any money, and, even if they had, they couldn't have counted it without us!

All of these investments spawned other smaller interests, such as a licensing and merchandising company to exploit the Hanna-Barbera cartoon characters and a company that designed amusement parks and choreographed shows that were a big thing in the parks in those days. I could go on and on, but the point is that all of these enterprises brought me in contact with people who became an important part of my life.

IN THE INTEREST of honesty and humility, I need to comment briefly on Taft Broadcasting's foray into the motion picture business. The motion picture business has been a siren song to scores of companies and individuals over the years. It is glamorous and holds out the dream of making a great deal of money on a small investment. The fact that neither of these notions is true hasn't seemed to deter anybody, and it did not deter us. I will mention only two of our projects, which are certainly the ones that stick out in my mind. The first was one of the few pictures that was profitable—*Running Man* starring Arnold Schwarzenegger—and it was quite profitable. We may have made a little money on a few of our early low-budget efforts, but *Running Man* probably allowed us to claim a break even in our movie efforts. The other movie, however, should be a lesson for anyone who dreams of success in Hollywood. It was what we thought was as close to a "can't-miss" investment as one could imagine. Adapted from a Pulitzer Prize-winning novel called *Ironweed,* it starred (can you believe this?) Jack Nicholson and Meryl Streep! We had visions of Academy Awards and riches beyond measure! So, what happened? It was a financial failure, not because anybody did anything wrong—Nicholson and Streep were magnificent, and the book was faithfully transferred to the screen.* The problem was very simple—it was a dark, depressing story, and the public just plain did not like it. This was enough for me and my associates. We exited the movie business with a few scratches and bruises but modest losses and a significant amount of learning and experience. That's the last movie we made.

---

*Although the picture did poorly at the box office, it was highly acclaimed. Nicholson won the Los Angeles Film Critics Association Award and the New York Film Critics Circle Award. He and Meryl Streep were both nominated for Oscars.

IN THE MID-1980S we made a very large acquisition of television properties from the Gulf Broadcasting Company. The price tag was $755 million, a big number even today. We acquired a number of big-market TV properties, including stations in Fort Worth, Houston, Tampa, Phoenix, and High Point, North Carolina. This was a major step in the growth of Taft Broadcasting Company. We were, of course, very excited but would probably have been less exuberant if we'd realized that this acquisition would lead to the end of the company we had worked so hard to build.

I had an interesting experience while negotiating the deal with Gulf that I'm not sure I have ever shared with anyone. We were in the Gulf corporate headquarters trying to finalize the deal. Unbelievably, although we were prepared to offer $755 million, Gulf was insisting on $765 million. We were getting nowhere in resolving the dispute, and Grant Fitts, the CEO of Gulf, said, "Charlie, let's go into a separate room, and you and I will settle this between ourselves."

When we were alone Grant said, "I really need the price to be $765 million." I pointed out that $755 million was what our board had approved, and I simply couldn't go higher. As the argument went back and forth, I had a very strange experience. One half of my mind was engaged in the dispute; the other half was saying something like this, "Charlie, do you realize what's going on in the other half of your brain? You're talking about spending $755 million! You are just a little boy from a little town in the southeastern Ohio hills. What on earth do you think you're doing talking about whether a deal should be $755 million or $765 million! Are you serious?!"

Fortunately, the negotiating side of my brain took over and we concluded the deal, but I have never forgotten that "out of body" experience!

THIS SEEMS LIKE a good spot to share briefly my thoughts on the "art" of negotiating. I have always had very strong feelings about the right way and the wrong way to negotiate. Over the years I have been engaged in countless negotiations, some as a lawyer and some as a principal, but my approach has always been the same.

I approach a negotiation as a discussion that leads to *making a deal*. As a result, I have always felt that respect for the other party and a willingness to compromise were essential ingredients. If one does not treat the other party with respect and courtesy it is, obviously, harder to reach an agreement. Similarly, if one is unwilling to compromise, it is hard to see how an agreement can be successfully reached. It's like the old saying goes—a successful deal will not totally please either party.

I am very opposed to the opposite approach, the approach that sees negotiating as "winning" and humiliating your adversary. Again, negotiating should not be about winning, but rather reaching a satisfactory agreement and maintaining a relationship with the other party that will permit you to remain friendly and respectful in the future. I have never been more convinced about the rightness of my approach as I have been recently as we have watched the hopelessness and craziness of the negotiations in Washington over the debt ceiling and the so-called fiscal cliff. It has all been about "winning" or "losing," and insult and vitriol have made it impossible for the various parties to respect or trust one another in the future. To repeat one final time: The object of a negotiation should be to make a deal, not to prove your manhood!

By the way, I also think there is an "art" in conducting a meeting, whether it is a negotiating session or not. I will share some tips about what has worked best for me later in this book.

THE ACQUISITION OF the Gulf Broadcasting properties naturally drew a lot of attention, and one organization that was particularly attentive was the Robert Bass Group in Dallas. Shortly after the acquisition, the Bass Group began to acquire stock in Taft. When this became public knowledge, Carl Lindner, the well-known Cincinnati philanthropist and financial genius, approached me and expressed his concern that the Bass interests might take over our company and move it out of Cincinnati. He indicated that he would like to begin acquiring shares in our company to forestall this possibility. Once Carl and his group entered the picture, a bidding war developed between his company and the Bass Group, and, although we in management did not want to sell the company, the price being offered became so high that our legal responsibilities gave us no alternative but to support the sale of the company.

Let me explain this in more detail, because you might wonder why we in the management group didn't mount a strong effort to repel the takeover. The answer is simple though sad. Once the Bass and Lindner groups started bidding, everyone tended to lose sight of underlying values and became absorbed in over-bidding the other guy. When the Bass group started to acquire stock the price was around $50. When it became publicly known that they were buying, the stock price rose to around $62 a share. It was at that point that the Lindner group moved into the picture. As the price of our stock moved above $100 a share, I sat down with our senior management group and told them to determine what price a management-led group could afford to pay without risking over-paying and putting our limited personal resources at risk. They came back a few days later and told me that we could probably go as high as $120 per share but to offer anything above that would be foolhardy. Unfortunately, the bidding war took the price past $120 per share quickly and never looked back! When the final price reached $157 per share, we in the management group were squarely up against a legal doctrine—"fiduciary duty." We owed our shareholders a legal duty to accept what we believed to be the best price available, even if it meant losing control of the company. So, reluctantly we supported the sale of the company. Though we had deep regrets (and still do) that it had come to this, it is even clearer in retrospect that we did the only thing we could have possibly done.

Thus, in 1988, the Lindner group acquired the Taft Broadcasting Company.

The Company and Its People

MY YEARS AT Taft Broadcasting comprised the largest segment of my professional career. We had a phenomenal group of people in the company, at all levels, and we had a great time. As has been true whatever I have done and wherever I have been, I have been privileged to work with good people. As I point out repeatedly, no one has success without a strong "supporting cast." This has been true for me in each of my "careers." It was certainly true at Taft Broadcasting Company where, over a period of more than twenty years, I had a great group of executives, male and female, supporting me. It would be unfair for me to single out particular individuals because there were so many of them, and I don't know how I would ever pick and choose those to mention. I must, however, make two exceptions and mention Dudley Taft and George Castrucci. Dudley, the son of the founder of Taft Broadcasting Company, was a young lawyer with the Washington, D.C., firm of Koteen & Burt when his father was killed in November of 1967. Dudley later joined Taft Broadcasting Company and worked his way through a variety of roles, and we named him president of the company, my number-two guy. From the beginning, Dudley and I were friends and worked well together. But what is interesting and, I think, unique is Dudley's attitude as a member of the executive team. He could easily have felt entitled to run the company, and he could just as easily have taken advantage of the fact that his name was "on the door." He could have resented me for sitting in "his father's chair." He never did this and simply let his ability and his personality speak for themselves. He was an enormous asset to me and a credit to his father and his family. Our relationship was briefly strained during the Bass/Lindner battle for control of our company. Dudley, quite understandably, made a bid of his own for the company, but it was soon over-bid in the heat of the battle. I respected and admired his position, and I think he understood mine. We remain good friends and always will.

George Castrucci was Taft's chief financial officer for many years and succeeded me as CEO. He provided me with sound financial and business counsel and was particularly highly regarded by our financial advisors and security analysts.

The friendships and respect generated among our people have led us to have a biannual reunion of the senior management group in Cincinnati. It is always well attended and a continuing reminder to all of us of the great years we enjoyed together. I think one of the nicest things anyone ever said to me was when a Cincinnati friend said, "Do you realize that everyone in town wants to work for your company!" This may have been a bit exaggerated but I loved it.

Hanna-Barbera

Unquestionably the most "famous" part of Taft Broadcasting was Hanna-Barbera. In 1965, while I was still practicing law and representing Taft Broadcasting Company, the company had the opportunity to acquire Hanna-Barbera Productions. Taft owned the maximum number of broadcast properties then permitted by the Federal Communications Commission and determined that a primary area for expansion would be companies producing content for broadcast. Hanna-Barbera was seeking to be acquired, and it seemed a perfect fit for us. I made several trips to Los Angeles with Hub Taft and our investment bankers to negotiate and complete the acquisition.

I was in seventh heaven when we decided to buy Hanna-Barbera. I loved animation and I loved Hanna-Barbera, and here I was meeting with the great men themselves to negotiate the acquisition. Bill Hanna and Joe Barbera were represented by their agent, Jess Morgan, who became one of my very good friends and later served on the Taft Broadcasting board. Most of the meetings were held in a bungalow at the Beverly Hills Hotel. This in itself was culture shock to this small-town Ohio boy. With lush grounds, opulent accommodations, the world-famous Polo Lounge, and a constant stream of celebrities, it was very hard to keep my mind on matters legal!

The hardest time I had keeping my "legal bearing" came when I went to the Beverly Hills Hotel for one of our negotiating sessions, this time to meet with one of the senior partners in the large investment banking firm that represented Hanna-Barbera. He had asked me to meet him at his bungalow at the hotel. I appeared at the scheduled hour at the door and rang the bell. The door opened, and I was met by a stunningly beautiful woman in an equally stunning dressing gown. I quickly said that I must be in the wrong place, but she assured me that this was the right place and that the gentleman I was to meet was expecting me. I went in and heard a shout from the bedroom, "Charlie, come on in." When I went in the bedroom he was also in his dressing gown and was sitting up in bed eating breakfast. I suggested that it might be better if I came back later but he insisted that we could go right ahead with our negotiations. I obviously couldn't walk out, so I sat in an easy chair in the bedroom, opened my briefcase, and we began to talk. My concentration was further shaken when the young lady lay alongside him on the bed and listened intently to our conversation. This was a scene that could have been part of a Hollywood movie starring Clark Gable and Carole Lombard! (With me being played by somebody like Percy Kilbride.) Here were these two handsome people lying on the bed in the elegant bungalow with this young lawyer in his three-button Brooks Brothers suit sitting primly in the chair with his briefcase and papers on his lap.

It was, without doubt, the strangest negotiating environment that I ever found myself in before or since. But, we made the deal! Hanna-Barbera became part of Taft Broadcasting, and I began a life-long friendship with Bill Hanna and Joe Barbera, two of the most talented and engaging men I have ever known. Hundreds (probably thousands) of books and articles have been written about Bill and Joe and Hanna-Barbera, and it is not necessary—or indeed possible—for me to add significantly to this material. However, because we were such close friends I think a few stories will give you a better glimpse of these remarkable men.

First of all, they were successful and famous even before Hanna-Barbera was formed. They were cartoonists at the MGM Studios where they created the classic *Tom and Jerry* cartoon, which won a number of Academy Awards. Though it is now hard to imagine, MGM decided in 1957 to close its animation studio, apparently not seeing a strong future in animation. So, Bill and Joe were out of work at a critical point in their lives. They managed to scrape together enough money to open their own studio. They had a bit of money themselves, and the rest came from Harry Cohn, the legendary head of Columbia Pictures, and a well-known Hollywood director George Sidney. As always, Harry Cohn was a shrewd bargainer, and, in return for his investment, Hanna-Barbera agreed to distribute its product through Screen Gems, Columbia Pictures' distribution arm. This deal lasted for many years and was very lucrative for Screen Gems. At the same time, they did an outstanding job of handling the Hanna-Barbera product.

Success came quickly. Bill and Joe created and perfected a technique called "limited animation." This was exactly what the phrase implies—the animators drew far fewer frames (called cels) than the classic Disney animation required. The theory was that, while people loved Disney's intricate animation, entertaining and funny shows could be created by limiting the amount of animation and, as a result, significantly reduce the cost of production. This latter point was critical in the equation because limited animation could be produced at a price that would be attractive to the major television networks.

The first cartoon turned out by the studio was *Ruff and Reddy*. After that came *Huckleberry Hound, Yogi Bear, Quick Draw McGraw,* and many others. At one point Hanna-Barbera was responsible for some 80 percent of all animation seen on the three networks on Saturday morning. And, greater things were still ahead with the creation of *The Flintstones, The Jetsons,* and *Scooby Doo,* to name just a few.

The partnership of Bill Hanna and Joe Barbera was a very unique one. First of all, it lasted for some fifty years, a phenomenon in a town where fifty days would be a lengthy partnership! Moreover, it brought together two men who were very different in many ways. Indeed, I believe that is precisely why the partnership survived and prospered for so long. Joe Barbera had a great explanation for the longevity of the partnership. In receiving an award from the Academy of Television Arts and Sciences, Joe commented that many people had asked him over the years why the partnership had lasted so long. He said that he was going to reveal the real reason. He said, "The first week we were together we had a huge fight. We haven't spoken since!"

While obviously this was a great line from Joe, the truth is even more interesting. Although both men were immensely talented, it is hard to imagine two more different individuals. Joe grew up in New York City and was the consummate "city boy." He loved the glamour of Hollywood and show business. He and his wife, Sheila, moved in the same social circles with Zsa Zsa Gabor and James and Pamela Mason. I once asked Joe to describe himself in one sentence. He smiled at me and said, "I like room service." What a wonderful response.

Bill Hanna on the other hand was an outdoorsman. His family moved a lot when Bill was young and almost always lived in areas where he could indulge his passion for the outdoors. He was very much into scouting and became an Eagle Scout. He and his wife, Vi, lived their entire married lives in the same modest home that they built in North Hollywood and chose not to be part of the Hollywood "scene." Bill's passion, other than the outdoors, was music. He had a beautiful tenor voice and was part of a barbershop quartet that competed nationally. He used these musical talents to help write many of the songs for the company's cartoons, including *The Flintstones* theme song.

It was this very difference in these two men that allowed the partnership to endure and prosper. They simply did not get in each other's way. Joe was the artist and gagman as well as the "pitch" man for selling their product to the networks—and, by the way, the best I have ever seen! Bill, on the other hand, was the production genius and would see that the ideas generated by Joe and his staff reached the screen. Most of their careers came before computer animation, and the process of creating an animated show was tedious and demanding. It was in a very real sense a "hand art." Individual scenes were hand painted on cels, individually photographed, and then put together in the form of a continuum. This was hard enough, but the process was made even more difficult by the need to precisely time the dialogue and music to the sequence of scenes. This is why animation, in its traditional sense, was so expensive. The genius of Bill and Joe was to limit this whole process without affecting the story or quality.

Naturally, when a company like Taft Broadcasting Company acquired a creative enterprise like Hanna-Barbera, there were questions about the possible difficulty of managing creative talent. Happily, this turned out to be no problem at all. Bill and Joe were just plain good guys and became part of our company with enthusiasm and grace. The people in our other divisions—television, radio, and theme parks—loved Bill and Joe. They were a genuine asset to our company, not just financially, but personally as well. We had a meeting of our senior executives each year, and Bill and Joe always attended and were very much part of the gang. The Hanna-Barbera studio on Cahuenga Boulevard in Hollywood was a busy place. But, it was also a very happy place. I have not done a scientific study, but I truly believe that animators live longer than most of the rest of the human race. Bill lived to be ninety-one, Joe to ninety-five, and there are many other examples. If this is true, it's no coincidence. I firmly believe that laughter is good for your health and creating laughter is probably even better!

Speaking of healing laughter, Bill and Joe came up with an idea for a "Laugh Room" in several children's hospitals. The rooms were filled with funny cartoon drawings, and the television played endless funny cartoons. The doctors said the results were wonderful. The children loved the room, and it definitely seemed to help them with their problems.

There may have been another reason the Hanna-Barbera studio was a happy place. One day an actor who was the voice of a popular cartoon character was expressing his unhappiness about something. One of the studio executives said, "I'm sorry if you're not happy, but since you are only an animated character, if you become too obstreperous all we need to do is erase you!" Sobering thought!

One last line that I have never forgotten. One day at lunch, the subject turned to the animator's place in the Hollywood firmament. It was generally concluded that animators were respected for their talent, but one of the guys pointed out a significant negative. Producers and directors gain the favors of beautiful young starlets by simply saying, "Honey, I can get you into pictures." Our colleague said that somehow the women weren't as excited when you said, "Honey, I can get you into cartoons!" However that may be, it was a very upbeat bunch, and our involvement with Hanna-Barbera was nothing but happy!

The Jack Nicklaus Sports Center

Another nationally known part of our company was what we originally called the Jack Nicklaus Sports Center at Kings Island. The complex consisted of an 18-hole championship course and a 9-hole executive course, all designed by Jack. Building a golf course was not part of our original plan for the Kings Island complex. However, sometimes things happen for odd reasons. When Interstate 71 was built, it cut through large sections of farmland in Warren County, Ohio. When we acquired the land needed to build Kings Island, one of the parcels included a piece of land (more than three hundred acres) on the other side of the interstate highway. We really didn't have any interest in it but were compelled to buy it to get the bigger parcel on which to build the amusement park. We decided to build a golf course on this property, and Jack Nicklaus, an Ohio boy, was at the peak of his playing career and just beginning to design golf courses. Choosing Jack as the architect was an easy choice: he didn't disappoint. He designed and built a good, playable public golf course, which was precisely what we wanted. Over the years the course hosted PGA, LPGA, and Champions Tour events, making it, I believe, the only public course in the country that hosted tournaments on all three major tours.

I have many happy memories of the golf course at the Nicklaus Center. Two that stand out involve two well-known personalities—Johnny Bench and Evel Knievel. One day I was playing in an outing at the Sports Center in a group that included Johnny Bench, the great Cincinnati Reds Hall of Fame catcher. Johnny is a superb golfer and can hit the ball out of sight, literally! We were having a very pleasant round when we came to a hole where out in the fairway was a stake in the ground that indicated the hole was a long-drive contest hole. Here's how a long-drive contest works: One particular hole is chosen as the contest hole. If, on that hole, you hit a drive that you think might be in the running as the longest drive of the day on that hole, you walk out to a little placard that is attached to a stake in the ground. You write your name on the placard and put it back into the ground at the point where your drive came to rest. If, during the day, someone else in a group hits a drive that goes farther than yours, he or she writes his or her name on the placard and reinserts it where his or her ball ended up. So, at the end of the day you simply look at the last name on the list and that is the winner.

Johnny stepped up to the tee and said, "My reputation is at stake. I've got to fly that marker"—which he promptly did, his ball coming to rest quite a distance beyond the last best effort. He walked out, took the placard on the stake, and wrote "Johnny Bench" on it, then took it to the spot where his ball had come to rest and put it back in the ground.

When we finished the round, we came in and talked to my colleague Burch Riber, who was running the event, and Bench said, "Well, I think I won the long-drive contest." Burch looked at him blankly and said, "What long-drive contest?" Johnny said, "The one on number fifteen." Burch said, "We didn't have a long-drive contest." Johnny said, "What do you mean? There was a placard in the ground." Burch replied, "That must be from the other group that's having an outing out here today. And, by the way, they're having awards and cocktails in the next parlor." The rest of us are all breaking up with laughter, and I said, "Bench, you signed a placard for the other outing, and some guy is in there right now saying 'who the hell wrote Johnny Bench's name on this thing—this is ridiculous.' You've got to go in there and explain what happened and apologize to those people." Of course, we didn't really mean that, and Johnny had no intention of doing it. It was a harmless mistake. I'm sure the rightful winner got his due, and we all had a great laugh with, and on, Johnny.

Another "happening" at Kings Island is worth sharing. Kings Island had a huge parking lot. Daredevil Evel Knievel approached us wanting to do one of his famous motorcycle bus-jumps in the parking lot. I don't recall now how many buses he planned to jump, but it was a lot! We liked the idea because we knew it would draw large crowds and give national publicity to Kings Island.

So the deal was arranged. Evel came to town and spent a week or so before the jump getting ready. One day, after I'd gotten to know him fairly well, he said he wanted to play some golf. (He was a very good golfer.) I agreed and suggested that we play at our Jack Nicklaus course right across the interstate highway from Kings Island. Evel thought that was fine and we agreed to meet the next morning. That night I was speaking to a friend and told him that I planned to play with Evel the next morning. He warned me that Evel was a big bettor and would bet on almost anything, and he added, "His bets are not small!" The following morning the course was a little sloppy because it had rained during the night. But, it was quite playable and so we teed it up and were on our way. After decent drives on the first hole, each of our second shots into the green plugged in mud in front of the green—four or five yards short of the putting surface. As we walked toward the green, Evel turned to me and said, "I'll bet you a thousand dollars that my ball has more mud on it than yours." I was speechless, but managed finally to say, "Evel, I'm not a betting man, and I'm certainly not a good enough golfer to bet you. Let's just have fun today." We did have fun and I kept my wallet in my pocket. By the way, Evel went on to make the bus-jump on national television in front of some twenty-five thousand people. He was an incredible guy, and I'll never forget the time we spent together.

The Jack Nicklaus Sports Complex also included a tennis stadium. It had a modest beginning, but has over the years grown into a superb facility that seats over 11,400 people in center court and is the home to one of the most prestigious tennis tournaments in the world, the ATP Masters Series-Western & Southern Open.

There is an interesting story behind this tennis event and the stadium itself. There was a professional tennis tournament held in Cincinnati in the 1960s that was a good event but not a particularly prominent one. Its sponsor, Bob Harpenau (who was a good friend of mine), decided he would no longer stage the tournament. The organizers of the event needed a new home and approached me to see if Taft Broadcasting Company could help. I agreed that Taft would build a temporary five-thousand-seat stadium at its old amusement park on the Ohio River, Coney Island. We did this and the event was a big success from the beginning and continued to grow over the next couple of years. At this point, working with the ATP (Association of Tennis Professionals), we agreed to build a permanent stadium at the Jack Nicklaus Sports Center. During the course of this process we became close with the top executives of the ATP, Donald Dell and Bob Briner, who, along with the players, were in the process of reorganizing and restructuring the tour. We reached an agreement by which we would share proceeds from the event at Kings Island with the ATP to establish and fund a pension plan (which, amazingly, they did not have at that time). Later, as the restructuring of the tour was finalized and a limited number of so-called Super Series events were designated, our tournament became one of those coveted Super Series—now called ATP World Tour Masters.* This was done largely because we had such a good relationship with the ATP and had helped them start their pension program. As a result of a new stadium, a great location, and the Super Series designation, the event has grown in size and prestige ever since. It is one of the best in the world.

I don't want to leave this subject without commenting on the genuine pleasure it was for me to make this arrangement with Donald Dell, who remains a good friend to this day. At that time he was the head of ProServ, a firm that represented many athletes, especially in the tennis world, and he was one of the founders and certainly the leader of the players' association. Donald had been a Davis Cup player and captain, and in his own right was a formidable force in the growth of professional tennis. I doubt if everyone who dealt with Donald found the experience "fun." He was a very tough negotiator and direct and blunt in his approach. However, we developed a very solid relationship and it produced results. As I mentioned, we remain in touch and have been his guests at the U.S. Open on several occasions. One memory particularly brings a smile to my face. Donald and his wife, Carole, attended our daughter Allison's wedding in Jackson Hole in 1997, and Donald played golf for what I think was the first time in his life. As with many fine athletes, he took to the game, and I hope he still plays now and then.

---

*Coveted because the top players are required to play in this category of events.

I MAY MAKE an enemy by telling this next story, but I hope not! I will begin by saying that Tom Callahan was—and is—one of the finest sports writers I have ever seen, and I've seen a lot of them. I got to know Tom when he was a sports writer for the *Cincinnati Enquirer*. He went on to be senior writer at *Time* magazine and sports columnist at the *Washington Post*, and is a recipient of the National Headliner Award. He also wrote the *New York Times* best seller *Johnny U.* Now, after having said that, I can't imagine that he will get angry with me for this story.

As we were completing the course, getting ready to open in the summer of 1972, one day Jack Nicklaus told me, "Charlie, we're going to have a PGA Tour event next year on this course." I almost had a fatal heart attack. I said, "Jack, this is a public golf course, not designed for tournament play, and we are not ready—the grass and the trees are barely coming up. You can't be serious." Jack replied, "I am serious. Any golf course can be a tournament golf course if you let the rough grow high, cut the fairways narrow, and make the greens fast. He went on to say, "Beman [Deane Beman, the PGA Tour Commissioner at the time] owes me one, and we're going to have a PGA event." And, we did.

I might say parenthetically that we had a PGA Tour event for four years, and it was a genuine success (Jack won it in one of those years). At the end of four years we decided to change tours because we had the opportunity to host the LPGA Championship, one of that tour's majors. We had very good reason to move from the PGA Tour to the LPGA. Our place on the PGA Tour schedule was in October. The weather normally was good, but the competitive environment in the Cincinnati sports world was not good. What finally motivated us to make a move was the year the Cincinnati Bengals were playing the Cleveland Browns and the Cincinnati Reds were in the World Series—on the weekend of the tournament! Talk about a tough competitive environment!

So now the stage is set for my Callahan story. Tom, when he learned that we were going to have a PGA Tour event on the brand-new course, was not impressed. He took a very dim view of hosting a PGA Tour event on a public course that had barely opened and felt that it would be an embarrassment for the players. Naturally, I was not pleased with Tom's attitude or the publicity that it generated. I knew that our golf course was better than Tom gave it credit for. So, I had an idea—a devilish one to be sure.

I called my friend Bill Keating, the publisher of the *Cincinnati Enquirer*, and told him that I would like to have Tom play in the Pro-Am before the tournament and that he could do so as a sponsor's guest. I can't remember whether I let Bill in on my little plan or not, but in any event, Bill agreed that Tom would play. What no one knew at the time was that I would load the draw so Tom would be paired with Jack Nicklaus. I casually let Nicklaus know before the Pro-Am that Tom had not been too kind to the course in a recent article. Jack said, "Is that so? Well, let's see how today goes."

Tom did not have one of his best days. Being paired with Jack turned him into glue (as it would anyone) and his score was, shall we say, on the high side. Tom was simply overcome by being paired with the greatest player in the history of the game, and Tom's game suffered from that exposure. Tom was good-natured about it, but admitted later both publicly and privately that he had underestimated the course and that it was certainly considerably more of a test than he had realized.

So there, Tom, you have my little secret. You probably knew this or learned of it a long time ago. But I think we all turned out better for it, and I believe to this day that you are one of the best sports writers ever!

Conducting a Taft annual shareholders meeting. The person in charge of flowers got a bit carried away.

Dudley Taft and I show off a rendering of Kings Island shortly before it opened.

Dudley Taft, George Castrucci, Stan Ausbrooks, and me taking an early ride on the first Kings Island roller coaster.

With Carl Lindner and Johnny Bench at a party at the farm of the "Ribs King," Ted Gregory.

Taft Broadcasting sponsored the LPGA Championship at its Kings Island course. Nancy Lopez won in 1978. The prize money was $22,500. Today it is $375,000!

Playing golf at Kings Island with Dinah Shore and my old pal Bill Keating, publisher of the Cincinnati Enquirer.

Real fans paint their faces!

Bob Hope and many other celebrities visited Kings Island and the Jack Nicklaus Sports Center.

With President Nixon and Bill Morton at the National Football Foundation dinner.

Here I am with Bob Lintz, Carl Lindner, "Ribs King" Ted Gregory, and Dodgers' manager Tommy Lasorda.

Jack Nicklaus showing the members of the Cincinnati Commercial Club the fine points of the game on the tenth tee at the Camargo Club.

Receiving an award from Jack Nicklaus with an unexpected guest.

Taft Broadcasting and Jack Nicklaus worked together on many projects.

The river entrance to Coney Island. A very long time ago!

SPEAKING OF BILL KEATING and golf, one experience is, I think, truly unique. Bill once invited me to be his guest at the member-guest tournament at the Cincinnati Country Club. Like most such events it was divided into five nine-hole rounds, each against a different opponent. Bill and I managed to lose every round, probably the only pairing to do so. At the awards dinner, after all the prizes had been awarded, the master of ceremonies announced that there was one additional prize: Bill Keating and Charlie Mechem had been named the most "congenial twosome." This brought a lot of laughs and taunts but we accepted the "award" enthusiastically.

The Ribs King

Whenever I think about the Jack Nicklaus Sports Center I think about Ted Gregory, the famous "Ribs King" of Cincinnati and one of the great characters I have ever been privileged to know. Ted was Greek and when he and his charming wife, Mattie, came to Cincinnati, they started a restaurant that ultimately was called the Montgomery Inn. Everything that the Montgomery Inn served was terrific, but it soon became best known for its ribs. They were and still are the best! What really made the Montgomery Inn famous was that Bob Hope often stopped by when he was in town. He was so taken by the ribs that for many years he had them sent to his homes in Los Angeles and Palm Springs to serve at dinners and parties.

Ted owned a farm adjacent to the Jack Nicklaus Sports Center, and during the years when we hosted the LPGA Championship, Ted and Mattie would entertain the LPGA players at the farm. A lot of tour caddies went to the Montgomery Inn and, during my years as LPGA Commissioner, I had a ribs party each year for the caddies. We would have the ribs shipped to one of our tournament sites and it was always a great party.

Over the years Ted and I became very good friends. I would see him whenever we went to the restaurant and also ran into him frequently in downtown Cincinnati. He always had a lighter on a loop around his neck as a ready light for the big cigar that was his constant companion. Although I have scores of happy memories of times with Ted, my favorite has to do with his plan to build another restaurant on the Ohio riverfront between the Reds' and Bengals' stadiums. One day when I ran into Ted in downtown Cincinnati, he told me he hoped to build the restaurant but some in his family were very skeptical of the project and were understandably nervous that it would not be successful, given all the competition it would face. Ted was concerned that he would not be able to persuade them that it was the right thing to do. Some weeks later I ran into him again and asked about the status of the project. He smiled and said that it was going forward. I told him how pleased I was and wondered how he had overcome the family's concerns. His answer was one I never forgot. He said, "I decided to have a family meeting. The vote was 8 to 1 against building the restaurant. But, I was the 1—so we're gonna do it!" As usual, Ted was right on the money. The restaurant has been a huge success. One final note about the Gregorys: Mattie was as understated as Ted was overstated. She was obviously his anchor and played a very important role in the success of their businesses. I'm sure Ted would be the first one to point out that he was a very lucky guy to have married Mattie!

There were many benefits to having Ted Gregory as a friend. Among them was the opportunity to meet Bob Hope. As I mentioned earlier, Bob was a big fan of Montgomery Inn ribs and made occasional visits to Cincinnati to do benefits or appearances. One day he was at the Jack Nicklaus Sports Center and it fell to me to ride around the course with him in a golf cart, which, of course, I was thrilled to do. He was very gracious and complimentary of what was going on. We stopped to talk to people, including people taking pictures and press people. At one point, we were talking to a group when I made some remark that elicited a great deal of laughter. I don't remember what it was, but I do remember a big laugh from everybody. Bob turned to me and said without cracking a smile, "I tell the jokes around here!" I think he was kidding—but I'm not entirely sure!

Jack and Barbara Nicklaus

For me, the greatest thing about Taft's involvement in the Jack Nicklaus Sports Center was the opportunity it gave me to meet and get to know Jack and his amazing wife, Barbara. Allow me to pause in my narrative to share some of my favorite memories of Jack and Barbara.

When I was first approached about becoming Commissioner of the LPGA it was mid-1990. Judy Dickinson was then serving as president of the LPGA Players Association, and Judy called me to say they were looking for a new Commissioner and my name had been suggested. I told her I was flattered, but wasn't sure I wanted to be Commissioner at this point in my life. However, I promised that I would certainly consider it. One thing led to another and ultimately I was offered the job.

I wanted to be sure this position was right for me and, just as importantly, that I would be looked upon favorably in the golf world. So, I resolved to talk to a few people I thought would give me some straight answers. One of these people was Jack Nicklaus. I went down to Jack's office in North Palm Beach and explained to him that I had the opportunity to become Commissioner of the LPGA and wondered if he thought it made sense for me to accept the position. Jack smiled, looked me right in the eye (as he always does), and said, "I think it's a great idea, Charlie. In fact, I'm the one who recommended you!" I was stunned. I had no idea he was involved. Needless to say, this had a fairly substantial bearing on my decision to take the job!*

Now for the second Nicklaus story. In September 1982, I asked Jack if he would come to the Camargo Club, the great golf course near Cincinnati designed in 1923 by Seth Raynor, and be part of an outing of the Commercial Club, a businessperson's club of which I was a member. Jack said he would be glad to do so and so it was arranged. I picked Jack up at the airport and as we were driving to Camargo, he reminisced about earlier times when he had been there. He admired and respected this splendid golf course. He had qualified on several

---

*My good friend Burch Riber, I later learned, had also recommended me.

occasions at Camargo for the U.S. Amateur and U.S. Open, but it had been some years since he had been at the course. Incredibly, he could remember virtually all the holes. There's one hole with a white mailbox about 325 yards from the tee, which makes it a good target line for your drive. As Jack was reminiscing about the course he said, "Is that mailbox still there on number thirteen?" I had to struggle to keep the car on the road. I had never seen anything quite like his recall of a golf course—especially one he had not seen for many years. But I have since learned that this is not uncommon for Jack, and I guess none of us who know him should be surprised.

Now, the "rest of the story," as Paul Harvey would say. Later that day, after all the players had finished their rounds, we gathered around Camargo's tenth tee, which is quite near the clubhouse, for Jack's clinic. By this time most of the members were enjoying a cocktail, and, naturally, a few members were enjoying more than a few. When Jack demonstrated how you should always be able to get a sand wedge up in the air, he pointed out that the flange of the club fit quite nicely under the golf ball, so that if you hit it properly, the ball would go high in the air, just as a sand wedge was supposed to. At this point one of the fellows in the front row said with slurred speech, "Yeah, that all sounds great, but it won't work on hardpan!"* Jack turned to a waiter who was walking by with a steel serving tray, one of those almost indestructible trays waiters use to carry drinks to and from a crowd. Jack asked to have the tray. He put it on the ground and proceeded to hit five or six balls, beautiful, lofted sand wedges off the surface of the steel serving tray. Then he turned to the somewhat embarrassed questioner and said, "Is that hardpan enough?"

In the "old days" (circa the 1970s and 1980s) Jack and Barbara Nicklaus had a dinner party at their home in Florida for Jack's "partners."

---

*Hardpan is defined in http://golf.about.com as follows: "Any spot in fairways, rough or other playing areas other than hazards where the ground is very hard due to compacting of the soil. With a hardpan lie, the golfer has a difficult time getting the club under the ball to take a divot. The club, upon striking the hard ground will often bounce up, resulting in many shots being 'thin.'"

These were people and companies that did business with the Nicklaus Companies. Taft Broadcasting Company was one of these companies, and Marilyn and I attended the dinner whenever we could.

At one such affair, Taft Broadcasting was honored as "Partner of the Year," and I received a plaque and silver trophy recognizing our efforts. After dinner, Barb pulled Jack and me aside and said, "I want to get a picture of you two holding the cup," but then Barb said, "I don't know where I put my camera—I am never without my camera, but I simply can't find it." So, she looked around and spotted another guest—a very pleasant Japanese man—who, of course, had a camera.

Barbara persuaded the man to take a picture of Jack and me, even though he spoke no English and we no Japanese. As Jack and I posed for the picture, holding the trophy, another Japanese gentleman stepped into the picture with us. As politely as we could, we tried to make him understand that only Jack and I should be in this particular picture. He stepped aside, but the man with the camera shook his head and refused to take the picture unless and until the other Japanese gentleman was part of it. It soon became clear that the picture was not going to be taken unless all three of us were in it. The three of us posed, and the picture was taken. When that was accomplished, the man with the camera was happy to take a picture of Jack and me together holding the trophy. The puzzle of the "third man" was solved before the evening ended.

It turned out that the third man who kept stepping into the picture was the boss of the man with the camera, and the man with the camera was not about to take a picture of Jack Nicklaus that didn't include his boss! As far as he was concerned, I was not even there! On my office wall, to this day, are both pictures—one with Jack and me and our new Japanese friend, and the other with just Jack and me with the trophy. We both are laughing as we remember what we have just been through to get that photograph made! I smile again each time I view these two pictures side by side.

We did a number of joint projects with Jack and his companies, including the development of the Jack Nicklaus Sports Center at Kings Island, partnering with him in the acquisition of the MacGregor Golf Company, and the production and distribution of the incredibly successful *Golf My Way* video in 1983. The idea for the production of an instructional video came from the agile mind of Ken Bowden, who for many years was Jack's right-hand man on all the publications and books Jack has published. Ken approached me and we discussed how Taft Broadcasting could be involved in the video. The arrangements began to take shape: Ken would write all the material, and Taft's Worldvision subsidiary would handle production and distribution. Kevin O'Sullivan, who ran Worldvision, was a golf fanatic and greeted this idea very enthusiastically.

We were convinced that we really were onto something, and we were optimistic that the product would be successful. It certainly was! The video broke all sales records and has become the most popular golf instructional video of all time. It has now been premastered into DVD format, a new app has been created so the digital application of the original reaches the new generation, and it is currently being formatted in a virtual golf simulator. I'm told that golfers like Greg Norman and K. J. Choi credit *Golf My Way* with helping them learn the game. There had been a few golf videos done by that time, but nothing of the scope we planned and certainly not by someone of Jack's stature. Our problem turned out to be Jack himself! Although I think he supported the project, he had difficulty seeing how he could work it into his incredibly intense schedule. At times it seemed he was leaning towards proceeding, and then he'd back off because of the time commitment it obviously required. One day Ken called me and said, "Charlie, I can't get Jack to commit to the project. You're the only one who might be able to persuade him to go forward." I told Kenny that I was flattered that he felt that way, but he and I both knew there was only one person in the world who could persuade Jack to do something he was not enthusiastic about. That person was Barbara Nicklaus. We needed her help!

So, we did a little plotting and planning. I noted from Jack's schedule that he would be playing in Akron, Ohio, at the Firestone Golf Course and that he would be there in just a few weeks. I suggested to Ken that Marilyn and I have dinner with Jack and Barbara and that, at the appropriate time, I would bring up the subject of the video and urge him to get on with it. If we strategized properly and explained to Barbara what we were doing, we hoped she would become our ally and urge Jack to go ahead.

The dinner at Firestone was arranged and we had a very pleasant conversation about a variety of things. I eventually turned the conversation to the subject of the instructional video and told Jack that we really needed to get going on it. Jack, once again, said he loved the idea but just didn't have time to do it. I tried to explain that I felt it would be highly successful because there really hadn't been a video up to that time by anyone who commanded the respect Jack did, and I was convinced that golfers would be eager to buy and use the video. Jack was still hesitant. At the absolutely perfect moment, Barbara spoke up. She said that she understood Jack's concerns and observed that she knew better than anyone how busy he was. But, what troubled her was that if Jack didn't get moving on the project somebody else would beat him to it. (Author's note: The reader can surely guess who "somebody else" might be!) Her comment sealed the deal. Filming started very soon thereafter.

There is another aspect of this project that I particularly remember. We were meeting in New York City in an effort to persuade a large company headquartered there to become involved in the video. Naturally, part of the discussion involved how the video should be priced. My memory is that a few instructional videos produced at that time were priced in the thirty-five to forty-dollar range. There was naturally some sentiment in the meeting to set our price somewhere in that vicinity. Jack, who attended the meeting, insisted that was a mistake. He pointed out that he was determined to make this an outstanding product and that its price should reflect that fact. He reminded us all that not only do people often judge a product by how it's priced, but usually associate a higher price with a higher-quality product. So, as I remember, we priced the first video at around eighty or ninety dollars—and the sales were sensational!

I had this very valuable lesson brought home to me again in a project at Kings Island. We concluded that it was a shame to have such a marvelous facility idle for eight months out of the year, and one of the ideas to remedy this problem was to open the park for several weeks before and after Christmas. We called it Winterfest and decorated the park beautifully in the Christmas spirit. We had a meeting to decide what admission price we should charge. Since we had no idea how popular Winterfest would be, there was some thought that we should allow people to enter free and content ourselves with making money on purchases they made once inside. However, someone in the meeting made the point that if you charged nothing you would be giving the impression that the attraction was not worth very much. Instead, by charging a few dollars you give the opposite impression, namely, that this is something worth paying to see. I have seen this situation a number of times over the years, and there is no question in my mind that charging a fair price reflects quality and enhances sales.

My friendship with Jack led to my being invited to become a member of the Captains Club of the Memorial Tournament, Jack's event held each year at Muirfield Village Golf Club in Dublin, Ohio. The club is made up of a number of men and women who have been deeply involved in the golf world. They are all better known and better qualified than I, and it has been a humbling experience for me to be part of the group. We gather each year during the tournament and have a meeting and dinner during which a number of significant issues are addressed and the honoree for the following year's tournament is selected. I think it inappropriate to discuss the subjects we consider, as

I believe these discussions should be private and confidential. Having said this, I hope Jack and the other members will forgive me if I make an exception to tell two stories that are simply too good to keep!

The first story involves Jay Hebert, who was a member of the Captains Club and who was a very close friend of Gardner Dickinson, Judy's husband and my good friend from our Loxahatchee Club and LPGA days. (Much more later on these days.) Jay and Gardner were two of the great professional golfers of the 1950s and 1960s. Gardner became a wonderful friend of Marilyn's and mine as a result of the fact that his wife, Judy, was president of the LPGA Players Association during my first two years as Commissioner of the tour.

Jay and Gardner were very close friends and had played together a lot. One night at the Captains Club dinner we talked about Gardner, and Jay said, "Charlie, I'm going to tell you a story about Gardner. When you next see him I want you to ask him about what I'm about to tell you, and I will tell you right now what he will say. He will say, "You heard that from that goddamned Jay Hebert and it's absolutely not true—never happened."

The story went this way: The tour was playing on a course in the South during a hot, dry spell in August. The course had deep rough, and this was in the days when many courses were not irrigated. It was, therefore, incredibly dry. Gardner, according to Jay, became infuriated with a poor shot he had hit and threw his club high into the air in anger (even Gardner's dearest friends acknowledged that he had quite a temper). There apparently was a power line running parallel to this particular hole, and Gardner's club hit the power line, shorted it, and as the live wire fell to the ground the rough caught on fire and, according to Jay, it burned up a sizable part of the golf course.

When I got back to Loxahatchee, where we then lived and Gardner taught, I couldn't wait to see him, and when I did I said, "Gardner, I heard an interesting story about you recently. He said, "Oh, what's that?" I said, "It's about the time you set a golf course on fire." He looked at me and said almost exactly the words that Jay had predicted: "You heard that from that goddamned Hebert and it's a lie." Now, I have no idea what the real story is here, but it is such a great story that I want to believe it's true!

One final word about Gardner. He could be a curmudgeon and he did have a temper, but he was a fine player, one of the best teachers the game has ever known, and a wonderful husband to Judy and father to their twins. He died some years ago and we truly miss him.

At a Captains Club dinner only a couple of years ago, Andy O'Brien, the delightful and talented senior vice president of marketing, licensing, and communications for the Nicklaus Companies, reminded me that we were very close to the thirty-second anniversary of the famous "Duel in the Sun." Perhaps the most famous golf match in history, the Duel in the Sun took place in 1977 between Jack Nicklaus and Tom Watson at the Open Championship at Turnberry in Scotland. Tom Watson is also a member of the Captains Club and was present at the dinner. Andy wondered if I would ask Jack if he would like to say something about that momentous event. I told Andy that I was reluctant to do so unless Jack was comfortable with my bringing up the subject. Andy went back to Jack's table and spoke to him and then gave me the thumbs-up. At this point I said, "Ladies and gentlemen, I am reminded that we are approaching the thirty-second anniversary of the Duel in the Sun, and we have the two players who were involved here in our midst. Jack, would you like to say a word?" Jack's response was unforgettable. He said, "Sure, I lost. That's all I've got to say." Naturally, this brought much laughter. When the laughter settled down, Tom said, "Well, I won and I'm more than happy to talk about it." We did indeed talk about it, and these two great players were both humble and gracious in their recollections, as you might imagine. It was one of those unforgettable moments that you wish had been recorded or filmed.

One of the happiest memories I have of Jack is one that shows a facet of his character about which not enough has been said. One weekend during the fall, Marilyn and I were houseguests of Jack and Barbara at their home in North Palm Beach. Jack and I played golf early in the day, and when we got back to the house we sat in the family room and turned on a football game. (Jack is a great fan of all sports and continues to be a rabid Ohio State Buckeye supporter.) All but one of Jack and Barbara's five children live close by, and before long various and sundry grandchildren began to arrive. Soon there were four or five of them on Jack's lap, hanging around his neck or sitting close to his chair, all smiling and laughing and obviously happy to be close to grandpa. As I watched this scene unfold, I thought how different this image was from the image of total focus and seriousness that was his golf course persona. I don't think there is a more accurate gauge of people than how their grandkids act in their presence. It was a Jack Nicklaus that I wished the whole world could see. Jack and Barbara Nicklaus are among the most generous, caring, and compassionate people I have ever known. They support causes in both Florida and Ohio that do enormous good for many people, especially children.

The Taft Board of Directors

NO ACCOUNT OF my years at Taft Broadcasting would be complete without talking about our board of directors. In a word, it was an extraordinary group. It included several members of senior management and a very impressive group of "outside" members. These included Senator Robert Taft; former Secretary of Commerce Bill Verity; Margita White, the first female member of the Federal Communications Commission; Bill Rowe, the CEO of Fifth Third Bank Corporation; Roger Howe, the founder and brains behind US Precision Lens; and my old pal from Taft Stettinius & Hollister, Charlie Lindberg. There were three other board members who deserve special mention—David Ingalls, Charlie Taft, and Neil Armstrong.

David S. Ingalls

Mr. Ingalls was the largest shareholder in our company and had a distinguished and fascinating background. He was the first Naval Air ace in World War I and ultimately ended up a rear admiral.* He had been a great athlete at Yale and later became a lawyer and newspaper publisher. He took a very deep interest in our company and was vice chairman. Two stories stand out in my mind. Uncle Dave, as we called him, typically did not say much in board meetings, but when he did speak, everyone listened! At one board meeting shortly before our Kings Island amusement park was set to open, I was enthusiastic (perhaps too much so) in predicting the future success of the park. When I had finished my rosy forecast, Uncle Dave looked at me and said, "That all sounds fine, but I think the only thing you have proven so far is that you know how to spend money!" This elicited smiles and laughter around the table. I was a little embarrassed but had to admit he was right. Happily, my prediction came true, and Uncle Dave was as happy about that as anyone.

The second story involves a very famous figure in American history, Captain Eddie Rickenbacker, who was an American fighter ace in World War I and a Medal of Honor recipient. He was also a racecar driver and automotive designer as well as serving as the longtime head of Eastern Airlines. During one of our board meetings, my secretary, Mary Deller, came into the meeting and handed me a note. It was highly unusual for Mary to interrupt a board meeting so I was apprehensive as I opened the note. As I read it, I understood why Mary had interrupted. Captain Rickenbacker was in the studio of our Cincinnati TV station to do an interview on one of our daily talk shows. As two of the legendary World War I airmen, Uncle Dave and Captain Eddie, obviously were good friends, I turned to Uncle Dave and simply said, "I was just handed a note that Eddie Rickenbacker is in our studio

---

*I highly recommend googling David S. Ingalls. You will find fascinating accounts of his World War I aerial exploits.

downstairs." Without a word Uncle Dave jumped up and quickly left the room. The other board members were confused until I explained that, on the first floor of our building, there was about to be a reunion of two of the great combat pilots of World War I. Naturally, we all went downstairs to see the reunion.

Charles P. Taft

Charles P. Taft was a truly legendary figure. Son of President William Howard Taft, brother of "Mr. Republican" Senator Robert Taft, and a distinguished political figure in his own right, most especially as Mayor of Cincinnati, he was a progressive and visionary thinker. Charlie, as everyone called him, was also a great outdoorsman and his trademark was his small car with a canoe strapped to the top! He was wonderfully outgoing and charismatic. He served on the Taft Broadcasting Company board for a number of years, and when he reached our mandatory retirement age, we recognized him in all the appropriate ways. We invited him to continue to come to board meetings (a custom normally offered to retiring board members and virtually never accepted), and he continued to come to every meeting! Not only that—he continued to vote! No one—certainly not I—had the courage to tell him that he had no voting rights. As he grew older he didn't say much at board meetings, but one day he brought us up short. We were discussing programming at our various television stations, one of which was in Cincinnati and was Charlie's favorite station. In the middle of our discussion Charlie boomed out, "I don't care much what you do, just don't replace the *Love Boat!*" This apparently had become his favorite show, and you may be certain it remained on the air, at least in Cincinnati!

Neil Armstrong

I have been blessed to have many good friends, but none better than Neil Armstrong. We first met when Neil retired from NASA's space flight program and returned to the Cincinnati area to become a professor at the University of Cincinnati. He lived on a farm near Lebanon, Ohio, not far from where Taft was then building Kings Island. I learned from a friend that Neil was curious about Kings Island, so I invited him to join me for a tour of the construction. After meeting him, I was so impressed that I invited him to become a member of the Taft Board of Directors, and he said he would consider it. I went to his office to issue a formal invitation, and he asked me a number of penetrating questions, which confirmed my feeling that he would be a superb board member. He accepted and I was never disappointed. Every board should be lucky enough to have Neil helping them shape strategy and make decisions.

I have had countless "Neil moments," but the ones I want to recount have nothing to do with his worldwide fame as an astronaut or his performance as a member of our board. Instead, they are experiences that simply brought a smile to both of our faces.

I don't consider myself in Neil's class except in one respect—our shared passion for the game of golf. In that exasperating game we shared a common handicap: we were both 18s. We weren't that good; in fact, I always said we were "brothers in mediocrity." But did we ever have fun! On one particular day, things were not going well for Neil. Finally, he hit a really great shot. Without jumping up and down and throwing his arms in the air, as I might have done, he simply said quietly, "Well, that's one in a row!" On another day, for fun I proposed that we not only allow a mulligan on our drives on the first hole, but that we also allow a "traveling mulligan" to be used anywhere throughout the eighteen. The round progressed and on about the thirteenth or fourteenth hole, Neil missed a one-foot putt. As I was about to record his score, he said, "I believe I'll take my mulligan here." "Wait a minute," I protested, "you can't take your mulligan on the green!" Neil's response was terse: "You said it could be used any place and I just used it." I had no response. Once an engineer, always an engineer.

Neil and his wife and Marilyn and I used to go to dinner a lot when we lived in Cincinnati. Inevitably, when we would go to a restaurant, someone would pull me aside and say, "Charlie, would you ask Neil Armstrong if I could get his autograph?" And I would always do this if I knew the person and, obviously, if Neil didn't want to do it, he didn't. One night we went to a restaurant where I knew the maître d' very well. After we were seated, I excused myself, supposedly to go to the restroom, but instead pulled the maître d' aside. I said, "Look, let's have some fun. After a few minutes, come over to Neil, lean over, and whisper in his ear that several people in the restaurant would like to get Mr. Mechem's autograph and would Mr. Armstrong please ask Mr. Mechem if that is okay!" The maître d' pulled this off brilliantly, and Neil and the rest of us got a good laugh. Incidentally, no one really wanted my autograph!

I have always felt that an out-of-control ego is one of the most dangerous things that can befall anyone. Thanks to my family and my colleagues, I have always been surrounded by people who didn't let me take myself too seriously. Here's one of the best examples I can remember. I was playing in a wonderful celebrity golf outing, Bogie Busters, in Dayton. I was not a celebrity by any means, but I knew the organizers of the event and was invited to join in the fun. As I finished my round and walked off the eighteenth green, a young Boy Scout sitting near the green approached me, handed me a program, and asked for my autograph. I was naturally surprised but flattered, and I signed my name. The young man very politely said, "Thank you very much, sir." I replied, "You are certainly welcome, but it is I who should thank you. I am not often asked for my autograph." The young man said, "Oh, that's okay, sir. I was just waiting here for Neil Armstrong!"

I HAD THE great experience of giving tours of Kings Island to two of the world's best-known astronauts—Neil Armstrong and Wally Schirra.

Each produced a memorable line. When we arrived with Neil for his first visit, I told him that we had a lot of great rides and asked which ones he would like to try. Though his response was not as historic as his first words from the moon, I remember them just as well. He said with a smile and a twinkle in his eye, "Nothing too dangerous." Wally Schirra was one of the original crew of Gemini astronauts. As Wally and I strolled through the park, we passed a looping roller coaster that went forward through a wild series of dips and turns, then stopped and did the same thing in reverse! I asked Wally if he would like to try the ride, and he said, "No." I kidded him and told him I was amazed that, with everything he had done, he wouldn't ride this ride. He said, "You don't understand. In everything I've done in the space program, I was always going forward." None of this backwards stuff for Wally!

NEIL ARMSTRONG MAY be the most modest man, given the magnitude of his accomplishments, I have ever known. This is not a false modesty designed to create an image of a mysterious, unapproachable person. Rather, he simply regards the things he has done as things anyone with the proper background and training could also do. For example, when I asked him if he was apprehensive, troubled, or concerned on the Apollo XI moon shot, his answer was that he really was not. The astronauts had faith in their equipment, and they had trained exhaustively to accomplish precisely what they accomplished. In other words, they were simply doing exactly what they had expected to do.

ANOTHER EXAMPLE CAME when my friend Dudley Taft and I were talking to Neil about his days as a test pilot when he had flown practically everything that existed with wings—and sometimes without. Dudley, a very fine pilot himself, mentioned the craft known as the X-15, which always looked to me like a rocket with small wings. The pilot flew the craft to its apogee, at which point the fuel was exhausted. Thus, in order to land, the pilot needed to fly the plane in what is called "dead stick"— meaning that the plane needed to be flown and landed without any power, an extremely difficult procedure. Dudley remarked to Neil that flying such a craft back to a safe landing must have been a very harrowing experience. Neil answered simply, "Not really. You just couldn't make any mistakes." This was not said in a boastful way at all. Rather, it was just a statement of simple fact from someone who knew what he was doing.

EVERY YEAR FOR quite a few years, Marilyn and I traveled with three couples to various vacation spots. One year we spent a week in Tuscany. Among our traveling companions were Neil and his wife. I was always designated as the trip planner for reasons not entirely clear to me. However, I relished the task and was forever poring over guidebooks to find something fun and exciting to do every day.

As I was going through various options, I learned that the little town of Vinci—the birthplace of Leonardo—was a relatively short drive from where we were staying. Everybody agreed this was a place we should see, so we loaded up in our rented eight-passenger van and made our way to Vinci.

It was a charming little village with a small museum to honor its illustrious son. As we were touring the museum, we came upon a display of a number of Leonardo's inventions. The replicas were most unusual, made of wood, and, of course, much smaller than the originals. While we greatly admired what we were seeing, we really had no idea what the inventions were or how they worked.

But, our befuddlement didn't last very long. Neil began to describe each replica and explain how it worked. This went on for about ten minutes and was obviously fascinating. When he finished we turned around and were surprised to see twenty or thirty people behind us who had obviously listened to the explanations. I am convinced to this day that they had no idea who Neil was and simply assumed that he was a tour guide or an employee of the museum. With his characteristic modesty he made no effort to inform them of his "credentials."

Roger Howe

Roger and I had been very close friends for a very long time, and we both love to laugh. This story has to be one of my biggest laughs! Roger and I shared the same doctor who treated us for high cholesterol, and that doctor prescribed similar medication for both of us. I don't remember the name of the medication, but it was a small pill and was to be taken each night after dinner. One night Marilyn and I were at a dinner party at the Howes'. It was a wonderful party and the dinner was superb. The meal was topped off by a hot fudge sundae. When mine was set in front of me and I reached for the spoon to attack it, I noticed sitting next to the spoon was a cholesterol pill. Roger obviously wanted to be sure that the hot fudge sundae didn't do any damage. Undoubtedly, it was the most interesting dessert I have ever had.

Roger's sense of humor is engaging and offbeat. Here's a good example: When Roger and his wife, Joyce, were visiting us at our home in Jackson Hole, Wyoming, for our daughter Allison's wedding, we were standing on our back deck looking at the majestic and imposing Teton Range—a truly glorious sight! For those who have not seen the Tetons, they jut abruptly and sharply out of the earth with virtually no foothills leading up to the high mountains. As we stood there and looked out, Roger turned to me and said, "Gee, Charlie, if you didn't have all those big hills out there you'd really have a terrific view!" I don't think I will ever look at the Tetons without remembering that remark.

Bernie Koteen

Even though he was not on our board of directors, Bernie Koteen,* one of our most influential advisors and a wonderful friend, was the company's communications legal counsel. Bernie was the only Federal Communications lawyer that Taft ever had, and we could not have done better. He was not only a superb lawyer but was highly respected by the members of the Federal Communications Commission. But, beyond all of that he was an incredibly funny man. Three of his classics will make my point.

One time we were involved in a complicated negotiation, and we decided to make a bold proposal that we hoped would conclude the deal. The proposal made us nervous because we were perhaps "giving away" more than we should, but we felt it might be the best way to get the deal done. After we had submitted our proposal, Bernie looked at me and said, "Charlie, our problem now is—can we afford to take *yes* for an answer!" I have never forgotten this line and have used it more than once since.

On another occasion we were discussing the wisdom of guaranteeing a loan. Bernie had little regard for "guarantor." He said, "You know what a guarantor is? It's a schmuck with a pen."

Finally, and perhaps most memorable, we were discussing someone with whom we were negotiating. Bernie had little respect for the wisdom and depth of this individual. He said, "Charlie, it's just sad, but down deep he's shallow."

---

*Bernie passed away at age ninety-seven on February 22, 2013, after a remarkably long and productive life.

Some Taft Memories

THERE ARE, OF COURSE, many more wonderful memories of my Taft Broadcasting Company days. Here are a few.

The Car Key

As anyone who listens to radio knows, there are often contests for listeners to participate in and, hopefully, increase the station's audience. One such contest, which I remember vividly because of its unexpected result, happened at WKRC radio in Cincinnati. At the time I was the company's lawyer, and I received an anguished call from the station manager. He explained that the station was running a contest in which the winner would receive a brand-new luxury car. The station had hidden a key to the car somewhere in the Cincinnati area, and each day the station gave listeners clues leading to the location of the hidden key. But, things had taken an unexpected turn. To publicize the contest, salesmen would occasionally drive the contest car with a large sign on top of the car advertising the contest. The problem was that when one of the salesmen went on a sales call, he left the actual key in the ignition. When he came out after completing his call, a fellow was standing beside the car waving the key in his hand, announcing that he had found the key!

The station manager said to me, "What on earth can we do? The guy found the key, but not the hidden key." I told him that I thought this was indeed a problem because there was obviously no question that the man had indeed found a key. So I said, "I think the only thing you can do is to call the guy and tell him what a great joke he has played on the station and give him some kind of a prize." The station manager replied, "Okay. But when I tell him what a great joke he has played on us, suppose he doesn't laugh?" Happily, and somewhat surprisingly, the guy did laugh, and the whole matter had a happy ending.

By the way, as funny as this was, it cannot begin to rival the greatest radio contest fiasco in history. Though it had nothing to do with Taft Broadcasting, it is simply too good a story not to share. Apparently, a television station in a Midwest market got an idea for a turkey giveaway on the day before Thanksgiving. The idea was that a helicopter would fly over a specified location, toss out a lot of live turkeys and when they flew to the ground, whoever captured them could keep them. There was only one small problem. Turkeys can't fly! I will leave the rest of the story to your imagination.

Those Damn Baboons

Perhaps the story that got the greatest national attention is one that, although it had a happy ending, gave us a great deal of embarrassment. This may be the most bizarre incident that ever occurred during my years with Taft Broadcasting Company. In 1976, we had a section of the Kings Island theme park called Lion Country Safari. This area featured wild animals of all sorts from all over the world, and it was extremely popular. One day the people running the park told me they were acquiring fifty baboons to become part of Lion Country Safari. They pointed out that baboons were very popular animals and would be a big hit. I remember someone in our group pointing out that baboons were also very dangerous animals, especially because of their strong jaws and sharp teeth. We were assured there was no way they could escape from the compound, protected as it was by two fences topped with barbed wire.

As I recall, things went fine for a couple of days, and then, to our dismay, the baboons escaped! Naturally, I was not pleased by this and demanded an explanation. The explanation is still funny after all these years. It was explained that the baboons escaped like soldiers in World War I who went "over the top." That is, a couple of baboons would throw themselves on the barbed wire fence, and the others would simply run over their backs and jump to freedom.

Though funny now, it wasn't very funny then. We had fifty mean baboons roaming Warren County! After a week-long search they were recaptured but again went AWOL. It took three more weeks until they were rounded up again. This part of the story is also amusing. All sorts of efforts were made to recapture the baboons, some very complicated and high tech. Eventually, the baboons came back when some smart fellow suggested putting bananas in a large cage and trapping the baboons as they came into the gate! Very low tech, but it worked! In any case, the episode ended amidst many red faces and apologies. As I now recall, a couple of the baboons were kept on display for the season with a sign that read: These are the baboons that made monkeys out of us.

The Duke

One of my dearest friends for many years has been Charlie Lindberg. Charlie and I first met at Yale Law School where Charlie was a couple of years ahead of me. Later, when I joined Taft Stettinius & Hollister, Charlie was already there, and we renewed our friendship. When I left the law firm to become Chairman of Taft Broadcasting Company, Charlie took over my lawyer role and became the company's general counsel. We have spent many hours together over the years, and Charlie was an integral part of the growth of the company. We still see one another occasionally and share adjoining offices as retirees of Taft Stettinius & Hollister.

Charlie has reminded me of a very funny episode that occurred when we were having lunch in the Beverly Hills Hotel, undoubtedly on some Hanna-Barbera business. We were meeting with one of the senior partners of our investment-banking firm, Loeb Rhoades. During lunch the fellow from Loeb Rhoades started making noises that at first were unintelligible but soon he was sputtering out, "Charlie, Charlie—the Duke, it's the Duke—he's right next to us." Sure enough, John Wayne—all six feet four inches of him—was at the next table. Though I don't remember, I suspect that there was very little business done for the rest of the meal!

Houston, We Have a Problem

Bill Hansher was the vice president of engineering at Taft Broadcasting almost from the beginning of its existence. Bill was very good at his job, but he was a curmudgeon. However, we all overlooked this side of Bill because he was so good at his job. Bill began to have a heart problem at some point in the 1970s and was told that he should explore the possibility of open-heart surgery. At this time, open-heart surgery was dangerous business and about the only surgeons in the country who were doing it were the noted Dr. Michael E. DeBakey and Dr. Denton A. Cooley, both in Houston. Bill visited one of them (I can't now remember which) and elected to have the surgery. When he told me about it, I wished him all the best and urged him to let me know what we might do to be helpful. Though he did not suggest it, we decided that it would be a nice gesture if we covered Bill's travel expenses and a few other items. We directed our travel agency to take care of flights to and from Houston. Unfortunately (and hilariously, as it turned out), since the date of Bill's return was obviously not certain, the travel agency got him a one-way ticket! They should have simply made it an open return, but they didn't. When he got the ticket, Bill came charging into my office waving the ticket and said something like, "What the hell is this about?" I professed (with complete honesty) that I had no idea what he was talking about. When he finally settled down, I figured out what had happened and we both laughed about the whole episode. I assured Bill that we were not making any judgments about the result of the operation and that, even though he could frequently be a major pain in the neck, we honestly wanted him to return from Houston. He did!

A Very Long Ride

One of the rides at our old Coney Island amusement park was a Sky Ride, where small gondolas moved on heavy cables from one end of the park to the other. These were very common and popular rides in the amusement parks of the 1950s, 1960s, and 1970s. When we built Kings Island, we moved a number of rides from Coney Island to the new park, and the Sky Ride was one of them. On a late afternoon in early summer, a major thunderstorm swept through Kings Island. Unfortunately, the gondola ride was in operation when the storm hit. The wind caused one of the gondolas to hit one of the support pylons, which jammed and stopped the entire ride, leaving several of the gondolas "swinging in the breeze." As often happens after such a storm, the weather turned cold and rainy. The closest fire department was immediately called, but when they arrived it became clear that their hook-and-ladder truck could not reach all of the gondolas. (The fire department did have what might be called "harpoon" equipment, which was then used in an incredible manner to shoot blankets up and over the support wire to be dragged into the various gondolas.) Since the hook-and-ladder truck could not reach the highest levels, the Fenton Rigging Company of Cincinnati was called since they had a "cherry picker" that would be capable of reaching the highest gondola. That was the good news. The bad news was that this huge equipment could only travel at about five miles per hour, so it took several hours before it arrived at the park. Meanwhile, the weather was getting colder and wetter. The evacuations were going well, but there was one particular car that was causing great concern. In that car were a woman and her young son. That was bad enough, but it turned out that the woman was about eight months pregnant! There was obviously genuine concern about her condition when she reached the ground, so park authorities were prepared to meet her with more blankets, a wheelchair, an ambulance, etc. The cherry picker brought the woman and her son down in a cage-like contraption, and they reached the ground successfully. What happened next amazed everyone. The door swung open, the woman came striding out of the elevator with her arm around her son, spotted her anxiously waiting husband, and said, "Henry, get me out of here; I'm freezing my ass off." Obviously, she had survived the ordeal with courage and fortitude. Happily, that was the end of the episode, and everyone breathed a great sigh of relief.

A World-Class Traffic Jam

The second themed amusement park that Taft built, Kings Dominion, is located between Richmond, Virginia, and Washington, D.C., on I-95. A very interesting thing occurred there at the grand opening from which I learned important lessons. We had given the park a tremendous amount of publicity, and there was huge anticipation in the area leading up to its grand opening. On the day the park opened, I got a call from the general manager, Denny Speigel, saying something like this: "Boss, I've got good news and bad news. The good news is we have incredible crowds. The bad news is that traffic is backed up for miles on I-95, and we have a lot of unhappy people, including the police and the Highway Patrol." Obviously, I could do nothing about this, and Denny could do very little about it. Of course, the traffic jam eventually worked itself out. But, the problem didn't end there. So much publicity was given to the traffic mess that people stayed away from the park for many weeks, and our attendance suffered. Eventually, people came to realize that traffic jams were not an everyday occurrence, and the rest of the park season proceeded quite satisfactorily. I learned two lessons from this episode. First, you can "over-hype" anything. Second, since Kings Island had gotten off to a very sluggish start we assumed that the same would be true at Kings Dominion. Obviously, what happens in one situation may well not repeat itself in another.

Odd Man Out

In connection with the Canada's Wonderland theme park project, we established a relationship with one of Canada's largest and most prestigious banks. One day we went there for a meeting, which was held in their new headquarters in downtown Toronto. After our meeting, the chairman of the board said he was anxious to show us his board of directors room. We went into the room and it was indeed spectacular—very tasteful and not ostentatious. There was one thing that was immediately striking—the board table was huge. When I commented on this, the chairman explained that the board was quite large and that a table of that size was necessary. He then went on to say, however, that they had figured out a way to use the room for smaller meetings. He then pushed a button on the back wall, and every third seat moved back on a track into the nearest wall where a panel opened and the seats disappeared inside. The table then, at the touch of another button, contracted into a much smaller table. It was an absolutely amazing thing to see, but I couldn't help but have an irreverent thought. I suggested that this would be a unique way to advise a director that his services were no longer needed. Press the button and have him moved backward into the wall. I doubt that this was ever done, but it sure would have been fun to watch!

Riverbend

The story of Taft Broadcasting's involvement in the Riverbend Music Center on the banks of the Ohio River is a classic example of how sometimes very unexpected things can happen when the stars are properly aligned and the wind is right.

Two of my very good friends in Cincinnati, David Joseph and Jim Ewell, came in to see me one day. I didn't know the reason for their visit, but I soon learned they were heading up an effort to build a summer home for the Cincinnati Symphony Orchestra, and they had come to ask for a contribution from our company. I had a brainstorm, one of those flashes of light that are probably wrong more often than they are right, but this one was right and was a win-win situation. Taft owned the famous old amusement park on the Ohio River east of Cincinnati—Coney Island. We had just built Kings Island, which was off to a great start, but we were concerned about keeping Coney Island alive and relevant because it had such a warm spot in the hearts of Cincinnatians.

So, I told David and Jim that maybe we could make a deal. We would give them enough land at the Coney Island site to build a summer home for the symphony. Moreover, we would donate $1 million to kick-start the project. In return we asked that the facility be named for the founder of our company, Hulbert Taft, Jr. The name that was finally decided upon was The Hulbert Taft, Jr. Center for the Performing Arts. Obviously, this proposal benefited our company by bringing a whole new life to Coney Island, but it was also of enormous appeal to David and Jim for obvious reasons. We made the deal. The summer home was built with widespread support, especially from the Corbett Foundation. Called Riverbend, it has become a very important part of the Cincinnati scene, and I am very proud of our company's role in helping it get started.

The Wrong Number

A fellow named Sam Johnston was an important part of Taft Broadcasting Company for many years. He managed several broadcast properties and then went on to be the senior Taft executive at our Los Angeles operations. Sam probably came up with more great lines than almost anyone I have ever known, but one line was truly classic. Four of us were flying in a small private plane from Buffalo to Toronto. The plane had no radar or pressurization. This would not have been any problem on a nice day, but we ran into a very serious thunderstorm. We were being bounced all over the sky with lightning bolts flashing all around, and we couldn't go any higher (no pressurization) or find any alternative course (no radar). We just had to plow ahead. We were all scared to death but tried not to show it. One of our colleagues, who was seated in the front row with the pilot, turned to Sam and me, who were seated in the back. He said something like, "We've got to calm down. It's all in the hands of fate. If your number's up, you go—if it's not, you don't." Sam gave him a very skeptical look and said, "That may be true, Gene. I just don't want to go on *your* number." Terrified as we were, we all broke up laughing— and we made it to Toronto!

Gun Control

The next two stories are embarrassing and humbling but must be shared.

Whenever I need to dampen my ego, I simply think of all the things I am *not good at*. Sadly, it is a lengthy list that includes golf, skiing, chess, and bridge, to name just a few. However, without question, topping the list of things I do poorly is hunting. I lay all the blame for this inadequacy on the shoulders of my father and his father, neither of whom hunted! As a result, that left me open for the ridicule and jibes of my friends when I was compelled to undertake this "sport." Two examples will be enough for you to understand my plight.

Every year for many years, Dave Ingalls, Taft Broadcasting Company's largest stockholder, invited me to join a group for bird (dove) hunting at his huge plantation in north Florida. He usually invited six or eight of us for several days of golf, hunting, and a great deal of eating and drinking. I could handle the eating and drinking and could hold my own in golf, but I dreaded the hunting part. A low point came one day when we were all lined up in the field at assigned spots to be ready when the birds came out. Each of us had a local fellow with us who looked after us and went to fetch birds as we shot them and they fell to the ground. One day I blazed away for quite some time without bringing down a single bird. Finally, more by luck than skill, I hit one and I looked around for my helper to go get the bird. I was horrified when I found him sound asleep! You can imagine how bored he must have been and how hopeless he viewed the situation when you realize that he fell asleep amidst the constant sound of gunfire. My partners were merciless in their attacks!

The second incident is one that Marilyn never lets me forget. Although this story is actually not a Taft Broadcasting story, I can't help but relate it as one more example of my "skill" in hunting. At the annual board retreat of the Mead Corporation (I was privileged to serve on their board of directors for twenty-four years) at its timber farm in southern Georgia, hunting was a big deal, and I was practically the only one who didn't really want to hunt. However, I was finally talked into a wild-turkey shoot, and Marilyn went with me. A fellow showed me how to handle the shotgun that I was given and took us to a very secluded spot in the woods and told us that we should quietly wait and almost certainly a turkey or two would come around the end of the dirt road not far away. After a fairly short wait, a turkey did in fact appear, and I waited until my "assistant" told me to fire. I hit the bird but only winged him, and he turned and began to run down the road (wild turkeys are not good flyers). So, I began running down the road after him, firing my shotgun like a machine gun, but without much success. To add to this insane scene, Marilyn was running behind me crying because she really didn't want me to hurt the bird. Finally, I put enough shots into the bird to mercifully end its life or, maybe more likely, it had a heart attack from running so far. In any case, I brought it down. At the end of our meetings, we were invited to take home anything we had shot. The folks in the kitchen would pack everything up in ice and make it easy to take home. But my bounty never made it back home. Marilyn didn't want a reminder of the frantic chase down the road and, besides, she pointed out, there would be so much buckshot in the bird that it wouldn't be safe to eat without serious dental risks.

Some Pig!

Of all the funny things that happened during my days at Taft Broadcasting, I don't think that any brings a bigger smile to my face than the story of Country Boy Eddie. Taft's television station in Birmingham, Alabama—WBRC—had an entertainer named Country Boy Eddie, who was on at the crack of dawn every day. He was an incredible entertainer and garnered ratings that were astronomical—often reaching unheard-of sixty-plus shares of the audience tuned to television. His popularity was so great that the station preempted its networks' morning shows and turned the time over to Eddie. His style was a blend of cowboy and country music and down-home talk and humor.

One year we scheduled a meeting of the Taft Broadcasting Board of Directors at WBRC to give them a first-hand look at Taft's most profitable broadcast property. While we were there, Nick Bolton, the station's general manager, asked if I would do him a favor. He explained that they were having a little party that evening to honor Country Boy and his twenty-fifth anniversary with the station. Nick asked if I would attend and present Eddie with a plaque. I said I would be delighted. So that evening I presented the award to Eddie, telling him it came from the board of directors of the company. He thanked me and seemed very pleased. When I got back to Cincinnati the next day, I had a call from Nick Bolton, who could hardly contain his laughter. He said that Eddie had come into his office earlier that day and told Nick how pleased he was to be honored, but he said, "What *is* the board of directors?" Nick said, "Well, Eddie, these are the people that set the strategy and policy of the company, declare dividends, and make all of the important decisions." Eddie said, "I see, but why were they here at WBRC?" And Nick replied, "Because we are the most profitable station in the Taft chain." Eddie thought a minute, and then said to Nick, "Oh, I get it. The tall hogs just came to the trough."

I had never heard the phrase "tall hogs," but I have certainly never forgotten it. And, indeed, as I write these lines, I am looking with great fondness at a photo that Eddie sent me later, on which he had written, "To Charlie, my good friend, the tallest hog at the trough." I'm not sure I was ever the tallest hog at any trough, but I sure knew a lot of tall hogs over the years!

What Time Is It?

As the CEO of a major broadcast group, I often attended Network Affiliate meetings. As the name suggests, these were meetings of the affiliated stations of one of the three major networks—NBC, CBS, and ABC. The meetings were multi-day affairs, principally for the purpose of introducing the network's new fall schedule and being brought up-to-date on major issues by the top network brass. There were also lavish dinners and entertainment. At one such meeting, the final dinner was held in the ballroom of the Century Plaza Hotel in Los Angeles. The guest of honor and principal speaker was Henry Kissinger. Probably because I was the "ranking" network-affiliate official in attendance, I was seated next to Dr. Kissinger. I, of course, wanted to make a good impression and not do anything foolish. But it was not to be! Earlier that day I realized that I had lost my wristwatch. I simply could not locate it. I mentioned this to my good friend Bernie Koteen (Taft's communications attorney—and the best in the business), and Bernie said, "No problem. I always carry an extra wristwatch and you can borrow mine." Sounded like a good idea at the time. As I sat down to dinner, I introduced myself to Dr. Kissinger and for fifteen minutes or so everything was going swimmingly. Then, I heard a strange noise. At first, I couldn't identify it, but then I realized that it was coming from me, more specifically from my wrist. My borrowed watch's alarm was going off! It wasn't an ear-splitting noise, particularly with the normal noise of the conversation throughout the ballroom. But, it certainly was audible. I thought, "If I can turn it off quickly, no one will notice. There will be no problem." There were two problems. First, I had no idea how to turn it off, and second, I was trying to do it by reaching behind my chair with both hands and trying to turn it off with my right hand. Things were further complicated by the fact that I had on a suit and tie, so I was trying to reach up under the sleeve of my jacket to shut off the damn thing. All the while, I am trying to carry on an erudite conversation with one of the most famous and brilliant men in the world. Frankly, it was taking on all the earmarks of a Marx Brothers comedy. It became clear after a few frantic moments that I simply couldn't pull this off. So I bit the bullet, brought my arm up to table level, confessed my sins, admitted I had no idea how to turn the watch off, and looked for help. Quickly, a couple of other people at the table told me how to turn the alarm off.

Dr. Kissinger got a good laugh, and I managed to return to some semblance of normalcy. A memorable moment, to say the least.

Johnny Mac

As I mentioned earlier, the ATP Tennis Tournament grew from humble origins to the superb international super event that it is today. It was not uncommon in the early days of the tournament for players to stay in the homes of local families. One year, my dear friend Paul Flory, the tournament's outstanding director, called and asked if Marilyn and I would host a player. We said we would be delighted. Paul's housing chairman called Marilyn to let her know that seventeen-year-old John McEnroe would be our guest. John had become famous by making it to the semi-finals at Wimbledon just a week or so before. On Sunday afternoon at the beginning of tournament week, there was a knock on our door. We opened the door and there stood John McEnroe, who had been almost unknown to the tennis world until Wimbledon a few weeks before! John was a typical seventeen-year-old in shorts and a tennis shirt and with a large head of curly hair. John had already begun to gain a reputation for his performance on the tennis court—not only his play but his temper. Throughout this particular week, thanks mainly to several lectures from our oldest daughter, Melissa (who was the same age as John), he behaved quite well. But that isn't the point of this story. That week, as anyone who has lived in Cincinnati will understand, was incredibly hot and humid. Naturally, when John came back to the house after playing a match, he was tired and hot and dehumidified! The house we owned at the time was a large, rambling home set back in the woods and had no central air conditioning. Thus, one day when we came home, we looked in the kitchen and saw that John had obviously found the best way to cool off. He had the refrigerator door open and was sticking his head in up to his shoulders, cooling off! I know John has been criticized over the years for his behavior on the tennis courts, and certainly with justification. But I will only say that he was a real gentleman during the week he was with us. I will also say that there is no one I would rather watch play tennis—especially doubles, where net play is so critical—than John McEnroe. I assume that his earnings since that week have been such that he no longer needs to rely on putting his head in the refrigerator to cool down!

I'm Sitting Where?

For a number of years Taft Broadcasting Company had a relationship with the National College Football Hall of Fame. One of the high points of the year was a black-tie dinner in the Grand Ballroom of the Waldorf Astoria in New York City to induct that year's honorees into the Hall of Fame. It was really an incredible dinner, not only because of its sparkle and glitter, but because it attracted an unbelievable array of past and present football players. In addition, it attracted a number of great military officers and the five-tier dais was a who's who of football and the military.

One year the event organizers called to tell me that I would be seated next to President Richard Nixon. This was a stunner! This was after he had resigned the presidency in disgrace and had spent a year or two at his home in New Jersey in virtual seclusion. But he had elected to come out that night because he was a great football fan and had been supportive of the National College Football Hall of Fame for many years. I suspect he also viewed this occasion as a great opportunity to begin his "comeback," as he would be with friends and supporters. I thanked the organizer of the dinner for giving me a heads-up, and then I started thinking: "What in the world will I say to him? Obviously it's not 'how are things?' or 'how's the old gang?'" I was really concerned that I not do anything to embarrass him or to be supercilious in making small talk. Providence came to my aid. I went to a bookstore that day for something—I can't remember what—and in browsing (one of my favorite pastimes), I found a section featuring President Nixon's books. He had written several, but one I was not familiar with was called *Leaders*. I bought the book and that night began to read. It was an absolutely fascinating book. It profiled a number of world leaders that he had known and that he thought were in the first tier of talent and ability. It was a diverse and sometimes surprising group, including Winston Churchill, Charles de Gaulle, and Douglas MacArthur. I finished reading the book on my way to New York City for the banquet. After the cocktail hour, we all sat down for dinner and the program. I was seated with President Nixon and Bill Morton, a good friend and the former head of American Express, right next to the podium. We had some small talk about the dinner and some of the honorees, and it was all perfectly pleasant. Then came a few introductions, salutes, tributes, and the master of ceremonies then said, "Enjoy your meal." It was at this point that I launched what I hoped would be a successful approach. I said, "Mr. President, it's so good to see you here. I hope you're feeling well." He said that he was and that he was doing a lot of reading and writing. I then said, "I just came across your book *Leaders*, and I was absolutely fascinated by it." I didn't have to say much more during the evening. He talked to us at length about the book and the various people in it, and, frankly, it seemed to energize him. In any event, what could have been a long and very awkward evening, turned out to be a delight, thanks entirely to my fortuitous trip to the bookstore!

A Rose Is a Rose Is a Rose

My family and I had the great good fortune of living in Cincinnati during the heyday of the Big Red Machine. Everyone has his or her candidate for the greatest ball club ever, and mine is the Big Red Machine. But, be that as it may, we had the chance to watch Pete Rose play ball for a number of years. I have no intention of getting into the Hall of Fame controversy that continues to surround Pete, but one thing is clear: he was one of the greatest and most exciting baseball players who ever lived. During my years with the LPGA, Pete was doing an evening radio sports show from a restaurant in South Florida near where we were playing a tournament. I got a call that Pete would like me to appear on his show and do an interview. I said I would be delighted, and I appeared at the restaurant, where we had a spirited question and answer, back and forth, session. As the interview came to a close, Pete said to the audience, "Ladies and gentlemen, we're going to take a commercial break now, but when we come back I've got a question for Charlie that I think he's going to find very interesting, and perhaps you will too. Stay tuned." We went off the air and I looked at Pete and I said, "Are you going to give me a clue?" Pete said, "No, I want to hit you with this and get your answer without your having had a chance to think about it." I said, "Fair enough." So, we resumed and Pete said, "Charlie, it's certainly good to have the LPGA here in South Florida. You've got a lot of great players out there. By the way, I'm told that the LPGA Hall of Fame is generally regarded as the most difficult Hall of Fame in all of sports to get elected to. Why is that?" And I said, "Well, Pete, it's because the criteria for induction into the LPGA Hall of Fame are totally objective. There's no subjectivity whatsoever. There are no sportswriter votes, and no fan votes. It's based solely on your record—the number of events you've won, what events they were, and things of that kind." Pete smiled and said, "Oh, I see. So it's based entirely on your play on the field. Nothing else matters?" I said, "Pete, that's absolutely right." And Pete said, "Don't you think that's the way it ought to be in every sport?" End of interview, end of program. Point made!

Again, everyone has his or her own view on whether Pete Rose should be in the Hall of Fame. But I do believe the point he made that induction should be based solely on your performance on the field is a pretty sobering argument.

Pete was, of course, totally obsessed with baseball, but for many years his "other" sport was tennis. Along the way, for some reason, Pete began to dabble in golf. I had occasion to play with him once or twice, and he was the same Pete—over the top, total immersion in attempting to succeed, determined to excel. What I noted after watching Pete swing a few times was that he was not following through. He was using his wrists, much like he did when batting, to punch at the ball. This, of course, works in baseball and doubtlessly had much to do with his breaking Ty Cobb's all-time hit record. However, in golf, if you don't follow through and simply punch at the ball, it will automatically and inevitably go to the right—not so much a slice as simply a push. After watching Pete, I said, "Pete, I'm a lousy person to give golf instruction, but I do know certain basics, and one of those is that you've got to come off your back foot and follow through in order to consistently hit the ball straight." Pete looked at me and smiled and said, "Charlie, I have spent my entire career on my back foot; it's too late for me to change now!" Hard to argue with that!

My Friend Marge

Marge Schott was a character. There is simply no other way to describe her. And, I use the term with great fondness. In spite of some regrettable gaffs—which got incredible coverage all over the world because of her ownership of the Cincinnati Reds—she was a generous, caring person. Still, you could never be sure what to expect from Marge. I spent quite a lot of time with Marge over the years, but one meeting stands out.

Marge had had a run-in with Major League Baseball and was required to turn over operations of the ball club to a third party for a period of time. There was, naturally, a lot of speculation as to who this person would be. Even though I was Commissioner of the LPGA at the time—a full-time job if there ever was one—a certain movement (spearheaded by a newspaper columnist and a sports talk show host) began in Cincinnati to "draft" me for the job. Naturally, I was flattered, but I was not at all sure that I was interested. Nevertheless, when Marge asked me to meet with her to discuss the matter, I decided that there was nothing to be lost by talking with her. We met in a private room on the third floor of the Queen City Club, the distinguished business club located in downtown Cincinnati. When I arrived, Marge was already there, and I gave her a hug, sat down across the table, and waited for her to begin the conversation. She had what looked like (and I'm sure was) a martini and was puffing on a cigarette. I say this to set the scene, not to be critical—a lot of people smoked in those days, and a martini at lunch was hardly unheard of. But it was her opening line that floored me. She looked right at me and said, "Well, what's it going to take to get you, honey?" When I recovered my ability to speak, I said, "Marge, I'm not sure I'm ready to be got!" I was much more interested in knowing what the parameters of the job would be and what authority the person in the job would have, but we really never got by what it was going to take "to get you, honey." Nothing ever came of this and, in retrospect, I'm very glad it didn't.

During my LPGA days, I traveled all over the world for various tournaments and other functions. As I look back on those travels, an amusing fact emerges. Wherever I happened to be, even in Europe, Australia, or Japan, when people learned that I was from Cincinnati, Ohio, inevitably they asked two questions. First, "Do you know Camargo?" The reputation of this magnificent golf course and its legendary designer—Seth Raynor—were known by golfers everywhere. The second question, in quite a different vein, went something like this: "Do you know Marge Schott? What is she really like?" Obviously, the first question was much easier to answer than the second. It was very difficult to describe and explain Marge. I would simply say that we were good friends and that, although she frequently said the wrong thing at the wrong time, she was at heart a generous and good person.

The Wildest Ride Ever!

Reminiscing about Marge Schott makes me think about the many wonderful friends I had in the Cincinnati business community. That, in turn, reminds me of one of the funniest and craziest escapades I ever endured with my Cincinnati business buddies. Every year the C & C Club of Cincinnati (a combination of two business clubs, The Commercial

Club and the Commonwealth Club) has an outing that lasts three days and is always held at a resort that offers all sorts of activities. One year (probably in the late 1970s or early 1980s) the outing was at The Greenbrier in West Virginia and was held in the spring, probably around mid-May. Virtually all of the top business leaders in Cincinnati signed up for these outings, particularly if it was at the Greenbrier. I remember people like Dr. Charlie Barrett (one of Cincinnati's premiere physicians and the CEO of Western & Southern Life Insurance Company), Dean Fite (CFO of Procter & Gamble), Bill Keating (former U.S. congressman and editor and publisher of the *Cincinnati Enquirer*), and many others. Among the activities that were offered was one that was described as "a raft trip," and quite a few of us signed up. Many of the guys, particularly the older ones, I am sure envisioned a leisurely float down one of the many beautiful rivers in the area.

We traveled by bus from The Greenbrier to the headquarters of the rafting company. We were told to go into a rather large room where we were greeted and told to go into one of the adjoining rooms to "put on our wetsuits and helmets." That direction naturally raised some eyebrows. We couldn't figure out why we would need wetsuits and headgear for floating down a tranquil river. We didn't have to wonder for long!

When everybody was in his gear, the bus took us to an area on a fairly high ridge, and the rubber boats were unloaded. We looked down and saw the river quite some distance below roaring through a canyon. It turned out that this river was one of the great whitewater rivers in the world—the Upper Gauley. Indeed, I note that it is currently ranked number two in the United States and number seven in the entire world for difficulty. It was running particularly strong because the spring rains had raised the water level and made the whole course even more "exciting." We couldn't figure out how we were supposed to get the boats down to the river, when the guide pointed to a large pipe probably two or three feet in diameter that ran down the hill to the river. He told us to put our raft on the pipe, and four or five of us would get on each side of the raft and let it slide down the pipe till we got to the river. There were quite a few of us so there were five or six boats that had to be taken down to the river that way. The slope was steep and rocky, and it was not a simple task to get the boats down to the water. Now, I need to stop and emphasize that I was probably one of the youngest people on the trip. Most of the guys were in their fifties and sixties, and a couple even older than that.

We got the boats in the water and away we went—and I mean *away we went!* The rapids were treacherous and the current was very fast. All of us were scared to death but had no choice but to forge ahead. Over the course of the next forty-five minutes or so (it seemed much longer!), we met the Upper Gauley at its best. Several times we had men overboard, who were fished out of the water, but finally we got to the end and made a hasty retreat up the hill and back to the bus. Happily, no one was seriously injured, although there were lots of muscle strains and bruised body parts. But, our relief at simply surviving made all the hurts easier to deal with. We went back to The Greenbrier, immediately found the bar, and everybody celebrated the fact that we were still alive!

There is a fascinating postscript. The raft company was actually headquartered in Cincinnati, and several months later I happened to run into the head of the company at some function. When we met one another and I learned what he did, I asked him about our trip. He laughed and said, "We had no idea who your group was. We assumed it was a bunch of young guys out for a thrill ride. I have to be honest with you: when I saw your group getting off the bus and walking into the office, I turned to one of my colleagues and said, 'Oh shit!' I was convinced there would be multiple injuries and heaven knows what else." But, we all survived, and the story of the infamous ride down the Upper Gauley is still talked about by those of us who are still around.

A Truly Great Man

John Smale was one of my dearest friends. John had a distinguished career at Procter & Gamble and rose to become its chairman and chief executive officer. He is a man of incredibly strong character and principles, and I have always admired him.

At the same time, we have always had great fun in kidding and teasing one another. One of the most memorable examples was a bet that we made when John learned that Marilyn and I would be going to the Super Bowl in 1989, the year the Cincinnati Bengals played the San Francisco 49ers in Miami. A month or so before that game, John and his wife were at our home for a dinner party. When he learned that we would be going to the Super Bowl, he loudly declared he wasn't sure whether I was a rabid enough fan, and, when I asked what he meant, he said that a really rabid fan would paint his face orange and black to show support for the team. I replied that I would gladly do that, but not for nothing! He pulled out his wallet and tossed a one-hundred-dollar bill on the coffee table and indicated that it was mine if I painted my face, but if I didn't, he expected the one hundred dollars back, along with a like amount from me.

I was determined to win the one hundred dollars and to demonstrate my fanatic devotion to the Bengals. So, I painted my face, sent a copy of the picture to John, and kept the hundred dollars! I had my daughter take a picture of me so that John could not protest that I was not being totally truthful. The picture is included in this book.

Sadly, the Bengals lost in a fabulous game that was decided when the great Joe Montana marched the 49ers all the way down the field in the last two minutes to score the winning touchdown. Sad as I was with the outcome, I was one hundred dollars richer and that helped ease the pain.

One of the most unforgettable stories involving John Smale took place in February of 1990, when Marilyn and I traveled to Moscow with a trade delegation from the State of Ohio, led by then Governor Dick Celeste. It was a fascinating trip during which we met many Russian businesspeople and made a side trip to Riga, the capital of Latvia. I spent most of my time meeting with animation studios and amusement park operators and developers. It was a fascinating visit, but the high point really had nothing to do with the trade mission itself.

Shortly before we left, I got a letter from a senior executive at Procter & Gamble, inviting us to be Procter & Gamble's guests for a concert by the National Symphony Orchestra, which was to take place on February 13 at the Moscow Conservatory. This was not to be an ordinary concert. It would feature maestro Mstislav Rostropovich conducting his first performance in his native land since he was forced to leave in 1974. We attended, along with Governor Celeste and some senior executives from Procter & Gamble, including John and Phyllis Smale and John and Francie Pepper. The concert was held in the Bolshoi Hall of the Moscow Conservatory. It was a large hall with several balconies, very similar to the design of many of the great classical music halls around the world. There were several thousand people there, and it was a "happening" if there ever was one. *Time* magazine, in later reporting on the concert, put it this way: "The scene at the staid Moscow Conservatory last week had all the trappings of a rock concert, minus the rock. Shouting and clapping, fans pressed toward the stage, dropping red carnations on the podium. The maestro blew kisses to the standing-room only crowd—which included Raisa Gorbacheva." But the crescendo of the evening came at the very end. When the orchestra had completed its program, the audience insisted on encores. Finally the maestro returned for the fourth encore and, without announcing to the audience what the selection would be, led the orchestra into a literally spine-tingling rendition of the "Stars and Stripes Forever." There were perhaps forty or fifty Americans in the crowd and, following the old custom, we stood and began clapping rhythmically to that stirring Sousa march. Though it was unlikely that many of the Russians knew the song, they knew it must be special if all the Americans were on their feet. Then, what happened was electric. The entire audience, including a number of Army officers in full regalia, got to its feet and joined us in clapping along with the music. It was an absolutely extraordinary moment. As *Time* magazine reported: "'That was great,' said one wildly applauding young woman in the balcony. 'What was it?' Well might she ask: The parting piece was John Philip Sousa's 'Stars and Stripes Forever.' After sixteen years in exile, the man once branded a 'renegade to the motherland' was home again." To my great delight, I found there is a YouTube clip of this incredible moment. It is well worth your time to check it out. Just google "Rostropovich Returns to Moscow."

There is a sad postscript to this profile. John Smale passed away on November 19, 2011. We remained in touch and close friends until the very end. Indeed, I was blessed to visit him just a few days before he died. We had a wonderful conversation about a lot of different things. His mind remained very sharp and his range of interests very broad. When I left him that evening I think we both knew it might be the last time we would see one another. I have never known anyone for whom I had—and have—greater respect.

With a Name Like Smucker's

During my Taft years I was privileged to serve as a member of the board of directors of the J. M. Smucker Company for twenty-five years. It is one of the most remarkable companies in the history of American business. Not only is its trademark slogan—"With a name like Smucker's it has to be good"—one of the most well known, but, in my judgement, its reputation for high-quality products is unsurpassed. I was asked to join the board by its legendary CEO, Paul Smucker, part of the third generation in a family line that has directed the company since its founding in 1897. Paul was as highly respected and admired as his company. Though modest and self-effacing, he had a wonderful way with people and a puckish, engaging sense of humor. My favorite story captures Paul as well as anything I know. It happened at a Smucker annual shareholders meeting. Shareholders meetings are usually very dull affairs, but in recent years, they've become noisy and rancorous, with shareholders putting managements on the hot seat. But not at a Smucker's meeting! They were always held at or near Orrville, Ohio, the company's birthplace and headquarters. As a result, the room was filled with friendly faces and satisfied shareholders and employees. It often seemed that everyone knew everyone else.

One year, during the question-and-answer period, a woman got up and asked Paul a question. She noted that they had known one another since they were in grade school together and that she had always loved the company and everything it stood for. But, she said, "There is one little thing." She said, "Paul, all of your jams and jellies are put up in such large jars. We older folks, especially those of us living alone, just don't need such big containers. Couldn't you put up your jams and jellies in itty-bitty jars?" The audience laughed and applauded. As I sat there, I thought, "Wow, how is Paul going to handle this one? It was a good question. And it was asked by a lovely lady and an old school friend." Paul smiled, looked out at the audience, and said, "Mable, you're right. We've known one another for many years, and I respect your judgment. It's a very good question that you've asked, and let me try to answer this way. We could, indeed, and maybe should, put up our jams and jellies in itty-bitty jars. But, Mable, if we did, then we'd have to pay itty-bitty dividends!" The audience roared, Mable smiled, we all tipped our hat to Paul, and the meeting went on. A classic Paul Smucker moment, and there were many more like them.

Dave Thomas—One of a Kind

Another unforgettable character that I met during my Taft days was Dave Thomas, the legendary founder of Wendy's. He and I became very good friends and played golf together on a number of occasions. Our friendship began because we both ran sizable Ohio-based companies and found ourselves coming together frequently. Dave was one of the most interesting people I ever knew and, without doubt, one of the most generous. His was a classic rags-to-riches story, moving from short-order cook in an Indianapolis restaurant to the founder and inspiration of one of America's largest restaurant chains.

Early in our acquaintance, Dave said he would like to see Kings Island. So, we invited Dave and his wife to meet us one evening at the park for dinner. We had a delightful visit and Dave then said he would like to walk around the park. Over the next hour or so we strolled through the park, and Dave asked me a lot of questions about Taft Broadcasting Company. I answered all his questions as best I could, and he seemed to be impressed with what we were doing. As we were completing our walk, Dave, who never beat around the bush about anything, stopped, looked me directly in the eye, and said, "What would it cost to buy your company?" I was stunned. Naturally, I was flattered that he was interested, but we really had absolutely no interest in doing anything but continuing to grow the company in the direction we had already set. As politely as I could, I explained this to Dave and he understood. Dave and I were friends for the rest of his life and did a lot of fun things together. However, I will never forget that totally unexpected offer to buy our company. Kings Island was an impressive place to host visitors. One day a friend who ran a large company met me at the park for a tour. When we finished he commented on Taft's ownership of TV and radio stations, Hanna-Barbera, and amusements parks and then gave me a wink and said, "Do you get paid in your job?" His point was obvious!

Dave loved having money and loved doing things with it. My favorite story involves a visit that Marilyn and I made to Dave and his wife at their home in Ft. Lauderdale. I had not seen Dave for a year or so, so I asked, "Well, what's new?" Dave said, "I've got a yacht." I said, "You've got a yacht!? You don't even like the water." He said, "Yeah, but this is such a great boat. It's 120 feet long!" I said, "Dave, why and how did you buy a yacht?" He said, "I was going to play golf one Saturday, and it was raining, so I couldn't play. I was driving along and I noticed this boat store so I went in and I just bought this yacht. Come on, you got to see it." So we toured his yacht, and it was unbelievable. I don't remember what the size of the crew was, but it was sizable. Everything about it was just incredible. About six months later, Dave and I visited again, this time at my club, Loxahatchee, in Jupiter, and I said, "Well, are you getting a lot of use out of the yacht?" Dave said, "No, I don't have a yacht anymore." I said, "Well, what happened to it?" "Oh", he said, "I just didn't use it much, so I traded it for a golf course." I said, "Traded it for a golf course!?" He said, "Yes, it's a little course up in the Carolinas, and I'm really having fun with it." I have no idea whatever happened to that golf course, but the likelihood is that Dave traded it for something else.

One of my favorite Dave Thomas stories happened at a time when the LPGA was playing an event in South Florida and struggling to raise money for the event and to sell playing spots in the Pro-Am. Dave had invited me to play golf with him that day at Adios in South Florida—a truly superb golf course. On our way to the golf course, I was telling Dave about my difficulty in selling Pro-Am spots at the event. Dave said, "Maybe I can help." When we got to the course, we walked into the locker room—it's Saturday morning, probably mid- to late morning— and there were the usual gaggle of guys playing cards at several different tables, either before or after their golf games. Dave stood in the center of the room and said, "I want you all to meet my friend Charlie Mechem. He's the Commissioner of the LPGA Tour, and they're playing a tournament just a few miles from here. Charlie's having trouble selling Pro-Am spots. I want every one of you guys to buy at least one. That'll really help Charlie out, and it'll help women's golf out." These guys all blinked a couple of times, raised their hands to say that they would help out, and went on with their card games. They immediately committed to a dozen or so spots in the Pro-Am. It wasn't a lot of money, but it helped me out enormously, and several of the guys probably made their investment back several times over in their card game. It was another classic Dave Thomas act. Sadly, Dave is gone, but my memories of him—including those related above and countless more—are among my most treasured.

Happy Birthday

One of the most exciting things that happened during my years at Taft Broadcasting Company was the surprise birthday party that Marilyn, my friend Burch Riber, and several others cooked up to celebrate my fiftieth birthday. We were having a meeting of our senior management team and their spouses at our Kings Island amusement park in early September of 1980. After the business sessions, a dinner was scheduled in the beautiful International Restaurant that looked out over the park. When we walked in, it turned out to be a surprise party for me, and, boy, was I ever surprised! It was a wonderfully warm and happy affair, and many people had a turn at the microphone. Perhaps the most unusual part of the night was orchestrated by Joe Barbera. He had arranged for Sammy Cahn, one of the great lyricists in the history of modern music, and his songwriting partner at the time, Burton Lane, to be at the party. Sammy had rewritten the lyrics to a number of his famous songs to tie into my birthday and party. Some of the songs he'd customized included: "The Tender Trap," "On a Clear Day," "It's Magic," "It's Been a Long, Long Time," "Love and Marriage," "Time after Time," and "All the Way." Sammy and Burton Lane sang the songs. It was truly an unforgettable moment.

To give you an idea of Sammy's poetic license, here's a lyric sung to the tune of "Love and Marriage":

> *Charlie Mechem! Charlie Mechem!*
> *Gives you anything if you beseech 'im*
> *Listens to the birdies*
> *That's why Taft owns Palos Ver—dees!*

I am not an easy person to surprise because I am a nosey sort. But Marilyn sure got me that night, and it was wonderful!*

---

* Taft owned Marineland of the Pacific on the Palos Verdes Peninsula. You can see another example of Sammy's wonderful lyrics, as changed for my party, in the Appendix.

A Radio Legend

Taft Broadcasting Company began with a single radio station—WKRC. So, perhaps it is fitting that I end this section with a story about a great WKRC radio personality.

In the 1950s and 1960s, Stan Matlock dominated Cincinnati radio. Happily, he dominated it on Taft's station, WKRC. Stan called his show "The Magazine of the Air," and it was precisely that. He shared stories and anecdotes, almost all of which he wrote and that covered a very wide scope of subjects. He wove these bits and stories into the day's news, weather, sports, and music. John Kiesewetter, the longtime columnist for the *Cincinnati Enquirer*, did a great story on Stan after Stan's death at age seventy-eight. John quoted Stan's wife, Louise, as saying, "He loved to write. I think he considered himself a writer, more than a broadcaster." Typically, Stan drew 50 percent of the total listening audience—an unbelievable share then and now.

I admired Stan greatly, and we were very good friends. His was one of the first calls I received when the announcement was made that I was to become CEO of Taft Broadcasting. We talked often, and I always tried to listen to as much of his show as possible. The anecdote that I want to share has a moral, but we will get to that later. One day Stan came into my office, and we sat down to talk. Stan said that he had been thinking a lot about his future and wondered if he would be better off to leave his "on the air" role and become a part of management. I couldn't contain my surprise, and I told Stan that I couldn't imagine why somebody enjoying such phenomenal success would think about walking away from it into some probably dull management position. Stan was equally frank in his response. In essence, he said, "What do I do if people stop smiling and listening?" I told Stan that this was an understandable concern but a very unlikely one and that I thought that he should continue to do what he did because he did it as well as, if not better than, anyone anywhere. Happily, Stan stayed on the air and his legacy lives on. I said there was a moral. It is probably less a moral than simply an observation on human nature. Part of being successful and staying successful is, I think, never taking your success for granted and never being totally confident that your success will automatically continue. Frankly, all of the highly successful people I have known have always harbored something of a fear that their "audience" would stop watching and listening. Not a bad thing to keep in mind. In a word, it is called "perspective."

A Final Word

It is impossible to adequately sum up my years at Taft Broadcasting Company. Maybe the best way to put it is that I had great fun with great people as we built a broadly based international entertainment company. I always was and always will be proud of what we accomplished together and the way we accomplished it.

Who are those guys with Charlie? Seriously, one of my proudest moments representing the broadcast industry at the White House.

Golf with Pete Rose, my daughter Allison, my good friend Dick Johnston, and his son Chris.

A shot of Doug McCorkindale (CEO of Gannett), Dave Thomas, Patty Sheehan, and my good friend Bill Keating.

Playing golf with Paul Smucker, P & G CEO Ed Artzt, and LPGA pro Cindy Rarick.

Joe Barbera at a Taft management meeting. Was I really holding my nose?

My biggest and brightest piece of jewelry—the Phillies 1983 National League Championship ring.

A tennis event at Kings Island attracted the top players. Here I am with Jimmy Connors and Tournament Director Nelson Schwab.

Bill Keating and me with Paul Flory at the ATP Tournament supporting the sponsor!

Golfing with Neil Armstrong and LPGA player Kim Saiki. Neil and I were not great players, but we loved the game!

My Pro-Am colleagues at an LPGA event at Kings Island in 1979. Governor Jim Rhodes, President Gerald Ford, Nancy Lopez, me, and Cincinnati Enquirer publisher Bill Keating.

Handing Pat Bradley the winner's check of $45,000 (!!!!!) at the LPGA Championship Tournament at Kings Island, June 1, 1986.

Sammy Cahn performing at my fiftieth birthday party. A true genius at work!

Country Boy Eddie. He taught me about the tall hogs.

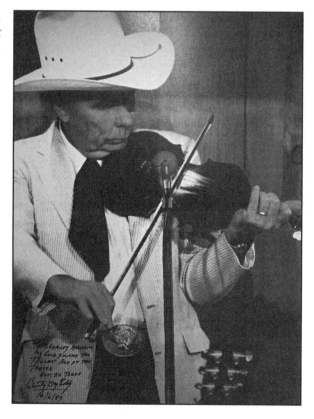

A BRIEF INTERMISSION

AFTER THE SALE of Taft Broadcasting Company, Carl Lindner asked me to stay with the company for a couple of years, and I agreed to do so. It was not an easy two years for a couple of reasons. First, I had been "the boss" for over twenty years but no longer had that authority. As I said earlier, I have always felt that I have my ego reasonably under control, but it was simply not an easy transition. Second, the Lindner folks needed to sell a number of Taft's properties to help pay for the acquisition. This was quite understandable but difficult for those of us who had assembled and grown the properties that made up our company.

I want to make one thing very clear. All of us from Taft Broadcasting Company were treated graciously and with respect by the Lindner people, from Carl Lindner on down. Craig Lindner, Ron Walker,* Jim Evans, Tom Mischell, Sandy Heimann, Bob Lintz, and the others were a pleasure to work with and became and remain good friends.

After my two years with the new company, I returned to my old law firm, Taft Stettinius & Hollister. My former colleagues and new friends could not have been nicer, but after a year or so I knew this was not what I wanted to do with the rest of my business career. First of all, I had simply been away too long—over thirty years—and I felt I could not advise and counsel clients without a lot of re-education and re-learning the law. In short, I was simply not prepared to be a practicing lawyer. Second, I simply was not comfortable in a firm as large as Taft had become. This is no criticism of large firms; most of the great law firms in the nation had become quite large. Rather, I had begun as the twentieth lawyer at the Taft firm thirty years before, and that was the environment and culture that was attractive to me. So, I was in a quandary and didn't quite know what to do. That all changed with one phone call!

---

*Ron Walker was one of the most pleasant and intelligent people I have ever known. I think he and Jim Evans were the only two people to be part of the inner circle of the Lindner enterprises who were not Lindner family members. Ron was very helpful to me in making the transition from the old Taft Broadcasting Company to the new. We became very good friends, and I was deeply saddened when he died prematurely at age fifty-nine.

CHAPTER XII

The LPGA

THAT PHONE CALL came from Judy Dickinson, the president of the LPGA Players Association. Judy and I had never met, but we both belonged to the Loxahatchee Club in Jupiter, Florida. How Marilyn and I got to Loxahatchee in the first place is an interesting story.

When our life reached a point where we could seriously consider having a second home, I talked to Jack Nicklaus about a golf course that he had just designed in Scottsdale, Arizona. While on a trip to the Phoenix area, I took a look at the course—and it was magnificent. I thought it would make an ideal place to spend some time in the winter. When I got home I "announced" to the family that I had found an ideal spot for a second home. They unanimously and enthusiastically endorsed my idea for a winter home but equally emphatically told me that I was looking in the wrong part of the country. They wisely pointed out that it was two thousand miles and three time zones away from Cincinnati, which would pretty much rule out brief visits. Since I was still active in business and the kids were in school, short trips were the only kind of visits that we would be able to make for a while.

As we continued to discuss the matter, it was increasingly clear that we should look in Florida where, in fact, most Ohioans go when they are seeking warm weather. So, I went back to Nicklaus who once again had a suggestion. He said that another one of his recent course designs was near Jupiter, Florida, and was called the Loxahatchee Club. To make a long story short, that's where we ended up and spent many happy years before moving to Orlando. We made a number of good friends, especially a gentleman named John Berger, who became our very good friend and remains so today. He is a remarkable man—warm, friendly, a world-class fly fisherman, and a fine golfer. Loxahatchee was a great place for us to live and a wonderful spot to entertain LPGA players, sponsors, and potential sponsors over the years, and it will always have a warm spot in our hearts.

A quick aside. One of the best things that happened while living at Loxahatchee was the chance to get to know Joe Namath. Broadway Joe was a member at Loxahatchee and was around the club a lot. I had always been a great fan of his and enjoyed getting to know him. He was very approachable and lots of fun. Joe had two daughters and he doted on them. When I first knew him they were very young girls. After we moved from Loxahatchee, I didn't see Joe for a number of years, but I ran into him at a charity function in Los Angeles. We both got one another up to date on our lives, and then I asked him how the girls were. He said, "Charlie, they are still the joy of my life but they are teenagers now, and I don't always understand them." Then he looked at me and said with complete sincerity, "Charlie, it seems to me that women are just wired differently!" I laughed out loud and said, "Joe, knowing your reputation, I would have thought you had learned that years ago!"

Our discussion turned to football. I asked Joe who he thought were the two or three best quarterbacks in the history of football. His answer was not at all what I expected. I thought he would list names like Unitas, Montana, Graham, Van Brocklin. Instead, Joe said it is impossible to answer that question because you would have to understand and evaluate the strength of the offensive line that protected the quarterback as well as the skill and number of his receivers. In other words, the quarterback might have a record that either enhanced or did not do justice to his ability simply because of those who surrounded and supported him. This made ranking them by skill levels completely unfair. This, by the way, is a pretty good lesson for life in general, not just for ranking quarterbacks. You are never better than the people that surround you and support you.

ALTHOUGH, AS I said, Judy Dickinson and I did not know one another, we had several mutual friends, one of whom was Jack Nicklaus. Judy told me that the LPGA had recently parted company with its Commissioner and that several people had recommended me as a possible candidate for that job. Judy wondered if I had any interest. I replied that I hadn't given the matter any thought and so did not really have a point of view. She suggested that I come to Florida and meet with her and her husband, Gardner Dickinson, one of the great PGA pros of the 1950s and 1960s. I went to Florida and spent a couple of hours at Loxahatchee with Judy and Gardner. It was a very pleasant meeting, and we both asked a lot of questions. As I flew back to Cincinnati that evening, I began thinking that the LPGA might be a very interesting next move for me. I was approaching age sixty and, as I have indicated, didn't feel that qualified or ready to resume a legal career. So, I began to think about the LPGA opportunity in a serious way.

When I got home, I talked to Marilyn, and she shared my view that it was something worth thinking about further. Therefore, I called Judy and basically said that I had some interest in the position but was not ready to go through an interview process in which I would be competing with other candidates. I said they should go ahead with their search, and if I turned out to be "the guy," Judy should let me know and we could talk further.

A number of weeks went by, and I largely forgot about the matter. Marilyn and I went to London for a long weekend, and the first night we were there I got a call from Judy basically saying that I was "her guy," and the search committee and the LPGA board wanted to interview me. She said the search committee and the board were meeting in New York in a few days and wondered if I could stop in New York on my way back to Cincinnati and meet with the committee and the board. That's exactly what we did.

Marilyn and I checked into the Waldorf in New York City where the meetings were being held, and I met with the search committee at around five in the afternoon. I must confess that I was a little smug about the interview, thinking that there would be a lot of fluffy questions and that it wouldn't take very long. Was I ever surprised! The committee was made up of players and a few board members and was almost totally female. They grilled me intensely, wanting to understand why a sixty-year-old man thought he could lead a woman's organization. One of the questions asked was, I believe, the smartest and most penetrating question that could have been asked. One of the board members, Mary Jo Jacobi, said, "Mr. Mechem, how long were you the CEO of Taft Broadcasting Company?" I replied that I had held that job for more than twenty-two years. She then said, "How many secretaries did you have during that time?" I couldn't help but smile, and I told her that was the most revealing question that could have possibly been asked under the circumstances. But I said that I was happy to respond that the answer was *one.* Everybody laughed and that was the end of the interview.

The one secretary to whom I referred was Mary Deller, who had also been Hulbert Taft, Jr.'s secretary. Mary was terrific! In subsequent years I have had only two other secretaries—now referred to as executive assistants. The first was Ellie Allen, who sometimes substituted when Mary was away and then worked with me with both enthusiasm and skill during my LPGA days. My other assistant is Gretlyn Thomas, who continues in that role today and, as I note at the end of this book, is importantly responsible for it ever seeing the light of day.*

I then was asked to meet with the full LPGA board for dinner. After being at dinner for a couple of hours and being asked more questions,

---

*I don't want to overlook my assistant in Daytona Beach when I was Commissioner of the LPGA. She was a delightful young woman named Chris Lundy, and she took very good care of me during those frantic days.

the board chairman observed that since it was after midnight on my biological clock (having just come from London) he thought it was wise for me to relax, go to bed, and they would be in touch with me later. I took that advice, went to our room, and went to bed. Not more than an hour later the phone rang, and I was informed that they had decided to offer me the job. Since many of the key participants were leaving early the next morning, they asked if I could join them and work out an agreement. I said that I could, and I got up, dressed, and went back to the meeting room.

It didn't take long to finalize our understanding. It was agreed that I would be announced as the LPGA's new Commissioner and would formally begin on January 1, 1991. As it turned out, they wanted me to begin sooner, and I moved into the job in the late fall of 1990. I was at the starting line of what would turn out to be a combination of a marathon and a sprint.

THE MAIN REASON I started in the job before January 1 was that the annual meeting of the Tournament Sponsors Association (now called the Tournament Owners Association) was being held in Phoenix in November, and everyone felt it would be helpful if I could attend that meeting. I'm awfully glad I did!

At the meeting I gave a talk telling people a little bit about my background and sharing some preliminary thoughts I had for the LPGA. The speech went well, and I was pleased to have the opportunity to meet the members of this organization. Obviously, the tour can only exist and prosper if it has solid tour sponsors and if they are positive and enthusiastic about their sponsorship. As I was leaving the stage, the executive director of the organization approached me and said there were a few sponsors who wanted to talk privately with me. They had assembled in a small room at the back of the main assembly room, and he escorted me to the meeting. Four or five of the biggest and most influential sponsors were seated around the table. We exchanged some pleasantries, and then they delivered their message: turn this organization around within a year, or we will be looking for other ways to spend our sponsorship dollars. This was no idle warning. At that time, the Senior Tour (now called the Champions Tour) was beginning to gather real momentum, and a disenchanted sponsor could easily turn to a Senior event or, of course, a regular PGA tour event. The people in the meeting made it clear that they did not want to leave the LPGA, they loved it, and they had great respect and affection for the players, but they simply needed to see some changes. Rather than being discouraged by this, I felt it was a shot of adrenalin and gave me the impetus that drove me to make a decision that would have a major impact on my time at the LPGA.

That decision was to personally attend every LPGA event. I decided this was the right thing to do for several reasons. First, it gave me a chance to introduce myself. Next, it underscored the importance of each event to the tour, and finally, it gave me a chance to get to know, both professionally and socially, the players, the tournament director and his or her staff, and the senior executives of the sponsoring company or companies. Many times I was asked to play in the Pro-Am tournament that preceded the main event, and I found this very helpful in my efforts to meet sponsors and players and get to know them better. I have many happy memories of these Pro-Am events.

ONE YEAR DURING the playing of the LPGA Championship at Taft Broadcasting's Kings Island golf facility, I invited my dear friend Bill Keating, who was then publisher of the *Cincinnati Enquirer*, to play in my group at the Pro-Am. I wasn't sure who would be in the group, but I knew we would have fun. To my horror, I learned that we would be playing with Nancy Lopez and President Gerald Ford. I don't remember now why President Ford was in the vicinity, but he was. On the day of the Pro-Am, we gathered on the first tee. There must have been at least five thousand people in the gallery—just a few more than normally watch me play! To say that I was nervous would be a colossal understatement. To be honest, I was scared to death. And, my buddy Keating, was equally unnerved. But, there was nothing to do but take a swing and hope for the best. I really think that I closed my eyes when I swung but miraculously my drive went reasonably well, as did Bill's drive. Nancy, of course, striped one right down the middle and a long way. President Ford then hit a drive that would turn out to be his signature shot for the day off the tee: a line drive, head high, into the gallery. The good news is that his aim got better as we went along and no one in the gallery got hit. The even better news is that his line drives—or at least the possibility of one—completely took the pressure off Bill and me!

All in all we had a great day, and I experienced what I had heard before and saw on several occasions later: Gerald Ford was a wonderful man, a fine athlete, and totally down to earth. It was an honor to be with him and hear what he had to say and see firsthand why he had been the perfect person to succeed Richard Nixon.

ANOTHER SPECIAL PRO-AM memory involves Dr. Jim Andrews, who is one of the most respected and prominent orthopedic surgeons in the world. He has operated on scores of world-class athletes who trust him to "fix" what ails them. My exposure to Jim, however, came in a very different way. Jim's organization, Alabama Sports Medicine, was an important sponsor and supporter of the LPGA during my time as Commissioner. We got to be very good friends and played together in several Pro-Ams. Jim loved the game and our skills were very similar, namely we were high-handicap golfers. The thing I remember most distinctly about Jim's game was the lightning-like speed of his swing. In golf lingo it was

"Zorro-like." I once told Jim that if he wielded a scalpel the way he swung a club, I wasn't at all sure that I wanted him to operate on me!

One particular experience stands out. We played together in a Pro-Am at the Dinah Shore Tournament in Palm Springs. I don't remember who the pro was, but Jim and I were both playing well, and, with our combined high handicaps, our team was in good shape. On the seventeenth tee Jim said to me, "Charlie, we've got a chance to win this thing. But, I have to leave the minute we finish eighteen because I have a plane to catch to get me back to Birmingham tonight. I will be in surgery much of tomorrow morning, but I really want to know how we come out. Here's a phone number you can call to get a message to me." I promised to do so, and that night I went to the awards dinner and learned to my delight that our team had in fact won the event. I called the number Jim had given me, and the fellow who answered was expecting my call and was delighted to learn of our victory. He said he would certainly pass the word on to Dr. Andrews.

The next morning at about 6:00 Pacific Time, my phone rang and I sleepily answered it. It was Jim Andrews and his excitement was very apparent. He said, "We won, we won. I am so excited!" I said, "Jim, it's six o'clock in the morning, and it's only eight in Birmingham." He said, "I've been up for hours, and I've already performed several operations. But I couldn't wait to call you and share the good news. So I thought I'd call while they're prepping the next patient because I don't know when I'll get the opportunity to call again." We laughed and cheered over the phone. When you are a high-handicap player, winning a Pro-Am, especially at a big event like "The Dinah" is a very big deal even for one of the world's great surgeons. I haven't seen Jim in some years, but I can almost guarantee that he remembers our victory and how excited we both were. Jim is a great surgeon, but an even greater guy!

OVER THE NEXT five years, I did indeed attend every event—some 190 of them. This approach to doing the job succeeded beyond my highest expectations. As I had hoped, it allowed me to meet senior executives of the sponsoring companies and that made a significant difference in strengthening the tour's relationship with the tournaments. Incidentally, I made many very good friends such as W. R. Howell of J. C. Penney, Jamie Houghton of Corning Inc., Herb Lotman, Dave Thomas, Dinah Shore, Jamie Farr, Jim Andrews, Sir Richard George, and Judy Bell (the first woman president of the United States Golf Association). Just as importantly, being there every week allowed me to get to know the players in a way that helped me immensely in keeping them informed and involved in our decision making. Many of these players remain among Marilyn's and my closest friends.

Finally—and this came as a pleasant surprise—my visits to tournament sites gave me a chance to talk with the local media and establish relationships with the writers and TV and radio people who covered the tournaments. It allowed me to get the LPGA's message directly to those people who could communicate it broadly. I had a built-in advantage in this respect because I had run a media company. It simply made my rapport with the media easier to establish and, I think, more valuable. Even more important in a broader perspective is that many of these media folks became and remain my good friends. The list includes Jaime Diaz, Tim Rosaforte, Larry Dorman, Christine Brennan, Jerry Potter, Jerry Tarde, Geoff Russell, Pete McDaniel, Patricia Davies, Lewine Mair, Jim Nugent, Jim Nantz, Judy Rankin, and Rich Lerner to name a few. This is not a name-dropping exercise: these people treated the LPGA and me fairly and honestly. We tried our best to reciprocate, and I believe the relationships we established and the mutual trust we built together were an extremely important part of improving the LPGA's public image. As I have indicated, this approach to my job worked so well that I continued doing it for all of my five years with the LPGA. I don't know how many air miles I logged during my five years, but I do know that most of the travel was on Delta Airlines, and I amassed nearly four million miles on Delta!

I must note one of the craziest things I ever did in my traveling with the LPGA: I flew to Tokyo for lunch! We were working hard to establish a new tournament in Japan. Everything seemed to be progressing well as we identified and negotiated a tournament deal with the new sponsor. Then our office received a call saying that the chairman of the sponsoring company wanted to have a press conference in Tokyo to announce the event, but he would not go forward unless I attended the press conference. Japanese sponsors put great stock in a Commissioner's presence at their events, believing, and I think correctly, that having the senior executive of the tour attend their events is a mark of the importance of the event. However, this was a new twist and presented me with a major problem. I had unchangeable commitments just before and just after the Tokyo press conference, and I asked my staff to explain this to the Japanese. It didn't work! They insisted that I attend. So, I flew from Pat Bradley's Hall of Fame induction in Boston to Tokyo, got a few hours of sleep, attended the luncheon and press conference, and flew home the same day. I know how crazy this sounds—and it was—but we got the tournament!

BUT I'M GETTING ahead of myself. My first task after officially becoming Commissioner was to analyze everything about the organization—budget, staff, tournaments (both existing and prospective)—and to begin to draw some conclusions about the strengths and weaknesses of the organization and what we needed to do to build it. Marketing any women's sports organization is a challenge. This shouldn't surprise anyone because it has been true for years. There are a number of causes, including the fact that most decision making is still done by men, and there remains a surprising amount of machismo among decision makers. But the LPGA had another problem in 1991. The PGA Senior Men's

Tour had by now gathered significant strength, and this meant that we were not only dealing with our normal competitors (other women's sports and the PGA Tour) but were now confronted with a brand-new golf tour and one that afforded a lower "price of entry" for anyone thinking about a golf sponsorship, not to mention the fact that it featured some of the legendary stars of the past—names like Palmer, Nicklaus, and Player!

This state of affairs, coupled with the bad press that the LPGA Tour had been receiving in the recent past, had had a real effect on the morale and outlook of the players. At the first general players' meeting after I became Commissioner, one of the players asked directly, "What do you think is our biggest problem?" I replied that I was still learning, but I had a pretty good idea that by far the biggest problem was that the players had what I called a "massive institutional inferiority complex." I went on to say that was the bad news, but the good news was that we could attack this problem on our own without relying on anyone else or being dependent on any outside circumstances. In other words, I was really doing nothing more than addressing an age-old motivational precept: you will never be any good if you don't believe in yourself. I told the players that I wanted them to stop worrying about the PGA Tour, the Senior Tour, and everything other than our own strengths. I wanted all of us to walk with our heads up and our confidence and pride on display. I am proud to say that the players embraced this philosophy completely, and I think whatever success I had over my five-year tenure was based largely on the players' attitude and performance. In the final analysis, the players *are* the tour. No matter how strong and supportive the sponsors are or the media or the fans, the players drive the success or failure of the organization. And that's as it should be.

A lot happened—and I mean a lot—over the next five years. We traveled all over the world, met thousands of people, and enjoyed *almost* every minute of it. It is impossible in this book to get into detail about these five years, but I would like to highlight several things.

NO CEO CAN be really effective without a great staff. Some CEOs will tell you (or imply) that they are the only real reason for their organization's success. This is egotism at its worst. A good staff not only will allow you to delegate many duties but, perhaps even more important, will challenge you when they believe you are wrong. The staff that I developed over the years is a source of great pride to me. I can't begin to mention them all but among my senior staff I would mention Jim Webb, my Deputy Commissioner, Ty Votaw, Cindy Davis, and Kathy Milthrope. Jim Webb served as interim Commissioner preceding my entry into the job and was a solid, experienced advisor during my years as Commissioner. Suzanne Jackson was perhaps one of the two most respected Rules Officials in all of golf, the other being the famous P. T. Boatwright. Tragically, Suzanne died of cancer after a valiant battle. I still remember her with great warmth and respect. I am especially proud of Ty and Cindy, since I hired them both. Ty began as our house legal counsel, worked up to become my assistant, and later became Commissioner. He is currently a senior vice president at the PGA Tour and one of Tim Finchem's most respected lieutenants. I hired Cindy to head the teaching and club professional division. This very important part of the LPGA had never before had any structure, and Cindy did a great job of bringing it into the mainstream of the LPGA. I promoted Cindy to several jobs as the years went by, and she became one of my principal advisors. She later ran the Arnold Palmer Golf Company and currently heads Nike Golf worldwide. As for Kathy Milthrope, although I did not hire her (she was at the LPGA before I was), she left the LPGA after I retired to take an important job at NASCAR but has now returned to the LPGA as its chief financial officer, a move that she and I discussed and I strongly encouraged. I remember someone telling me when I was a very young executive that you will ultimately be more proud of the accomplishments of the people that you helped to develop than you are of your own accomplishments. Frankly, at the time, I doubted that was true, but I have now lived long enough to know that it is.

A Look at Some of the Legends

WHEN I JOINED the LPGA, I was troubled to learn that not much time or effort had been made to keep in touch with the older players, including the legends of the game. I felt this was a serious mistake and decided to start meeting and getting to know the older players. Maybe this had something to do with the fact that I, myself, was an "older player," but it was more than that. I felt that we could learn much from them and that we would benefit from their visible support of the tour. As a result, I got to know a number of former players. Here are a few stories about those legends of women's golf that you might enjoy.

Patty Berg

Patty Berg was a golf legend. She was one of the original founders and the first president of the LPGA and remained a committed and active member of the tour until her death at age eighty-eight in 2006. I loved to be with Patty. Her spirit was unquenchable and she loved funny stories. One day we were chatting and I said, "Patty, what was the first prize money that you ever won?" Patty looked me in the eye and said, "Commissioner [she never called me anything but Commissioner], you'll be interested in this because my first money was in your hometown, Cincinnati, Ohio, in 1942." I said, "Patty, that's incredible, and I'm happy to know it, but tell me how much you won." Patty smiled and said, "I won fifty dollars." And I said, "Well, Patty, that's just scary to think that that was all you won, even though it was early in the 1940s after World War II had started. It still seems like a trifling amount of money." Patty laughed and said, "That's not the half of it, Commissioner. They paid me with a war bond!" For those of you who are too young to know much about World War II war bonds, a $50 war bond cost $37.50, but you had to wait ten years before you got your $50. Knowing Patty, I'll bet she collected that $50 ten years later!

As I have mentioned, Patty was one of the most revered and respected players in the history of golf—not just women's golf, but golf worldwide. Among the many wonderful things she did was hold countless numbers of clinics over the years, not only teaching people how to play the game, but dispensing her inimitable brand of humor and jokes. Patty would frequently take questions at these clinics. Now remember, at many of these clinics, there were quite a few people in the audience who knew little, if anything, about golf and certainly little, if anything, about the rules of golf.

I once said to Patty, "Of all the questions you've been asked in clinics, what is the one that amused you the most and stumped you?" Patty responded, with a grin on her face, "Commissioner, there is no doubt about the best question. It was: 'If the ball you whiff is not your own, is it still a penalty stroke?'" I must say, it is hard to think of any question that could be more amusing and yet possess a certain type of queer logic!

One last story involving Patty. I have been involved in many discussions and debates about which is the greater sport—golf or tennis. Naturally, I favor golf, even though I love tennis and follow it closely. However, I have found a way to silence (not completely, of course) the advocates of tennis. I say to them something like this: "You may say what you will, but here is the 'clincher.' There are literally thousands of jokes about golf, but there are none about tennis!" My point is simple: no sport can claim preeminence without jokes. This, of course, always brings an immediate protest from tennis advocates, but it never brings forth a tennis joke. I keep waiting to hear one, and if anyone reading this book knows one, I'd like to hear it! The closest I have ever heard came from Patty Berg. Patty knew of my challenge to find a tennis joke, and one day she said she had heard one. I told her to tell me the joke immediately. It went like this: A man left his house at dawn on Sunday morning and played thirty-six holes of golf, returning home at dusk. He was met at the door by his irate wife who said, "Damn it, Joe, I think you love golf more than you love me." Joe thought for a minute and then said, "You know, Betty, you're right, but I love you more than tennis!" I told Patty that I appreciated her offering, but I really thought this was a golf joke.

JoAnne Carner

Since golf started, centuries ago, a number of legendary players have crossed the scene. In my opinion, none were more interesting, more fun, or more talented than JoAnne Carner. One of the greatest amateur players in the history of the game, JoAnne Gunderson (her maiden name)—the great Gundy—distinguished herself to an incredible degree before she ever reached the pro ranks. But when she got there, she was no less awesome. Let me relate to you a couple of stories to give you a more personal look at this amazing woman.

The first story took place in Hawaii when we were playing an LPGA tournament at Ko Olina, a course on the western end of Oahu. It was a hilly course, as many of the Hawaiian courses are, and JoAnne was playing with two rookies. The rookies, naturally, were star-struck and intimidated by JoAnne. JoAnne was never cruel on the golf course, but she was quite aware of the power of intimidation and could intimidate without saying a word. The players holed out on the ninth green, and I happened to be standing on the tenth tee, which was up a fairly steep hill from the ninth green. JoAnne was smoking in those days (perhaps she still does), and after climbing the hill, she was obviously winded. The problem was that she had won the ninth hole and therefore should have been first to hit. Instead, being in no condition to hit the ball, JoAnne turned to the two rookies and said in her marvelous gravelly voice, "I don't give a damn who's got the honors; you two are up!" Naturally, the rookies hurried to the tee and by the time it was JoAnne's turn she was in good shape!

The second story involves both JoAnne and her husband, Don. They had a wonderful marriage. They deeply loved one another, but more than that, they thoroughly enjoyed the same things. Their boat, a cocktail at the end of the day, fishing, cruising to the Bahamas—just plain enjoying life and one another. Don never missed a tournament and was clearly JoAnne's greatest and most passionate fan. Toward the end of his life, sadly, Don had several physical ailments that left him virtually unable to speak and not able to get around very well. As one would expect, JoAnne devoted her life to taking care of him. She told me this wonderful story. Don had gone several weeks without speaking. JoAnne would take him for a drive every day in the hope that that might stimulate him to try to talk. One day they were driving around the neighborhood, and JoAnne came to a stop at a red light. Don turned to her, looked her over very carefully, and said, "You need a facelift!" JoAnne, flabbergasted, said, "You SOB, you haven't said a goddamn word in three weeks, and the first words you say are that I need a facelift! We're going home!"

"Big Momma"—the nickname given to JoAnne by another great LPGA player, Sandra Palmer—is in a class all by herself!

Althea Gibson

The great multi-sports star Althea Gibson had played on both the Women's Professional Tennis Tour as well as the LPGA. I reached out to her at her home in New Jersey. We had a nice visit, but it was clear that she was not a happy person. She was sad and somewhat forlorn. Her life had not turned out the way she wanted it to in spite of her phenomenal talents. After we had talked a while I finally said, "Althea, it has really been a privilege to talk with you. You have been a model and true sportswoman with everything that you have done." She then said something I have never forgotten. She said, "Commissioner, I appreciate your call but you must sense that my life is not a particularly happy one because, you see, I missed the gravy train not just in one sport, but in two!" Obviously, what she meant was not said with a sense of bitterness so much as a sense of resignation. She had excelled in *two* sports at a time when the financial rewards were minimal in both, to say the least! She nonetheless remains one of the greatest female athletes ever.

Louise Suggs

Louise Suggs is one of my all-time favorite people. She was one of the founders of the LPGA, the first woman elected to the LPGA Hall of Fame, and recorded over fifty victories in her LPGA career. She was a strong player. Bob Hope, who loved golf and played it quite well himself, called her "Little Miss Sluggs." When I set out to meet the players who had built the LPGA Tour, Louise was the first one I met, and we became good friends. In spite of some health problems, Louise remains active and committed to the LPGA and makes many appearances in support of the tour. She is a "fixture" at the Masters and, when she was young, was a close friend of Bob Jones, who helped her with her game. Some teacher!

Louise is beloved by the LPGA and its players. She continues to appear at many LPGA functions and events and has been a generous benefactor to the tour. I think one of the things that make Louise most proud is that the Louise Suggs trophy is presented annually to the LPGA Rolex Rookie of the Year. As for her golf skills, the legendary Ben Hogan once wrote, "If I were to single out one woman in the world today as a model for any other woman aspiring to ideal golf form it would be Miss Suggs."

Talking about Louise Suggs reminds me of another wonderful story. This is not a story in which I was involved but, rather, is one that Louise related to me. Years ago, there was a one-day tournament at a par three course in the Palm Beach area to which male and female pros were invited. In this particular year, Louise won the tournament, beating all the men and women, including the great Sam Snead. As Louise tells the story, Snead was very unhappy about the result. He confronted her in the parking lot and loudly voiced his displeasure about the condition of the course, how it was set up, and who knows what else. This did not amuse Louise in the slightest. Her response was something like this: "Sam, shut up! You've got no bitching rights—you didn't even come in second!" She said Sam turned and walked away, got in his car, and laid a trail of tire rubber as he squealed out of the parking lot.

Kathy Whitworth

There is simply no way to do justice to the career and personality of Kathy Whitworth in just a few lines. Her impact on the game and on the LPGA has been enormous. Perhaps the most important statistic is her eighty-eight tournament titles, more than any other professional golfer in history, male or female! She was the tour's leading money winner *eight* times, Player of the Year *seven* times, and won the Vare Trophy *seven* times—the most in LPGA history. Over the years she served the LPGA as president and in many other capacities. I have always thought of Kathy as the "conscience" of the LPGA: the personification of what the LPGA should always stand for—professionalism, class, humility, and dedication. I often asked Kathy for her advice and always found it useful. You don't win eighty-eight times without something special in your golf game. In Whit's case, other players have told me that it was her ability to visualize and shape shots as well as anyone who played the game. Whatever it was, it certainly worked! But most of all, I admired how widely she was respected by everyone in the game, especially the active players of the LPGA. There can perhaps be no better example of this than her being chosen to be captain of the American Team in the first Solheim Cup matches.

Marilynn Smith

One of the most charming people I met during my LPGA days was Marilynn Smith. Marilynn was one of the thirteen founders of the LPGA in 1950 and had a very successful career, winning twenty-one tour events and two major championships. But Marilynn's golf statistics only tell part of her story. She has been a wonderful ambassador for the LPGA and continues to do much good for many people. She sponsors a Pro-Am event at her home in Arizona that has raised a significant amount of money for charity. Marilynn and I remain in touch, and she is one of the most upbeat, positive people I have ever known.

Mickey Wright

Until Annika Sorenstam came on the scene, no one argued the issue of who had been the greatest player in women's golf history. Even her greatest competitors and rivals acknowledged that Mickey Wright was the best. Obviously, Annika's achievements created the women's version of the Hogan-Nicklaus-Woods debate as to who was the greatest. But, it is impossible and unnecessary to even deal with that issue. Comparing eras is useless and would be an injustice to both of these great athletes.

Shortly after I became Commissioner, I called Mickey Wright. I had read and heard so much about Mickey, and I knew she had walked away from the game at her peak and had never really looked back. She valued her privacy and was living quite happily in South Florida. When I called, I introduced myself and asked if I could pay her a visit. She was very gracious and we arranged to meet. I will never forget that first meeting: we talked very little about golf. Mickey had wide-ranging interests in current affairs, particularly the financial markets, and impressed me as highly intelligent and totally honest in the way she lived her life. After about an hour, I thanked her and said I needed to be on my way. Mickey said she had enjoyed our visit, but one thing puzzled her—I hadn't asked her to do anything! I smiled and said, "No, Mickey, I concluded that it would not be wise to meet you for the first time and then ask you to do me a favor." She smiled and said, "You made the right decision!" We both had a good laugh. Later, I did have occasion to ask a few favors, but never anything that was distasteful or intrusive. Let me tell you about one such favor.

During my years as Commissioner, the Centel Corporation sponsored an event in Tallahassee, Florida. The CEO of Centel was Jack Frazee, who was a devoted and active supporter of the LPGA and particularly wanted to do something for the older players. Together we came up with an exciting idea. The plan was to have a tournament within a tournament. We invited some of the "old-timers" to play in an event in which they would tee off before the regular LPGA Tournament commenced. In other words, if the first LPGA tee time was 8:30 a.m., all of the veteran players would tee off before that. I invited Mickey, but I knew that she avoided events like this, and I really didn't expect her to play. To my absolute delight, she agreed to play and was paired with Kathy Whitworth. (The event consisted of two-person teams.) By the way, for those of you who like statistics, that twosome had a total of 170 LPGA victories!

I had never seen Mickey play, but I had read a number of comments, including Ben Hogan's, that she had the finest golf swing they had ever seen. Naturally, I was anxious to see it first-hand. I noted that Mickey would be teeing off around 7:30 a.m. Figuring that she would hit a few balls before playing, Marilyn and I got up early and went to the driving range a little before 7:00 a.m. My first shock was to find some fifty or sixty LPGA players waiting to watch Mickey warm up. The second surprise was to see Mickey swing the club. It was effortless and perfect!

Once play started, two funny things happened. After watching Mickey play a couple of holes, one of the LPGA players came up to me and said in a startled voice, "Mr. Mechem, she doesn't have a yardage book!" I said, "No and she never did, nor did any of the other players of her era. She simply did it by 'feel,' and it seemed to work out pretty well!" The young player was incredulous. How could someone possibly play without a yardage book!

Later, another player came to me when Mickey's ball had come to rest near the rope line where the spectators were gathered. The player pointed to Mickey's clubs, and we all looked in her bag. There were her old Wilson clubs, which, in spite of their age, did not have a mark on them except in the middle of the "sweet spot." The toe and the heel were untouched. It was amazing!

Mickey played beautifully that day (including, as I recall, an eagle on a par five). After the round, she agreed to a press conference and was charming and forthright. All in all, it was a memorable day.

I remain close to Mickey and stay in contact with her. I treasure our friendship.

A Rookie Mistake

At the same time that I was establishing relationships with the older players, I was dealing with a problem that I observed among the younger players, especially the rookies. I felt that they really didn't know enough about the history of the LPGA, nor did they fully appreciate the hard work and dedication of our sponsors, especially the thousands of volunteers who gave of their time to insure the tournaments were the best they could be. Let me give you an example.

One day at an LPGA event I met Louise Suggs, the great LPGA Hall of Famer. I had invited Louise to meet me there so we could spend some time together. As we walked through the course, we passed the putting green, and I thought it would be nice to introduce Louise to a couple of players.

The first player we met was a rookie whose name I have since forgotten, and I wouldn't repeat it even if I could remember it. I introduced her to Louise using only Louise's name and not any specifics, because frankly I didn't think I needed to. The player was polite but dismissive, and her attitude made clear that she was anxious for us to move on so she could practice. We did, and a little later Louise and I separated and planned to meet again for lunch.

I went back to the putting green, and I walked up to the rookie. I said, "Well, Mary (or whatever her name was), how are things going?"

"Well," she said, "this is tough, this is the big time, and I'm working as hard as I can and hoping for the best." I said, "So, I bet you'd really love to win this tournament, wouldn't you?" "Oh," she said, "I can't think of anything that would please me more than to win a tournament." I said, "How'd you like to win fifty-eight?" She looked at me uncomprehendingly. I repeated, "How'd you like to win fifty-eight?" She said, "Commissioner, I don't know what you mean." I said, "Well, the lady that I introduced you to a little while ago won fifty-eight LPGA events. Her name is Louise Suggs and she's a Hall of Famer." Well, to the young woman's credit, she was horrified and immediately apologized to me and went off to do the same to Louise.

I think this story illustrates some important facts of life. And it's not a problem that is easy to solve. I think it applies to every sport, not just golf. The current participants in the sport don't have the memory, the regard, or the respect they should for those who went before them and made their current, very comfortable life possible. Now, this is not a blanket indictment; obviously, many do. But all too many don't. I think that every sport should support and implement programs and policies that encourage players to remember who gave them the life they are enjoying today. I hope that one little incident made that rookie more aware of the people like Louise who had gone before.

To begin to deal with this problem, we did a couple of things. One was to make sure that a significant portion of the orientation given to LPGA rookies at the beginning of the year was devoted to the organization's history. The second thing we did was to start a "Rookie Program." Each rookie was required to spend two full days at some point during the year as a tournament volunteer. Rookies were assigned to a particular tournament, and the tournament organization then assigned them to a volunteer job: it could be parking cars, working the media room, shuttling players, or similar jobs. The program had quite an impact on the rookies, who had no idea of the role volunteers played and how hard they worked. One of my favorite stories involves a rookie who was working a shuttle.

I was at a tournament (I think it was in Atlanta), and I was walking behind the ninth green when I ran across a rookie whose volunteer duty was to shuttle players the fairly long distance from the ninth green to the tenth tee. She would deliver players and then turn around and come back to await the next group of players. When I saw her, she had already been doing this for some hours, and she obviously wasn't thrilled with this duty. I walked over and asked her, "Well, how are you getting along?" She looked at me, not in an angry way so much as a pleading way, and said, "Mr. Mechem, I don't like doing this." I said, "You know, I'm sorry that you don't, but I'm not too surprised because there are a lot of things that the volunteers do that you probably wouldn't enjoy. But let me tell you something. You say you don't like doing this. I would only tell you that last week alone I had to do two or three things that I didn't like doing, and I have a hunch that next week it might be even more."

She looked at me for a minute and then smiled and said, "I think I understand your point." The point of this story is obvious. Professional athletes are living their dreams. Every day they "go to work" doing what they most want to do. They make up a fraction of one percent of all the people in the world who are doing as their life work the thing they enjoy most. It's always important to remind ourselves how lucky we are to be doing things that we enjoy doing, because we are in the vast, vast minority.

Doing Something for the Moms

OUR FIVE YEARS with the LPGA were both rewarding and fun. I say "our" because Marilyn was deeply involved throughout the whole five-year period, traveling to many events with me, entertaining players and sponsors at our home, and generally being supportive in every way. In retrospect, I think it was a good five years. I believe we strengthened the image and reputation of the LPGA, we achieved modest increases in prize money and the number of events, we established several events where the women and the men from both the PGA Tour and the Senior

Tour played together, and we established both the LPGA Foundation and the LPGA Child Care Center, just to mention a few of the accomplishments of which I am very proud.

The LPGA Child Care Center has turned out to be a wonderful benefit for the LPGA players who are also moms. Not long after I became Commissioner, Judy Dickinson told me that there was a crying need (pardon the pun) for some sort of child care for the players' children. More and more of the women were starting families—or wanted to—and child care was a major problem. It was a problem because the players who were also mothers were at the mercy of whatever commercial child-care facilities, if any, were available in the area where the tournament was being played. The players were also at the mercy of the opening and closing hours of those centers, because a player might need to be at the course before the center opened or need to arrive after it had closed.

Judy convinced me that as a women's organization, it was simply something we had to do. We brought our case to the LPGA board, and they enthusiastically approved going forward. When we left the meeting, Judy and I discussed next steps. I pointed out that we had sold the idea, and now we had to find a way to do it and do it right. That, basically, depended on two things: finding a sponsor willing to fund a child-care program and, equally important, finding someone whom the mothers and the children would like and respect to run it. I took on the first job, and Judy agreed to pursue the second.

I approached the J. M. Smucker Company, on whose board I had served for many years. I explained to them the need and pointed out that, in my judgment, doing something like this was totally consistent with the image of the Smucker Company. They agreed, and so the first problem was solved. Meanwhile, Judy had solved the second problem. She hired a young man , Tony Verive, who had been running a child-care center at one of our tournaments and whom many of the players already knew. He was trained as a teacher and was an absolutely wonderful guy.

So, we were off and running! We had established the first traveling child-care program in the history of professional sports. The best evidence of its worth and value is that the program still exists, although much expanded, and the Smucker Company remains the principal sponsor. Scores of players' kids have moved through the system and have loved it. Tony implemented the program so well that one child asked his mom, "How does Tony move that school building from one town to another every week?" He was referring to the fact that every week, at a different tour site, Tony arranged things so the room looked as nearly as possible like the room from the prior week. The kids loved Tony, and they loved the way he moved that building from one town to another!

Some Happy Memories

I HAVE SO many happy memories of my LPGA days. Here are a few.

Shortly after starting the job and concluding that we needed to improve the tour's image, I decided to create a group called the Commissioner's Advisory Council. The group had several purposes. One was to help me open doors that I couldn't open on my own. Another was to, in fact, give advice to me on significant decisions that needed to be made. And, finally, because of the prominence of the members, they added prestige to the image of the LPGA just by their association with us. The idea turned out to be even better than I had anticipated, and I believe the tour and I benefited significantly from the Advisory Council. We had some fascinating and interesting people on the Advisory Council, and I tried to get the group together once each year, typically at a tournament site. One of the members was Alice Dye, a delightful woman who had been a great amateur golfer and was married to Pete Dye, the incomparable and brilliant golf course architect. Alice, as I recall, attended every meeting of the Advisory Council, and Pete always came along.

Pete Dye is not only one of the greatest golf course designers and architects in the world, but also one of its great characters. I have known

Pete for many years. Pete would be the first to tell you that much of his success can be attributed to Alice. Alice was an outstanding amateur golfer in her younger days, and her knowledge of the game, as well as her keen intelligence, has made her truly a partner with Pete. Sometimes he uses this to his advantage. He once told me that all the holes that people complain about he blames on Alice; and the holes that are praised he claims for himself.

One of the funniest things that ever happened at an Advisory Council meeting happened at the Loxahatchee Club. We had lunch after the meeting, and spouses and companions of members were invited to join us. One of my good friends was seated next to Alice. He had not met her before, nor was he aware of her golfing background. In making polite conversation, he said, "Alice, do you play golf?" Alice responded that she did, and my friend then asked her handicap. With a twinkle in her eye she said, "I'm a three." Thinking she was joking, my friend laughed and said something like, "Oh, sure. I'll bet you are!" Several people sitting nearby heard the exchange and quickly informed my friend that she was indeed a three, at which point he was overwhelmed with embarrassment and apologized profusely. Alice took it gracefully, but it is something, I promise you, that my friend has never forgotten.

Another funny thing happened at that particular Advisory Council meeting, this time involving Pete Dye. Typically, at Advisory Council meetings I invited several LPGA pros to join the members of the Advisory Council in a round of golf after the meeting. Tammie Green was one of the pros who joined us at the Loxahatchee Club. I felt like I knew Tammie even before I first met her. One of the tour's top players, she came from a small town in southeastern Ohio, not far from the small town where I grew up. My town was a little bigger than hers, a fact that I never let her forget. In any case, she was by far the best-known and most popular golfer in the area where we both grew up. Tammie has a slow and easy gait and manner and was very popular among players and fans alike. As well as winning a number of LPGA events, she also served on the LPGA board.

Tammie was paired in the golf outing with Pete, and I walked a few holes with their group. Pete was wearing the worst-looking pair of golf shoes I had ever seen. They must have been twenty years old and hadn't been near a can of polish in fifteen of those years. They were some kind of orange-and-black mixture that I really can't describe. In any case, as we walked down the fairway, Tammie came over to Pete, put her arm around him, and said, "Pete, can I ask you a personal question?" Pete was a bit startled, but flattered at what sort of personal question Tammie might have. So, he said, "Of course, anything you like." Tammie then looked at him and grinned and said, "Pete, who shines your shoes?" We all did a double take and then really had a good laugh!

Let me tell you another story involving Pete that took place at that great golf resort Whistling Straits, which is owned by another one of the world's great characters, Herb Kohler.

Herb and I were playing Whistling Straits one day, and I was not aware that Pete Dye was in the vicinity, but he was, in fact, just across the road designing what came to be the River Course. Unbeknownst to me, Pete was standing on a knoll overlooking the ninth green when Herb and I hit our shots into the green. I hit one of the best three woods of my life that not only went long and straight but caught the contour of the land, which brought the ball down the hill onto the edge of the green. As we approached the green and Pete saw that I was the one who hit the shot, he called out, "Good God, if Mechem can reach this green in two, I'm going to have to redesign this hole! My reputation is at stake." I told Pete not to worry. All it proved was that even a blind pig can occasionally find a truffle!

I met many fascinating people during my LPGA days. One of the most interesting and impressive was a man named Dick Siderowf. I actually met Dick through his wife, Topsy, who worked for *Golf Digest*. Dick had won the British Amateur Championship twice and had won a number of prestigious amateur championships in the United States and around the world. I had two experiences with Dick that I shall always remember.

The first came on a day when we were playing golf at Dick's club in Connecticut, The Century Club. At one point during a round, I was marking my ball, and I asked Dick if he thought many players inaccurately and intentionally marked their ball slightly closer to the hole. Dick laughed and said that indeed he did. He told me about a fellow he played with who was consistently marking the ball closer to the hole. Finally, Dick said that he couldn't ignore it any longer, and he said something like this: "Pete, I am writing a book and it is about you." Pete (not his real name) said, "What do you mean? What would you write about me?" Dick responded, "The title of the book will be *My Friend Pete—Marking His Way to a Birdie!*"

The other Siderowf story came when we were playing in an outing at the great Laurel Valley Club in Pennsylvania. On one of the holes I had what for me was a great drive. Excitedly I turned to Dick and the other two members of our foursome and I said, "That's as good as I can hit it!" Dick quickly said, "No, no, no—never say that. Never let your opponents know that you can't do any better." As I think about it, this is probably a pretty good rule for living!

I **THINK THE** first call I received after it was announced that I was to be the LPGA Commissioner was from Deane Beman, then Commissioner of the PGA Tour. I had known Deane for some years, and our relationship had always been cordial. He was very kind in calling to congratulate me and to offer any assistance he might provide. I thanked him and told him I was sure I would be asking him for advice, which I did from time to time over the years. But, the story I want to tell actually has to do with Deane approaching *me* and asking for my thoughts and cooperation in a project. The World Golf Hall of Fame, located near St. Augustine, is a magnificent facility that tastefully presents the history of the game and honors its greatest stars. When Deane called me, however, the World Golf Hall of Fame was just an idea in his mind, but one to which he was clearly very dedicated. Deane explained to me his dream and stated quite simply that he needed and wanted the support of the LPGA because, quite obviously, the facility would not be representative of the game unless it also included the great female players. I laughed and told Deane that I couldn't help but needle him a little by saying that this was probably the first time in history that the Commissioner of the PGA Tour had called the Commissioner of the LPGA for help. I told Deane I thought it was a great idea, and, although I wanted to learn more about it, I was confident the LPGA would be an enthusiastic supporter and participant.

However, I told Deane that there was one condition critical to our involvement. I said, "Deane, the women need to be treated on an absolutely equal footing with the men. There cannot be a separate part of the building set apart for the women's 'section.' In every way the women players must be treated absolutely on a par (pardon the pun) with the men." Deane said he understood my "condition" and absolutely agreed that it would be honored. To his credit, Deane lived up to his word, and anyone who visits the World Golf Hall of Fame today will see ample evidence that he kept his promise. To say that Deane was as good as his word will not surprise anyone who knows him. He is a man of complete integrity.

ONE OF THE funniest incidents that occurred during my LPGA days was something that I had never seen before, nor have I seen it since. I was standing behind the ninth green at the McDonald's LPGA Championship at the DuPont Country Club in Wilmington, Delaware. The great Japanese player, Ayako Okamoto, in hitting her approach shot to the green, put a little too much muscle into the shot and it landed in the rough behind the green. The ball took a high bounce into the crowd of spectators, who were lined up five or six deep behind the green.

This in itself is not especially unusual, but what happened in this case *was* unusual. There was a man in the gallery wearing a Hawaiian-type sports shirt with a big breast pocket made even bigger by a pack of cigarettes. The ball bounced right into the man's shirt pocket and stayed there! Fortunately, he simply froze rather than running away or doing something equally troublesome. An official ran over and told him not to move and, believe me, he didn't. When Ayako arrived at the scene, everyone was laughing and she joined in the general mood. The official told her to simply pick the ball out of the man's pocket and take a drop where he had been standing. She did this and went on to play the hole as if nothing had happened!

NOW LET ME tell you a story that I wish had had a different ending. Marilyn and I were in Scotland attending the Solheim Cup when I received a call from Billy Payne, the brilliant impresario who went on to stage the highly successful Olympic games in Atlanta in 1996. Billy began the conversation by saying, "I need your help." I asked what I could do. He indicated that he was working hard to include golf in the 1996 Olympics and was confident that he could persuade the Augusta National Golf Club to host the event. He pointed out, however, that he didn't want to go forward with any serious efforts until he was certain that all the major organizations in golf were supportive. He was understandably concerned that the women of the LPGA might not be enthusiastic in light of Augusta's much discussed gender rules.

I told Billy that I understood the situation and that I would talk to our players and get back to him as soon as possible. I further told him that I had a hunch that our players would be supportive because they would view it as a way to showcase the talents of female golfers on this great golf course.

I promptly spoke with a substantial number of players, and my hunch turned out to be right. To a woman they were supportive because they were confident that women's golf would be significantly enhanced by the LPGA being involved in the Olympics at Augusta. I called Billy and communicated our enthusiasm.

Plans went forward and everything seemed to be going smoothly. Indeed, things progressed to the point that there was a major press conference on the famous lawn outside the clubhouse at Augusta. All the leaders of the major golf organizations were there, as was Jack Stephens, then the chairman of Augusta National. The plans were announced, everybody was thrilled, the press knew they had a big story, and all of us in golf were excited. Unfortunately, the plans later became enmeshed in Olympic politics, and the entire effort collapsed. Sadly, there was no golf in the Olympics in 1996.

I have a fascinating reminder of this whole matter hanging in my closet. Each of us at the press conference that day received a souvenir, a shirt with the striking new logo for the event that was supposed to take place. It was the Augusta flag placed squarely in the midst of the five Olympic rings. Sadly, this logo was never used and perhaps never will be. It is, of course, one of my prized possessions!

As a matter of interest and further detail, I have included in the Appendix the article from the *New York Times* reporting on these events.

Two postscripts:

In one of those fascinating quirks of history, Billy Payne is now Chairman of the Augusta National Golf Club and in my humble and unsolicited opinion the best since Bob Jones.

Happily, golf will be part of the Olympics in 2016 in Rio de Janeiro. The worldwide golf community, led by my good friend and protégé Ty Votaw, was successful in persuading the International Olympic Committee that it was time for golf to take its place in the Olympic games. It should be quite a show.

AS I MENTIONED earlier, shortly after joining the LPGA I created the Commissioner's Advisory Council. One of its members was Neil Armstrong. Neil loved golf and golf events, and I invited him to be my guest at an LPGA tournament. I knew the players would be thrilled to meet him, so I took him around the tournament site and introduced him to a number of people. One of these introductions remains vivid in my mind. The player to whom I introduced Neil was a delightful woman, one of my favorites. (Let's call her Betty.) I think I startled her a bit when I said, "I'd like you to meet Neil Armstrong." Her response was either born of shock or a very sharp sense of humor—or who knows what! She shook hands with Neil and said, "I'm so happy to meet you. You know, your name is exactly the same as the man who went to the moon." The only response I could muster was, "Betty, this *is* the man who went to the moon." This story swept through the tournament in a matter of minutes, it seemed, and is one many of the players remember to this day.

THE LPGA HAD a tournament in Lansing, Michigan, sponsored by Oldsmobile. Of course, Lansing in the early 1990s was a very important automobile center, and everything about the town reflected that. I arrived in Lansing for the tournament one year and learned that there had just been a spirited and somewhat controversial contest to decide on a name for the new Lansing Minor League Baseball franchise that everyone was very excited about. The name ultimately chosen in the contest was a beauty—the Lansing Lugnuts! Lugnuts, for those of you who don't know, are the nuts that hold the tires onto your car. I don't know why they're called lugnuts, but that's what they're called. Many people were happy about the name, but a lot of people weren't. The logo showed a whirling lugnut with a sort of sadistic little grin.

I had just arrived in town that day, and, of course, nobody realized that I even knew about this. I was so amused by the whole thing that at the Pro-Am dinner that night, when I was asked to make some remarks, I said how happy I was to be in Lansing and how I was always treated so well when I came there. But, I said, at dinner a little earlier a troublesome thing had occurred and I wasn't sure why. As I was eating my dessert, I bit down on something hard, and though it didn't break my teeth, it kind of frightened me. When I got it out of my mouth and looked at it, it was a lugnut! Then, I said, "Why in the world would there be a lugnut in my dessert?" (Of course, I was making this up.) Well, the whole crowd went crazy because, again, they didn't expect me to know anything about the controversy. There had been a lot of tension over the choice of the name, and when I said that, it seemed to relieve some of that tension. Anyway, I'll never forget it, and I have a hat hanging in my office today with the little Lansing Lugnut logo on it. A wonderful Lansing memory.

ONE OF THE most pleasant things that happened during my tenure as Commissioner was a Pro-Am tournament that President and Mrs. Gerald Ford hosted at their beautiful Club at Morningside in Rancho Mirage, California. Mrs. Ford, like Delores Hope (Bob Hope's wife), had long been a supporter and booster of the LPGA. President Ford, of course, was an avid golfer. Each year on the evening before the Pro-Am, President and Mrs. Ford hosted a small dinner party at their home. Since I was Commissioner, Marilyn and I were invited and were, of course, honored to attend. Part of the fun of the evening was the guest list, which always included people I was excited to meet.

At one of these dinners, we found our place cards and were happy to see that "Dandy" Don Meredith and his wife would also be at our table. I don't remember who else was at the table, but I do remember there was one place with a card for Peter Pocklington. At that time his name didn't mean much to me, but it certainly did a few minutes later.

We were all seated when Mr. Pocklington approached the table, stuck out his hand to me, and said, "Hello, I'm Peter Pocklington. I'm the guy who traded Wayne Gretzky." At first we were all a bit stunned. And then he said, "I just wanted to get that out of the way right up front because I know it will come up later in the conversation." We all got a big laugh, and I admired him for handling it the way he did.

I FEEL FORTUNATE to have had the chance to get to know and spend time with Karsten Solheim, a true genius, one of the great innovators in the history of golf, and the founder of Karsten Manufacturing. He was truly an exceptional person. If I had to choose one word to describe Karsten, it would be "strong." He radiated strength—both physically and mentally. But it was the softer side of Karsten that I had the privilege to see. Karsten, along with his beautiful and intelligent wife, Louise, and his son John, was the strongest supporter the LPGA has ever had. At one time PING sponsored three tournaments *and* the Solheim Cup.

My favorite memory of Karsten still makes me smile. Whenever he was at an LPGA tournament (and he was at many), he usually was up on the practice green with his newest putter design in hand (although his company designed and marketed the full line of clubs, the putter is where it all began with Karsten). At most golf clubs the practice putting green is located quite close to the first tee because after hitting balls on the driving range, players like to putt and get themselves mentally ready just before teeing off.

Karsten would walk onto the putting green and hand out his newest putter to various players and suggest that they put the putter in their bag for the day's round. He was sure that it would improve their performance on the greens. What made this amusing is that there is no way that a player would put a brand-new putter, which she had never used, in her bag for a competitive round. At the same time, this was Karsten

Amy Alcott, Judy Dickinson, Marilyn, and Gardner Dickinson.

With LPGA legend Patty Berg. Patty makes me look tall—the only time in my life.

*The great
JoAnne Carner.*

Speaking at the annual meeting of the Tournament Sponsors Association.

With Karsten and Louise Solheim at a Solheim Cup dinner.

Marilyn and me in Europe for the Solheim Cup.

Here is my Lansing Lugnuts logo ball cap. I still wear it!

CSM presenting Louise and Karsten Solheim with the LPGA's Commissioner's Award, 1994.

Nancy Lopez photographing Louise Solheim and Juli Inkster.

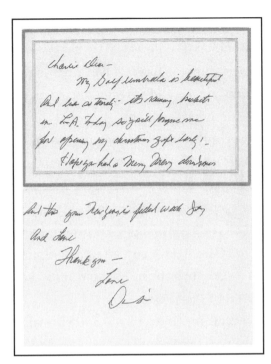

Dinah's thank-you note for her LPGA Christmas gift. She was one of a kind.

Our very special retirement gift! Two real first-class airline seats!

Solheim! He was not only famous, but he was beloved. No one wanted to turn him down so the players would find some way to try it—just not that day! I know that I speak for everyone who has ever had anything to do with the LPGA when I say that no one has had a greater impact on its growth and success than Karsten and Louise Solheim.

Another story that illustrates not only Karsten's strong resolve on all matters, especially on the "square grooves" issue, involves a meeting at NBC to discuss broadcasting the Solheim Cup. I was not at the meeting, but my good friend Jon Miller was. Jon has been a key part of the NBC sports organization for a number of years. Although we are quite a few years apart in age, Jon also went to Miami University, and I talked with him frequently during my years as Commissioner. I should note that Jon has always been a strong booster of the LPGA.

It was a large meeting with several members of the Solheim family, NBC sports executives, and the usual group of lawyers. The timing of the meeting is important because it took place during the heated dispute between the PGA Tour and the Solheims over the issue of the legality of "square grooves" on clubs.

As Jon tells the story, during lengthy meetings he had a habit of "doodling" on a sheet of paper to help pass the time. As this particular meeting stretched into several hours, he had a sheet of doodles, many of them involving members of the Solheim family. These were funny and harmless but not the sort of thing that Jon ever expected to share with anyone else. In about the third hour of the meeting, Karsten, who had said very little, got up and walked around the table and said to Jon, "Let me see that piece of paper." Jon's heart practically stopped, and he saw the end of his career flash across his mind. He said he looked in vain at his lawyers, who simply shrugged their shoulders. He had no choice but to hand Karsten the paper filled with doodles and wait for the axe to fall. Karsten took the paper, turned it over to the back side, which was blank, paying no attention whatever to Jon's "artwork." He then said, "Let me explain to you about square grooves," as he started drawing illustrations on the page. In other words, there was only one thing on Karsten's mind—not just during this meeting but during the entire time the contentious square grooves issue was working its way through the courts. Karsten viewed the PGA Tour's challenge as a challenge to his integrity, and it seemed to be uppermost in his mind all the time.

Jon, naturally, was enormously relieved that his career had been saved, but he was also impressed, as all of us who knew Karsten were, with Karsten's single-minded dedication.

IN 1994, THE SOLHEIM CUP was played at The Greenbrier in West Virginia. The week before, the LPGA played an event in Naples, Florida. We were anxious to get the players from Naples to The Greenbrier as soon as possible so that they could begin their preparation for what is the biggest week in their year. So, we chartered a 737 to fly them from Naples and land at the airport in Lewisburg, West Virginia, the closest airport to The Greenbrier.

Everything went smoothly; we got everyone on the plane and to The Greenbrier in good shape. When we taxied up to the terminal and walked down the steps to the welcoming party, we saw that they had big smiles on their faces. Now that in itself wasn't surprising; this was a very happy occasion. But they were laughing out loud, and that seemed a little much. They couldn't wait to explain.

It seems that just a short time before we landed an identical plane had landed and taxied to the terminal. The welcoming party greeted the arrival of the plane with flags, music from a local band, and all the trimmings. As the door opened and the women in the plane began to emerge, the welcoming party gasped! All the women were in plain dresses and were handcuffed!

A contingent of women prisoners bound for a detention center in Lewisburg had been flown in and landed just ahead of us. Apparently, the flag waving and the music stopped quickly when it was clear this was not the group they had anticipated. I don't have any idea what was in the minds of the women prisoners, but they must have thought it was a classy place they were going to, since they meet you with bands and flags. When our players learned of this, they were absolutely overwhelmed with laughter, and, ironically, it put them in a very good mood for what would be a very taxing week.

The Greenbrier was a phenomenal venue. Not only was the golf course great, but the accommodations were among the best in the world. Many of the players, particularly the Europeans, had never seen the likes of it before. The U.S. team won after a tough battle, but, as with every Solheim Cup, there really are no losers!

The remarks I made at the closing ceremony of the Greenbrier Solheim Cup sum up how I viewed this great international competition and its participants. Here's what I said:

> And so, the third playing of the Solheim Cup draws to a close. And what a fantastic one it has been—filled with all of the elements of a great sporting event—joy, sadness, elation, despair, emotion, patriotism, brilliant individual and team performance—and finally, inevitably, victory and defeat.
>
> But, try as I may, I can find no losers here. Instead, I find a great United States team that has played brilliantly, fought hard and won—and a great European team that has played superbly, fought tenaciously, but didn't win. I am—and I know all of you are—immensely proud of them both.
>
> To the Solheim family and The Greenbrier, our deepest and warmest thanks for allowing us this rich experience in this superb setting. And, my friends, we must not forget the unsung heroes—Executive Sports, the marshals, the scorekeepers, the drivers, all of the volunteers. The Pro Shop folks, greenkeepers, and course workers—and these quiet but critical participants—the caddies. And, to NBC—our deepest thanks and congratulations.

I said at the opening ceremony that—irrespective of the out-come—the ultimate winner would be women's golf, and indeed it has been so. To these two great teams, I would simply say that because of what you have done here the past three days, countless young women all over the world—and for generations to come—will walk a little taller, reach a little higher, act a little bolder, and think a little bigger. What an incredible legacy.

And so, I close by extending my warmest congratulations to the WPGET, to Captain Mickey Walker, and to this great European team. You have played with tremendous heart and skill. Many of you are my very good friends, and I am deeply honored by that.

And to Captain JoAnne Carner and the U.S. team—AWESOME! You have made us very proud. You have earned the single most important reward that anyone striving for excellence can attain—the unqualified respect of your peers and of all who watched you play. RESPECT. RESPECT. In the end, nothing else matters.

There is an interesting postscript to the Greenbrier Solheim Cup. A tradition had grown up that the victorious Ryder Cup team was invited to the White House to be congratulated by the president. I felt that the Solheim Cup team deserved equal treatment. Some weeks before the event at Greenbrier, I told my staff to contact the White House and see if an invitation could be arranged. In spite of our repeated prodding, we got no response. Finally, on the day before the matches were to begin, I had my staff convey the message to the appropriate staff in Washington that if we didn't receive an invitation in the next twenty-four hours, I would feel compelled in the Commissioner's pre-event press conference to explain that, although the Ryder Cup players were always invited to the White House, apparently our players would not enjoy the same courtesy. It will not surprise the reader to learn that an invitation came through promptly!

The day arrived for the White House visit, and everyone was very excited. Marilyn was with me, along with the twelve members of the team and its colorful and dynamic captain, JoAnne Carner. When we entered the Oval Office, President Clinton had the players line up in a wide semi-circle in front of his desk, and he went from one player to the next, congratulating each. But, the amazing thing was that he knew something personal about virtually every player. For example, when he came to Meg Mallon, who in a tournament earlier that year had good-naturedly thrown her putter into the lake after finishing her round to underscore what a bad putting day she had, the president shook Meg's hand and observed that he, too, had often wanted to throw his putter into a lake. Everyone had a good laugh. It was a classic example of President Clinton's famous ability to know the details of every subject he dealt with and of his amazing charisma.

EVERY YEAR AT Christmas the LPGA sent gifts to a number of its sponsors and supporters. One year, while I was Commissioner, the gift was a golf umbrella with the LPGA logo on it. Among the recipients was, naturally, Dinah Shore, who was one of the most recognizable names on the LPGA gift list. We never received thank-you notes for these gifts. We didn't expect to. They were just small acknowledgments of our gratitude to people who had given us support. The year we sent the umbrella I received *one* thank-you note, and it was from Dinah. Of all people to take the time to thank the LPGA, it's amazing that Dinah was the one. But, come to think of it, it's not amazing, because she was simply that kind of person. I still have the note. It reads: "Charlie dear—My golf umbrella is beautiful and ever so timely—it's raining buckets in L.A. today—so you'll forgive me for opening my Christmas gift early! Hope you had a merry, merry Christmas and that your New Year is filled with joy and love. Thank you. Love, Dinah." I'm not sure I know more than half a dozen people who would be this thoughtful and this warm. It typifies Dinah's whole career and why she was so universally loved.

Another story about Dinah shows what a good sport she was. David Foster, the legendary head of the Colgate Company, asked her to lend her name and support to the Women's Golf Tournament that David proposed to sponsor at Mission Hills in Rancho Mirage, California. If I remember correctly, Colgate was sponsoring Dinah's TV show, so Dinah was naturally anxious to help. As she told the story later, when David invited her, she simply assumed that it was a tennis tournament because she was an avid tennis player and didn't even play golf. She was more than a little surprised soon after to learn that it was indeed a golf tournament. But, with Dinah's ever-present enthusiasm and good spirits, she embraced the event totally and learned to play a very acceptable game of golf. By the way, this event continues as one of the LPGA's Majors. It was sponsored for many years by Colgate, then by Nabisco, and currently by Kraft.

I was privileged to announce at a dinner during the LPGA Tournament in 1994 that Dinah had been named to the LPGA Hall of Fame, the first time anyone other than a player had been accorded this honor. My remarks at the March 22, 1994, tournament gala dinner are included in the Appendix to this book.

IN NOVEMBER OF 2001, the LPGA was playing an event at Donald Trump's course in South Florida. Trump is a devoted golfer—and a good one. He was also a very strong sponsor and advocate for the women's tour. During the week of the tournament, the women's Chamber of Commerce of Palm Beach County sponsored a luncheon at which Donald was the guest speaker. Marilyn and I were invited, and I took notes as he spoke because I wanted to be sure to remember his comments. The subject of his speech was his "rules" for being a successful businessperson. Here they are, exactly as I wrote them down on my copy of the program. My apologies to Mr. Trump if I got any of them wrong, but I am confident that my notes are accurate.

- ✤ Think big

- ✤ Stay focused

- ✤ Be paranoid

- ✤ Maintain momentum

- ✤ Be passionate

- ✤ Go against the tide when you feel it appropriate— go with your "gut"

- ✤ Be lucky—some people are simply born lucky

- ✤ Get even—when "they" go after you, go after them

- ✤ Always have a prenuptial agreement

- ✤ Think like a winner

I thought these comments were delightful and insightful, and I kept that copy of the program with my notes.

IRONICALLY, THE EVENT that got the greatest media attention during my days at the LPGA was an event I wish had never happened. But, it did give me a platform to express certain things in which I deeply believed. During the 1993 McDonald's LPGA Championship in Wilmington, Delaware, a local reporter wrote a story with comments attributed to a well-known and respected reporter, Ben Wright. It quickly became a sensational story all over the country. It dealt with issues concerning the players' lifestyles, sexual preferences, physical attributes, and several other things that had nothing whatever to do with golf. Ben was one of the reporters covering the event, which was broadcast on CBS.

Marilyn and I were taking a couple of days away from the tournament that year because our oldest daughter, Melissa, was having her second baby in San Francisco. We intended to fly there and then come back to Wilmington for the weekend. We stopped in Cincinnati on the way, and when I phoned my office, I learned of the media "flap" that was growing bigger and bigger by the minute. Ben was denying what the reporter alleged he had said, and that, of course, made the story even juicier. There was really nothing to do immediately because we felt we should let the story play out a day or so before taking any position regarding it. I asked my office to schedule a press conference at which I would address the media on Saturday of that week.

We went on to San Francisco, made a quick visit to our new granddaughter, and hustled back to Wilmington, arriving late Friday night. On the way back I had a chance to think about what I wanted to say at the press conference. Meanwhile, the story grew and grew and became, literally, an international incident.

When I walked into the press conference on Saturday morning, I was absolutely stunned. It looked like a press conference at the White House. The room was filled with reporters and photographers. There must have been 150 reporters in the room. I realized later why it was such a huge story. It was not only a sports story; it was also a mass media story and a tabloid story. But, I had thought long and hard about what I wanted to say and was actually happy that there were so many media outlets to hear my comments.

The complete text of my remarks that day is in the Appendix of this book. But here is the gist. I pointed out that I was deeply disappointed with the entire affair. My disappointment stemmed from the fact that we were sitting in a room only a few yards away from where the greatest women golfers in the world were contesting one of their major championships. But, we were talking about something entirely apart from that. And, what we were talking about was, in my judgment, entirely irrelevant to what we were all about. The LPGA is an organization of professionals. The only thing that really should matter was how the players performed on the golf course. As a result of the hubbub that was going on around us, the performance of the players on the golf course had become a minor story. That, I felt, was totally wrong.

One postscript: Ben Wright and I had always been friends, and I hope that we still are, although I haven't spoken with him in years. I understand Ben has been critical of me for not defending him and supporting his position in the matter. I understand why he might feel that way, but I never felt that it was my role to support or criticize any of the "contestants" in this debate. I saw my job as speaking for and defending the LPGA and its players, nothing more and nothing less. I did that to the best of my ability. I wouldn't change a single thing I did or said that week.

IN SPITE OF tough times like this, I was sad that my "tour of duty" as LPGA Commissioner was coming to an end. There was an unexpected and funny result to my having announced on the day I was hired the date that I would be retiring—December 31, 1995. I really never thought any more about the repercussions that such an announcement might have until I attended the first LPGA event of 1995. That tournament gave me a retirement party—months before my retirement date! That turned out to be the pattern for the year, as similar parties were held at virtually every tournament I attended in that last year. I finally said at one such party late in the year that I had had the longest retirement of anyone since the Grateful Dead! But, it was great fun and a wonderfully thoughtful thing for these tournaments to do.

MY OFFICIAL RETIREMENT party was given by the tour and the players and was held in Charlotte, North Carolina, in October 1995.

It was an absolutely wonderful affair, and Marilyn and I were deeply moved. We received some marvelous gifts. Perhaps the most unusual was a pair of real first-class airline seats from the cabin of an airliner. The plaque read something like this: "Two first-class seats for a first-class couple." The only challenge was where to put them, but we solved that by keeping them in our home in Jackson Hole, Wyoming, for many years. It was a happy, wonderfully upbeat night with so many of our good friends around us. I remember being especially grateful that Tim Finchem, the Commissioner of the PGA Tour, and several of his associates attended. Tim and I were good friends and remain so today.

In my remarks that night, I tried to make the point that Marilyn and I had fallen in love with the players and everything they stood for. I reminded them of what I had told them about the "institutional inferiority complex" and that I was proud of how they had overcome that problem. The mood of the occasion was very light and happy, and I contributed to that feeling by telling them there were only two reasons I was actually happy to be leaving the job. The first was that I could stop treating my hair with Grecian Formula Gray and let it return to its normal dark, curly brown. Second, I could stop pretending to have an eighteen handicap and begin once again to play to my real scratch handicap! These comments were met with hoots and howls! By the way, there is one thing I wish I had accomplished during my LPGA tenure, but I just plain ran out of time. After playing a lot of golf over the years, and especially during my LPGA days, I was fascinated by how, when a person hits a bad shot and chooses to hit another, the second shot is inevitably a good shot. As a result, it has always been my dream to establish in golf the "second serve rule" from tennis! Just imagine how this would revolutionize the game and make it so much more enjoyable because, as I say, there are no bad second shots in golf—at least none that I have seen. It would be a simple rules change, and perhaps I should continue my goal of persuading the USGA and the R & A of the wisdom of this change. People who know how impatient I am with some of golf's arcane rules and policies might think I am serious about this. Much as I love the idea, I am just kidding!

The days at the LPGA were indeed happy ones, with very few exceptions. This was principally because of the people I met and worked with, including, of course, the players. I have many happy "player memories." Here are just a few. The names are in alphabetical order to protect the innocent—namely me!

Some Player Memories

Beth Daniel

Over my years at the LPGA—and since—Beth Daniel has become one of my good friends. Beth is, of course, a Hall of Famer and most deservedly so. It has always been accepted that she has one of the greatest—if not the greatest—golf swing on the tour and her record suggests that it is certainly true. Beth also served on the Player Board of Directors during my time at the LPGA and always took her work seriously and was very effective.

The first story I want to tell about Beth started when one day she said, "Are you going to be playing in the Pro-Am this week?" And I replied that I was. She said, "I'm not playing this week, but I'd love to caddy for you. What do you think?" I said, "I would love it," and arranged to meet her the following morning outside the pro shop so that we could hit a few balls and then go to the first tee. Beth said, "Charlie, don't take too heavy a bag." And I promised that I wouldn't. Before the next day dawned, I had a thought. I went into the pro shop and looked for one of those huge golf bags that are frequently found in pro shops for storing and displaying a great number of golf clubs. The typical display bag is probably one-and-a-half feet across and can hold probably seventy to eighty clubs. I talked to the pro, and he was more than cooperative. He helped me take the bag outside the shop complete with its seventy to eighty clubs, and I awaited Beth's arrival. As she walked up to me and said good morning, her eyes moved to the bag, and, I must say, her eyes became saucer-like. She looked at me and said, "What is this?" I said, "Well, I need a few more clubs than most players, and I figured this would be the best way to get around." By this time, I was starting to laugh so hard that the joke became apparent and Beth joined in. Needless to say, I got my regular clubs, put them in a Sunday bag, and Beth caddied for me all day. It was an absolutely delightful experience that I will never forget!

This next Beth Daniel story still makes me laugh, but I am not sure whether it makes Beth laugh! During my years at the LPGA, the Korean golf boom was just beginning. We had secured a new event to be played on an island just off the coast of South Korea, and we were very excited about it. I flew there for the opening of the event. In my preliminary meetings with the tournament sponsors and organizers, I was told that the sponsors wanted to start things off on a festive and patriotic note. They intended to put a red ball, a white ball, and a blue ball on the tees and wanted me to be one of the three people who would hit these balls to inaugurate the event. The chairman of the sponsoring company and a local dignitary would be the others. I told them that, while I would do almost anything to promote the event, this was not something that I was comfortable doing. I hastened to add that I would get one of our top players to take my place, and I thought that would probably be better anyway. They thought that would be just fine. I found Beth and asked her if she would stand in for me. She said she would be happy to help.

The big moment arrived, and I was standing on the first tee watching the proceedings. All three people lined up and took big swings at the three balls. Then, the "fun" began. It turned out that the three balls were fake and were loaded with smoke that billowed from the balls once they were struck, so red, white, and blue plumes of smoke lifted into the air. It brought forth great surprise and applause, and everyone seemed thrilled, except Beth. She was absolutely convinced that I knew what was going to happen and had "conned" her into doing it. I was finally able to convince Beth that I was totally blameless, and she joined in the laughter. It was one of the funniest moments I had ever seen at an opening ceremony, and I'm glad it didn't permanently affect my friendship with Beth.

Judy Dickinson

As I have indicated elsewhere in this book, Judy Dickinson was the president of the Players Association when I became Commissioner. Indeed, I had heard so many good things about her performance in that job that I made it a condition of my accepting the Commissioner's position that Judy would remain for another year as president. She and I established an immediate friendship and solid working relationship. She and her husband, Gardner Dickinson, became good friends of Marilyn's and mine. Gardner died several years ago. We miss him very much, but we stay in touch with Judy.

Judy and I had a lot of fun times, but perhaps the most hilarious was during a Pro-Am in San Diego where we played in the same group. We were paired with the comedian who had entertained at the Pro-Am dinner the night before. He was a delightful guy who kept us laughing.

That particular day I had the greatest putting experience of my life. I made something like ten or twelve one putts, some from a long way off! After four or five of these putts, the comedian began referring to me as "Mr. Wonderful"!* He became more demonstrative and vocal as each improbable putt found the hole. To this day, Judy frequently refers to me as Mr. Wonderful, and it is a warm and happy memory for both of us.

---

*"Mr. Wonderful" was a hit song written in 1955. The most popular version was by Peggy Lee. It was also the title song of a Broadway musical starring Sammy Davis, Jr.

Juli Inkster

Juli Inkster is a legend in her own time! A Hall of Fame golfer, a mother of two delightful daughters, married for thirty-two years to Brian, a terrific guy who has been the head pro at Los Gatos Country Club for over thirty years. In addition to her great play, she has found time to be deeply involved in the operation of the tour and serves as an unbelievable role model to younger players, many of whom are as old as Juli's daughters. Juli and Brian continue to be among Marilyn's and my closest friends.

I had the great honor of acting as master of ceremonies for Juli's Hall of Fame induction in San Francisco in April of 2011. Typical of Juli—one of the world's great jocks—the party was held at Giants' stadium, AT&T Park, in San Francisco with cocktails in the dugout! It was a warm and funny evening, and you could feel the love and respect in the room. Here is a summary of what I had to say.

I began by teasing Juli about both her age and the fact that it had taken her ten years from the time she was elected to the Hall of Fame to choose when and where she wanted to have her party. For example, I said that she had been around so long that even Bobby Jones had commented that Juli Inkster was one of his favorite players. As for taking ten years to have her party, I teased that she had thought she had to pay for the party, but when she learned that the LPGA would pick up the tab she immediately scheduled it.

I then made the following comments: I am very excited to share this evening with you. My years with the LPGA were among the happiest of my life, and it is so good to see so many of you who helped make it so. But, no one more than Juli Inkster.

I have known a lot of golfing greats—but none greater than this woman—for the honesty and completeness of the life she has led. In searching for a way to describe Juli in a word or two, I have settled on the phrase "abnormally normal." A wife, a mother, great family, a jock of the highest order, embarrassing dancer, and, by the way, a three-time U.S. Women's Amateur Champion and a Hall of Fame golfer. That, to me, is "abnormally normal."

My favorite story about Juli involves playing together in a Pro-Am in Phoenix—at the Solheim family's Club at Moon Valley. Like many of the Arizona clubs, Moon Valley was surrounded by large mountains, although the playing surface was fairly flat. On top of these mountains were built beautiful, expensive, and sprawling homes. As we were walking down one of the fairways, Juli looked up at one of the homes and then turned to me and said, "Charlie, if you owned one of those homes, I'd consider having an affair with you!" We all got a big laugh out of that, knowing what a prude Juli Inkster was when it came to her marital vows. Later that night, I had an idea. The next day I checked the starting times and figured out approximately when Juli would be walking down that same fairway during the first round of the tournament. I made my way out to that fairway and waited for her group to come through. As she walked by me, I waved, and she, of course, sent a friendly wave back. I yelled out to her, "Juli, do you remember what you told me yesterday about those houses?" She smiled and nodded. I said, "Well, I just want you to know I just bought the biggest house on that mountain!" We had a private laugh, and the round went on.

Nancy Lopez

I have known Nancy Lopez almost from the day she won her first major championship and went on to that incredible string of nine straight victories in her rookie year. We have become very good friends. We were even next-door neighbors for a short time at the Jack Nicklaus Sports Center, and I have stayed in close touch with her over the years. One of the most pleasant memories I will always have of Nancy is that she succeeded me on the board of the J. M. Smucker Company. And that leads to my first story.

As my retirement from the Smucker board approached, Tim and Richard Smucker (the co-CEOs of that superb company) asked me what I thought about Nancy Lopez coming on the board. They both knew Nancy because they had played in Pro-Ams with her over the years. Smucker had sponsored (and still does) the LPGA's Child Development Center, and one of the ways the moms showed their appreciation was to play in Pro-Ams from time to time with the Smucker folks.

I told Tim and Richard I would be flattered if she succeeded me, but I said, "You'll have to accept the fact that the collective golf handicap of the board will certainly go up when a great golfer like me is succeeded by a girl!" My crack about the collective handicap of the board going up needs a little explanation. I am a hacker—an eighteen handicapper—and always have been. Now that I have reached eighty (years, not strokes), I don't imagine that it will ever improve. I have frequently commented that probably no one in the history of the game has been exposed to more great players with less visible results than I. But, when it comes to love of the game, I'm a scratch!

They were "polite" in their response. I then turned serious and said that I thought it would be a great idea. They asked if I would call Nancy and see how she felt about the situation.

So, I called Nancy and told her that she was being considered and that I thought it would be terrific; she would do a great job and make a real contribution. Plus, she would be exposed in-depth to how a great company operates. I told her that Tim and Richard would be contacting her. They did—and formally invited her to join the board. Shortly after they talked with her I got a call from Nancy, who was very excited but also nervous. I asked her what she thought. She said, "I am very, very humbled, but I need to ask you something. Do you have to be smart to be on a board?" I laughed and responded, "Nancy, you don't have to be smart. I've known plenty of directors—some of big companies— who weren't very smart or who at least were so arrogant that it muffled their intelligence." Then I added, "Secondly, you are a very smart lady!"

Happily, she joined the board and has become a valued board member. She is obviously an immensely popular figure within the company, and my fears that the golf handicap of the group would suffer once I was gone turned out to be unfounded!

My next Lopez story happened when she was playing an event at the course Taft Broadcasting Company owned in Cincinnati. This particular day Nancy shot an incredible 62, but she was given a slow-play penalty (which, for those of you who don't know much about golf, is a two-stroke penalty) that made her final score 64. Nancy was distraught. I was watching the press conference following her round, and she was really in tears (of course, you must understand that if crying were an Olympic sport, Nancy would have more gold medals than Michael Phelps! She is so soft hearted, so tender, and very emotional). When the press conference ended and she came out, I took her arm and we strolled along. I said, "Nancy, for heaven's sake, don't be upset. Even with the two-stroke penalty you shot 64, and you're leading the tournament." She said, "Charlie, that's not what really upsets me." I said, "Well then, what is your problem?" She replied, "What bugs me is— how could I have been playing slowly? I only swung 62 times!" What a marvelous response—and how persuasive!

During my days at the LPGA, an incident occurred that involved Nancy and that made quite an impression on me in terms of how things get done (or at least used to get done) in Washington, D.C. There was proposed tax legislation in Congress that, if enacted, would have had a seriously negative impact on the major golf associations. The PGA Tour had strong and well-paid lobbyists, but they were not having much success in stopping or slowing the progress of the legislation. I was asked if the LPGA could be of any help, and I offered to call my old friend, former law partner, and former Commissioner of the Internal Revenue Service, Don Alexander, and seek his advice. I called Don, and after I had outlined the problem, he said he would call "Rosty" and then get back to me. By "Rosty" he meant Dan Rostenkowski, the most powerful person in the House of Representatives at that time. Don called me back a few days later and said he had spoken to Rostenkowski, and he told Don to have Nancy Lopez call him and review the matter, and then they could play golf together and, hopefully, resolve the problem.

So, I called Nancy and explained the situation. As always, Nancy was ready to help but she said, "Charlie, I don't know anything about tax law. I am a golfer!" I told her not to worry—that we would fully "script" her for her conversation with Rostenkowski. And that's what we did. After Nancy talked to Rosty and followed up, I presume, with a golf date, the difficult and contentious issue we were concerned with was resolved! This, I think, is lobbying at its very best!

I was honored to be the master of ceremonies at the Memorial Tournament Honoree Ceremony in 2011 at which Nancy was the honoree. This is one of the highest honors in the golf world, coming as it does at Jack Nicklaus's prestigious tournament. I've included my comments of that day about this amazing lady in the Appendix.

Meg Mallon

The LPGA has never had a more delightful player or wonderful talent (she won two U.S. Opens) than Meg Mallon. Meg's smile and friendly attitude were an important part of the LPGA's appeal during the years I was Commissioner. Meg also loved to tease me because my golf game was a fit subject to be ridiculed. One week we were playing in Toledo, and I was in the Pro-Am. We came to the tenth tee, which was right in front of the clubhouse. I had noticed a small balcony on the clubhouse behind the tenth tee, but never really knew what it was. I later learned it was the players' locker room, and several players were out on the balcony (unbeknownst to me) watching our group tee off on ten. Well, I teed off and took my usual slashing, flailing, rapid-fire swing and dribbled the ball about fifty yards down the fairway. A voice from the balcony, quietly but clearly, said, "Charlie, take it easy, it's already dead!" I looked up and there was Meg smiling and laughing. She, of course, was right: the ball was already dead, but that didn't stop me from trying to kill it again!

Meg's great career is being highlighted by being named the captain of the Solheim Cup Team in 2013.

Dottie Pepper

Dottie Pepper joined the LPGA just a couple of years before I became Commissioner. She won seventeen events, including two majors and earned almost $7 million. Since putting away her clubs, she has been a top broadcast analyst for the Golf Channel and NBC Sports. We have always been good friends, and I have counseled with her more than once on various business arrangements that she was pursuing. I believe she will be an increasingly respected and popular analyst in the years ahead. Dottie was one of the fieriest competitors the game has ever known. This worked both to her advantage and to her disadvantage. She was sometimes misunderstood, but never underestimated. Dottie and I have often laughed that the first thing she would say to me when I called her or saw her in person was, "Okay, what have I done wrong now?" That's an exaggeration, but there *were* times when I needed to "reason" with her.

One of these situations happened at the Dinah Shore Tournament while I was Commissioner. I got a call very early in the morning on Pro-Am day. It was one of the LPGA officials calling to tell me that Dottie had called and said she wasn't going to play in the Pro-Am that day. She really had no excuse and I'm sure she knew she would be fined for failing to show. But the problem was bigger than that. Her playing partner that day was to be Henry Kravis, the Henry Kravis of KKR who owned RJR Nabisco, the tournament's sponsor.

I called Dottie and, when she asked, "Now what have I done wrong?" I told her exactly what the situation was. I said that it was important that she play in the Pro-Am. She said she was tired and simply wanted to rest. I made clear that that was not an option and said, "Dottie, you're playing with Henry Kravis!" Her answer was, "Who's Henry Kravis?" I explained that not only was he one of the most famous financial figures in America, but, even more importantly from our perspective, his company owned the organization that sponsored our tournament. "Dottie, get out of bed, and go play in the Pro-Am because if you don't, we might lose this tournament!" Obviously, I didn't really believe that, but it worked—Dottie played!

Dottie has a great sense of humor. It was never better demonstrated than one Christmas when she came into the Cincinnati area to visit her niece and to play Santa Claus at the niece's school Christmas party. Dottie called me and said she had an idea for some fun. She would stop by my office (I was then chairman of Convergys and my office was in downtown Cincinnati) in her Santa Claus suit, ask to see me, and see how many people in the office she could fool. I loved the idea and encouraged her to do it.

She arrived on schedule. The receptionist called me and said, "Santa Claus is here to see you!" I walked out and greeted her and brought her back to my office where a curious group of my colleagues were gathered. Dottie never spoke, but stood near a desk waving and smiling. I asked if anyone could guess who it was. At first no one did. Then, one of the women said, "I know who it is—it's Dottie Pepper!" After much laughter, I said, "How in the world did you know it was Dottie Pepper?" The lady explained that the minute she looked at "the eyes" she knew it was Dottie. For those unfamiliar with many professional golfers, Dottie was well known for her sharp, piercing eyes that were rivaled only by the same kind of eyes that characterized Jack Nicklaus. There was an unbelievable sharpness and focus in those eyes, and any fan of women's golf would recognize them quickly. That is exactly what happened. All in all, it was an unforgettable moment.

Another story involving Dottie also involves Jack Nicklaus and is a very good example of the sportsmanship that Jack has exhibited throughout his life. The Wendy's 3 Tour Challenge began in 1992 and came about as a result of conversations that Jack and I had concerning ways to stage events that involved all three U.S. professional tours. The first Wendy's 3 Tour Challenge was held at the New Albany Links Golf Club near Columbus, Ohio, and had a star-studded array of contestants. The PGA Tour included Fred Couples, Raymond Floyd, and Tom Kite; the LPGA team was Nancy Lopez, Patty Sheehan, and Dottie Pepper; and the Senior Tour team was made up of Nicklaus, Larry Laoretti, and Chi Chi Rodriguez. On the last hole, Dottie had a putt that, if she holed it, would win the match for the LPGA. It was not a simple putt, being a downhill twister of some fifteen to twenty feet. Dottie told me later, as she was lining up the putt, Jack walked behind her and said, simply, "Why don't you just go ahead and knock it in!" Dottie did precisely that, and the LPGA won the first 3 Tour Challenge. Once again, Jack demonstrated a level of sportsmanship that no other athlete, in my opinion, has exceeded.

Patty Sheehan

I have many wonderful memories of Patty Sheehan, all of which make me smile. My favorite is the impersonation by Patty Sheehan of Patty Berg giving Patty Sheehan instructions on the essential elements of a good golf swing. I must point out that this impersonation was always done in good humor and with great respect for Patty Berg, whom all the players loved. Patty Berg was a tiny woman, and in her later years, like many of us as we age, was somewhat stooped, which made her even smaller and meant that she really couldn't stand up very straight. This, however, did not slow down the indomitable Miss Berg one bit. One day she approached Patty Sheehan and in that commanding, nasal voice of hers began lecturing

Sheehan on the golf swing. As Sheehan tells the story, Berg's stooped head was only slightly above Sheehan's waist as she wagged her finger at Patty and said, "The first important thing in the golf swing is posture—posture!" Sheehan managed to keep her composure. Later in life, Patty Sheehan developed her impersonation of Patty Berg lecturing on posture, and Berg loved Sheehan's impersonation more than anyone.

My other favorite Sheehan story involves a Pro-Am in which we played together in Hawaii. We were paired with the head of the sponsoring company, which was one of the largest television companies in Japan. We won the Pro-Am and looked forward to receiving our trophy at the Pro-Am dinner. As it turned out, we received much more than a trophy. It seems that the chairman of the sponsoring company had never won an event of this sort before, and he was unbelievably excited. He directed his company to televise the awarding of the first-place trophy for broadcast in Japan. This may be the only Pro-Am award ceremony in history that has ever been broadcast throughout a nation. A reporter interviewed us—and the whole nine yards! Patty and I were in stitches throughout the whole episode; it was great fun and very memorable!

Annika Sorenstam

I was Commissioner of the LPGA when Annika Sorenstam joined the tour,* and before I knew it, she won the U.S. Open at the storied Broadmoor in Colorado Springs. This came as no great surprise, because she was a very highly anticipated talent, as she had had a phenomenal amateur and collegiate career. The interesting thing about this particular story is how much I think it tells you about Annika as a person. The tournament that followed the U.S. Open, the one being played the following week, was what was then called "the JAL Big

---

*I will never forget our first meeting. I think she was a little intimidated by sitting down with the Commissioner, but she also was very shy. She has retained that understated, unassuming way about her but has become a poised and very articulate young woman. In any case, it has become an important milestone in our friendship.

Apple Classic," and it was played at a great golf course (Wykagyl Country Club) in New Rochelle, New York, just north of New York City. It was sponsored by *Golf Magazine* and was carried on NBC. Therefore, it was an extremely important event for our tour. The day after Annika won the U.S. Open at the Broadmoor, I began receiving frantic calls from various sources telling me that Annika had withdrawn as a participant in the JAL Big Apple Classic. Before long I had a similar message from Annika. I was, of course, very concerned. It meant upsetting an important sponsor, missing a chance to be on network television (we didn't have that many opportunities), and not playing an event in the largest media market in the world. So, I called Annika, fully prepared to be the tough, mean Commissioner that would shame her into playing. I reached her without difficulty. However, I was not prepared for what happened next. When she answered the phone, her voice was weak, and it was clear she had been in and out of crying spells. She said, "Commissioner, I know the problems that are being created by my not playing the JAL Big Apple Classic and missing a television opportunity. I would like to play there more than you know. However, I simply am not physically or mentally capable of playing. This U.S. Open win has taken everything out of me, and I can't even get out of bed." And then she said, "I will never play an event, no matter what it is, unless I feel that I can bring to it my very best game."

I have told this story a number of times both publicly and privately, and Annika has repeated it often as well. I think the reason it means so much to each of us is that we each learned something about the other as a result of the call. Obviously, I was not happy to disappoint a sponsor and the network, but I understood what was driving this young woman and how sincerely she felt about what she was doing. For her part, I think she learned that I did indeed understand, that I was sympathetic even though it caused me significant problems to be so.

The second Annika story is far more whimsical. After her first baby was born and she was settling into being a wife and a mother, we were chatting on the telephone one day and I said, "Now be straight with me; we're good friends and I want you to level with me. Do you really miss it; do you miss playing golf?" She was thoughtful for a moment and then gave me a classic Annika answer. She said, "If I could be dropped by helicopter onto the eighteenth fairway of a major championship tied for the lead with my playing partner and heading for the eighteenth green, I would love to come back tomorrow. However, that's not possible. And what it takes to put one in that position is not something I miss at all. I love being a mother, and I wouldn't trade where I am now for anything."

Annika's "stepping away" (her phrase) was widely received with regret, but with respect and understanding that she had other priorities in life, particularly starting a family, that were paramount. One sports writer (who shall remain nameless) was skeptical and even caustic in suggesting she was not serious, that she would not stay on the sidelines very long and would soon return to competitive golf. All that his column proved was that he really didn't know Annika very well.

The 1996 Solheim Cup was played at St. Pierre Golf and Country Club in Wales. The United States team won by an overall score of 17 to 11, but that totally obscures what happened. Going into the final day, the European team was leading 9 to 7, but the United States completely dominated in the singles matches, winning ten points to the European's two. The only European player to win her match was Annika Sorenstam. Two other European players halved their matches. The next day, a sports writer for one of the prominent British newspapers was irate. He complained that the European team had been mishandled because the captain did not play her two alternates until the final day, thus thrusting them into the action with no "warm-up." He made the additional point that since the regular players had gotten no rest, they were exhausted, and that's why the last day's matches turned out as they had.

Then he said something like this: "All of the players were exhausted by the final day except for the one who won—Annika Sorenstam. Annika was not exhausted simply because she walks directly from the tee box to the pin without ever deviating more than a yard or two from the center of the fairway. That, of course, is why she wasn't tired!" Whatever the reason, the record is what it is, and it was a phenomenal last day performance by TEAM USA.

Lori West

There may have been players on the tour who were better golfers than Lori West, but there is no question whatsoever that she was the greatest comedian on the tour. She had a marvelous sense of humor. We were playing in a Pro-Am in Youngstown, Ohio, one year and I was paired with Lori—always a delightful experience. We came to one tee, and as I teed off, I completely came "outside-in" over the ball and hooked it badly to the left—a perfectly awful shot! I turned around to Lori in complete frustration and said, "Dammit, Lori, my problem is I just had too many swing thoughts when I was hitting the ball." Lori looked at me for a moment, smiled, and said, "Did any of them have anything to do with golf?" I said, "Lori, I should fine you for insubordination to your Commissioner, but that is such an incredibly funny line that I am going to waive the fine."

Hall of Fame Parties

SPEAKING OF LPGA players, no history of my LPGA years would be complete without sharing with you what was among the most pleasant "duties" that I had during those years. The LPGA Hall of Fame is unique among sports halls of fame for one simple reason: there is absolutely no subjectivity in the selection process. Election is based solely on accomplishments on the golf course, except for the requirement that the player must have been an active LPGA Tour member for ten years. There is also a veteran's category, which contains some nonplaying criteria, but these criteria have never been used, to my knowledge. Quite properly, election to the LPGA Hall of Fame guarantees automatic election into the World Golf Hall of Fame. During my five years as LPGA Commissioner,

I had the unique opportunity to induct three players into the LPGA Hall of Fame: Pat Bradley, Patty Sheehan, and Betsy King. I also participated in the induction of Beth Daniel and Juli Inkster. Though I had no "official" role in her induction, I had the great privilege—and fun— of attending Amy Alcott's Hall of Fame party at the famous Riviera Country Club in Los Angeles, where Amy has been a member for many years. It was a delight to see Amy receive this well-deserved recognition. Speaking of well-deserved recognition, Hollis Stacy, one of the LPGA's all-time greats, was recently elected to the World Golf Hall of Fame. Hollis had an extraordinary career winning eighteen LPGA events and four majors—including, incredibly, three U.S. Women's Opens!

The LPGA has a long-standing custom that, when a player is inducted into the Hall of Fame, she is entitled to a party at a place and time of her choosing to celebrate the induction. It is not surprising, as I reflect on it, that each of the five induction parties I attended reflected to an amazing degree the personality of the player.

The Parties

Patty Sheehan's party was held in Reno, and the highlight of the evening had to be Patty appearing wearing a strapless, red gown covered with sequins! Patty was well known for her golf knickers and conservative clothes on the golf course but decided that she would make a complete reversal at her party. This was entirely appropriate because Patty was and is a free spirit and a truly fun gal. None of us who were there will ever forget that red dress!

Pat Bradley was always a lady, both on and off the golf course. She was conservative by nature but had a real streak of Irish good humor about her. Her party was in a ballroom at the Ritz-Carlton in Boston. Pat wore a beautiful evening gown, and the whole night was a wonderful reflection of Pat and her family, especially her beloved "Mama." It wasn't a formal evening by any means, but it was proper and dignified —just like Pat.

Betsy King had her party in a school gymnasium in Reading, Pennsylvania, close to where she grew up. Betsy is one of the most honest and caring individuals I have ever known. She is deeply religious, but tolerant of others and totally honest in her beliefs and convictions. Betsy's life since the LPGA has simply reinforced my view of her character as she is pursuing humanitarian projects in several parts of the world. Betsy's affair was simple and, at the same time, inspiring.

Although I was no longer Commissioner of the LPGA when Beth Daniel was inducted, she asked me to act as master of ceremonies at her party, which was held in her hometown, Charleston, South Carolina. I was obviously delighted to do so. I had a brainstorm, which, happily, worked out well, although it could have been a disaster. I rewrote the words to the song "Nothing Could Be Finer Than to Be in Carolina" and sang the song from the podium amidst much laughter and catcalls. I can't begin to remember all the words of the rewrite but I do remember the first few lines:

> Nothing could be finer than our girl from Carolina
> in the LPGA Hall of Fame.

> Nothing could be sweeter than our sweetie when we meet her
> at the LPGA Hall of Fame.

> All the great old players, thronged around the door offering words
> of welcome—echoing ever more.

My singing was great fun and I enjoyed it, whether anyone else did or not.

Juli Inkster's party was a real happening. It took place April 5, 2011, and true to Juli's roots as a sports "nut," it was held at the Giants' stadium, AT&T Park, in San Francisco, with cocktails in the dugout! I go into more detail on this party in my profile of Juli earlier in this chapter.

WHAT IS THE future for the LPGA Hall of Fame? I have little doubt it will remain an independent entity within the World Golf Hall of Fame. I do, however, suspect that the criteria will need to be looked at again, sooner rather than later. There is only one player even close to meeting the entry requirements at this point, and that's Laura Davies. Laura needs two more tournament victories or one more victory in a major tournament. The likelihood is that with the flood of young talent coming on to the tour (just as there is on the PGA Tour), it will not be easy for Laura to achieve her goal. And, it is precisely this wave of new talent that will likely drive a revision of the existing criteria. It will be very difficult for a player to dominate as Annika Sorenstam or Nancy Lopez once did.

But, if adjustments are made, I would be strongly opposed to changing the fundamental strength and character of the criteria—namely, that the only things considered are directly related to the play of the game itself. No sports writers' votes, no votes from other Hall of Famers—nothing but performance on the golf course.

Some Closing LPGA Reflections

AS I CLOSE this section on my LPGA days, it is perhaps appropriate to reflect briefly on why I think I enjoyed the LPGA job so much and why a sixty-year-old man was comfortable and confident leading a women's organization, a significant number of whose members were half his age. I think the answer is really quite simple. I have been surrounded by strong, accomplished women my entire life. My mother, my wife, my sister, my two daughters—all were important in molding my views, as was Dot Murphy, the treasurer of Taft Broadcasting Company, and a trailblazer in her own right, having been the first woman who set foot on the floor of the New York Stock Exchange. The other women I would put in this category include Lucie Salhany, who was vice president for programming at Taft Broadcasting Company and went on to become chairman of Fox Broadcasting and was the first female to shatter that particular glass ceiling; Cindy Davis (whom I speak of elsewhere in this book); and Judy Bell, the first female president of the USGA. I worked closely with Dot Murphy both as the company's lawyer and later as her "boss." At the LPGA I found the same kind of women. They were skilled, professional women—their profession just happened to be hitting the golf ball with incredible skill.

I jokingly said at my retirement dinner that the LPGA had turned me into the world's first sixty-year-old, gray-haired male feminist. However, this is stretching the point. I never ever really espoused feminist views, and I never suggested that the LPGA were entitled to any special privileges. My position was always that we simply wanted an equal opportunity, an equal seat at the table. We would take it from there. Having said that, I must quote a line from Timothy Leary that I have always loved. "Women who seek to be equal with men lack ambition." Another of my favorite lines (and, sadly, I don't know who said it) is "There really is no glass ceiling. Just a thick layer of men."

AS I WRITE this, the LPGA is enjoying solid growth under the leadership of its bright, hard-working Commissioner, Mike Whan. I am proud of the part I played in Mike's decision to sign on with the LPGA. Let me tell you about it.

During the LPGA's search for a new Commissioner in 2009, I received a call from the then board chair, Dawn Hudson, telling me they very much wanted to hire Mike Whan and wondered if I would take a call from Mike, as he had indicated he had some questions he would like to discuss with me. I said I would be happy to talk to him, and early the next morning he called. We quickly found we had much in common even though we had never met. Mike grew up in Cincinnati, went to Miami University (my old alma mater), and his mother had been executive assistant to one of my closest friends at my old law firm. So, we were pals before we even approached the subject about which he was calling!

Mike asked me a number of questions about the Commissioner's responsibilities, and then he came to what was his most important question. He said, "I have three kids who either are or soon will be teenagers. Can I do the job as LPGA Commissioner and still be a good father?" I must say that I was enormously impressed with the question. However, I probably didn't answer it as he might have expected. What I said was something like this: "I can't completely identify with this issue because my kids were grown and gone from home before I became Commissioner. I will, however, say this: I have never known a teenager to listen or pay much attention to anything that their father might say. However, they very closely watch what you *do*. You may not be aware or realize how closely they are watching. Therefore, if they see you working at something meaningful and something that you enjoy and see you making good things happen—that is what will be meaningful to them."

Mike understood what I was saying, took the job, and, from everything I know, has continued to be a great father. We have laughed about our conversation more than once when Mike would be heavily under the gun on some issue and learning—as every LPGA Commissioner has learned—that it is a very tough job. So, Mike would say to me, "Yours was the greatest sales job in history." I, with totally false modesty, would reply that I hoped I had been helpful and that I was certainly glad I had helped persuade him to take the job!

MY FINAL EVENT as Commissioner of the LPGA turned out to be another one of those surprise turning points in my life. It was at the Diner's Club matches at PGA West in the Southern California desert. We had put together an event that featured players from the PGA Tour, the Senior PGA Tour, and the LPGA playing a match-play event on the same golf course. I had learned that Jack Nicklaus and Arnold Palmer were playing together, and I decided to stop by the first tee to say hello and wish them well. When I did that, after an exchange of pleasantries, Arnie told me that he had been intending to call me and wondered if I would meet him after his round, as there was something he wanted to discuss with me. I had no idea what he had in mind but, of course, I agreed to meet him. As it turned out, my life was about to change direction once again.

A Word on the Future of the Game

BEFORE GOING ON with what became the next chapter in my "speckled" career, I want briefly to turn to a subject that is of great concern to me—the future of the game that I have come to love so much and that has been such an important part of my life. I need to make quite clear that these views are strictly mine and do not necessarily reflect the thinking of my many friends in golf.

Let's first look at it strictly from a business perspective. The golf industry, by and large, has not grown appreciably in the last decade. In my experience, any business with a record such as this would do three things. First, fire all the people who had been running the business. Second, immediately launch an in-depth study on why the business had not grown, and, third, explore every conceivable avenue that might help to reverse the trend. But, golf is not a business in the conventional sense and conventional remedies are not appropriate or workable. However, growth of the game is a subject that must be addressed.

A recent study by the National Golf Foundation simply confirms this disturbing trend. Although there was encouraging growth from the mid-1980s to the turn of the century, since the year 2000, to quote the

National Golf Foundation, "the number of golfers plateaued and has been slowly declining." The recent release from the National Golf Foundation reports a continuing decline in the business in 2010 but blames it largely on the recession. That may be partially true, but it should not be allowed to mask the deeper problem.

There are, of course, a number of reasons for this trend, some of which are beyond the control of anyone in the golf industry. For example, it seems clear that a significant part of the growth of the game in the 1960s, 1970s, and part of the 1980s was the explosion of golf courses being built as part of the nationwide residential development business. Because of the recession, that is no longer an area of expansion. But, I think there are other reasons why the game has been basically stagnant. To me, there are four principle reasons why the game has not grown in recent years.

First, the sheer difficulty of the game means that many people simply won't stay with it after giving it a try. Interestingly enough, in recent years, the number of people leaving the game has been about the same as those entering it.

Second is the cost of the game. Despite many laudable efforts by many golf organizations, accessibility, particularly to the minority communities, remains limited.

Third, and to me probably the most serious obstacle, is the length of time required to play the game in its present form. This is simply compounded by the slower and slower pace of play starting, alas, at the professional level. This particular problem has grown dramatically worse in recent years, and it is no longer a novelty to learn of, or be involved in, a round that requires five or six hours.

This third problem morphs into the fourth problem because of the fundamental change in our society. As a result of the age of technology, be it e-mail, texting, Facebook, Twitter, Google, and all the rest, society's attention span has gotten shorter and shorter, particularly among younger people. Today's young people are attempting to cram into every day and every hour far more than my generation ever even thought of.

We didn't think of it because it didn't exist. Therefore, a five- or six-hour round of golf—perhaps even a four-hour round—runs directly counter to today's lifestyle and our sound-bite society. I hope I'm wrong, but I simply can't see how, in its present form, golf can hope to lure today's young people. If you follow my reasoning and think it makes some sense, then it seems to me that the golf business must begin by thinking "outside the box" and considering nothing as sacred except, of course, the links at St. Andrews.

This leads to what I believe is the heart of the problem. I hope I can be forgiven for suggesting it. As I look at the lack of growth over the last two decades, I have to wonder how much the organizations that control the game really are focused on the growth of the game. I don't mean to imply that they don't love the game. Indeed, perhaps precisely because they do love it, they have been, in my judgment, unwilling to take the necessary steps to change it.

I have no magic solutions. I don't think there are any. But there are things that could be done if we are prepared to think "outside the box." More and more, responsible people are discussing these issues—such as twelve-hole courses, six-hole courses, special enticements for women and children to increase their interest in the game, courses with fifteen-inch holes, two sets of rules, Barney Adams Tour Link concept, Flogton, and many, many more.

All I'm really suggesting is the need to begin a serious dialogue among the principle organizations in the golf industry to consider what needs to be done to grow the game—or at the very least to stop the decline.* I would start such a dialogue with a completely clean sheet of paper and an understanding that every idea is encouraged. Such a dialogue would be based on the simple proposition that any business that

---

*I am aware that some of the major organizations in golf do not believe it is part of their "charter" to be concerned with the growth of the game. Rather, they see their function as "protecting" the game and/or insuring its integrity. Frankly, I don't see why these mandates, however laudable, should be interpreted to exclude the growth of the game. It seems clear to me that "protecting" the game should certainly include efforts to arrest its decline.

has been flat to down for the last decade or more simply must reverse that course or risk becoming increasingly irrelevant.

I must emphasize that I don't mean throwing away all of the things that have made the game great. I simply mean recognizing the obvious—the transformational changes in equipment, the vast difference in the skills of the people playing the game, and the fundamental changes in lifestyles in recent years. I sense there is a growing concern about this issue and that more and more key figures in the game see the need to attack this problem and to attack it soon.

There are some encouraging signs of a willingness to think "outside the box." Even more encouraging is that this thinking is coming from much respected names in the golf world. Leading this list is Jack Nicklaus. Jack began to notice a year or so ago that none of his grandkids (and he has twenty-one of them) were playing golf. Instead they were involved in soccer, lacrosse, and the tried-and-true sports like baseball, football, and basketball. He began to realize that there were two main reasons why his grandkids didn't seem interested in golf—the time it took to play and the lack of what one might call "golf parks"—places where kids could learn and practice their game for short periods of time. Jack has done several things at two of his best courses—Muirfield Village and the Bear's Club. He's introduced a twelve-hole course setup, bigger cups, and holes designed for players who are just learning or are short hitters. Obviously, not all of these innovations will work, but the important thing is to try them.

One organization that has really stepped forward in an effort to stimulate the growth of the game is the PGA of America. Under the able and enthusiastic efforts of its former president, Joe Steranka, the PGA of America has instituted a number of innovative programs and has energized its members throughout the country. The most recent organization to step forward is, somewhat surprisingly, the USGA. Long reluctant to believe that its mandate embraced the growth of the game, the USGA announced at its annual meeting in February of 2013 an initiative to address the pace-of-play issue. This is a welcome development, and the golf world will eagerly await the USGA's findings and recommendations.

There is a different, but related, wind blowing—the need to consider two sets of rules governing standards of equipment, one for professionals and one for amateurs. Often referred to as "bifurcation," this is a highly controversial, hotly debated subject.

I think one of the reasons that the subject is so controversial is that many people—when "bifurcation" is mentioned—believe that it is a code word for having two sets of rules governing the *play* of the game. This is wrong. Bifurcation properly defined means two sets of rules governing standards of equipment. Mike Purkey in a recent edition of GlobalGolfPost has clearly stated the difference:

> But where the USGA could really affect the temperature of the golf public is by making a different set of equipment rules for the professionals. Virtually every other sport does. We don't mind adhering to the same playing rules as the professionals, but equipment is another issue entirely.

The issue has been quietly talked about for years but is now gaining center stage with the proposal by the USGA to ban the so-called belly putters. Jaime Diaz, the editor of *Golf World*, has written a thoughtful and informative column in the February 4, 2013 edition of his magazine. Two excerpts from Jaime's column are worth noting:

> [Recently] the subject of bifurcation—one that golf's leaders has perennially either avoided or belittled— gained a new legitimacy and respect.
> Why now? Well, golf's problems have gotten more complex. The game's organizations are feeling the heat, and each seems energized to both re-mark and protect its turf. In such a tense time the proposed ban on anchoring [the putter] has acted as a trip wire.

> As Dawson [Peter Dawson, head of the R & A] tacitly acknowledged, bifurcation is not some crazy concept, but one that smart people can consider as a possible solution to a game that is increasingly cornered. That's why the term has endured in the shadows all these years, and why it's finally on the table.

One of the most respected golf writers, Jim Achenbach, put it this way after Bubba Watson's victory at the 2012 Masters:

> I find myself wishing that the USGA would be motivated by The Masters and by Bubba Watson. It could be time to seriously evaluate two sets of equipment rules—one for touring pros and highly skilled players, the other for amateurs. If we really want ordinary people to enjoy the game, one answer is to facilitate the long ball for everyday play. The rules makers, if they choose, could consider the relaxation of equipment standards for amateurs And the implementation of all the technology that is available.
>
> Some who oppose this bifurcation of the rules base their position on the argument that much of the charm of golf comes from a sense of history of the game and the passion of amateur players to identify with the professionals. It is often said that amateurs want to play the same game as the pros with the same equipment.

I think this argument fails for several reasons. First, in the seventy years that I have been playing and talking golf, never once have I heard a mid- to high-handicap player express this view—and it is the mid- to high handicapper who comprises the bulk of those playing the game. Second, it is a fantasy to think you are playing the same clubs as your favorite pro, even if his name is used to endorse the clubs. Anyone who knows anything about golf knows that the clubs the pros use and those that they endorse for amateurs bear very little resemblance to one another. Third, increasingly amateurs and professionals are not playing the same game. My good friend Larry Bohannan, the golf writer for the *Desert Sun,* put it this way:

There are high-schoolers out there hitting it 300 yards off the tee with drivers, and there are college kids hitting 340 yards with a driver. If you want to identify one area where the professional's game no longer resembles the recreational game played by millions across the country, it is in distance off the tee. While the average recreational player struggles to reach 200 yards off the tee, the average PGA Tour player is hammering it 320 yards anytime he wants.

A final word on bifurcation—and to me a compelling point. The simple fact is that amateurs and professional players do not play the same equipment and haven't for many years. As Purkey points out in his article, tour players have custom-made club heads and shafts and irons that are weighted and ground to a player's characteristics. So, it seems curious that so much heat is being generated on the issue of two sets of standards for equipment when, in fact, there are two standards right now!

One more comment on the importance and necessity of growing the game. One of the sports writers for whom I have always had enormous respect is Lorne Rubenstein. About a year ago he wrote a column that just came to my attention with the following heading: "Golf Is Stuck in the Past." The sub-headline reads this way: "Nothing wrong with tradition, but the eighteen-hole round in a time when few people have the time to play makes little sense." Rubenstein goes on to discuss the efforts that Jack Nicklaus is making to spur the growth of the game. Rubenstein notes that it is not surprising that Jack's grandkids are playing soccer, lacrosse, or basketball, because these sports are less expensive to play and it doesn't take four or five hours to get a game in.

Rubenstein also mentions something of which I was totally unaware. France was awarded the 2018 Ryder Cup in part because it pledged to build 106 nine-hole courses by the time the Ryder Cup comes around. Rubenstein's column ends this way: "Wake up golf. Wake up you people in the golf associations who claim to care so much about the future of the game. Wake up before you go down, down, down. By the way, you're on your way already."

It truly is time—indeed past time—to start thinking "outside the box." In any endeavor change is inevitable. Golf should be no exception.

Two of the LPGA's best—Dottie Pepper and Juli Inkster.

Beth Daniel as my caddy.
She tried to help me
—to no avail.

Patty Sheehan and I receiving awards for winning a Pro-Am tournament in
Hawaii. The awards ceremony was telecast back to Japan.

*Dottie Pepper at my office
as Santa Claus!*

The Solheim team and President Clinton in the Oval Office in 1994.

With Annika. Two golfers—one a superstar, the other totally forgettable!

At Juli Inkster's Hall of Fame party at AT&T Park.

Me with Meg Mallon.

Karsten and Louise Solheim have played a major role in the growth of women's golf.

The guy with the beard called me "Mr. Wonderful" because I had the greatest putting day of my life!

Spectacular sight at a Solheim Cup.

Making a Solheim Cup speech. I was not applauding myself.

Marilyn and me with Neil Armstrong and Bob Cantin at my LPGA retirement party.

*With Judy Rankin
at a Solheim Cup.*

With Nancy Lopez at my retirement party.

Another retirement party picture.

Captain JoAnne Carner with her legendary cap.

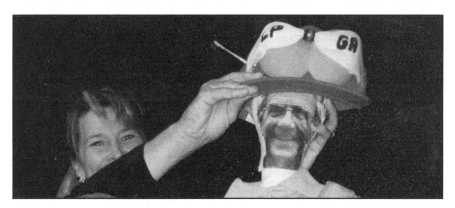

Judy Dickinson's hilarious gift at my retirement party.

At Pat Bradley's Hall of Fame induction. I flew directly from Boston to Tokyo for lunch.

A thorn between two roses.

Solheim Cup at Muirfield Village Golf Club with Judy Rankin as captain in 1996.

With Arnie and PGA Commissioner Tim Finchem.

ANOTHER BRIEF INTERMISSION

I NEED TO add a brief postscript before going on. Between my LPGA years and the next "adventure" with Arnold Palmer, I acted as nonexecutive board chairman of three Cincinnati companies—U.S. Shoe, Cincinnati Bell, and Convergys. U.S. Shoe was a diversified retail women's clothing company that also owned LensCrafters. Cincinnati Bell was, as the name suggests, the telephone company for the greater Cincinnati area. Convergys was an IT company that began as a division of Cincinnati Bell but which was spun off into a separate company in 1998. In each of these cases, my role was to manage the governance structure of the company and preside over the activities of the board of directors. Beyond that I acted as mentor to the presidents and CEOs, who, in each case, did not feel themselves ready to assume the role as chairman without a bit more experience.

One funny memory. When I retired as chairman of the board of Convergys, the company gave a very nice retirement dinner for Marilyn and me. Not all retirement dinners are pleasant, but this one certainly was. As I have mentioned, Convergys was an IT company and operated in areas in which I had no prior experience. Since my responsibilities as board chairman did not involve operations, it was not important that I had such knowledge. When I was asked to speak at the retirement dinner, I told the group how much I had enjoyed my involvement with the company and getting to know each of them. But, I said I had a confession to make that I really could not have disclosed until that precise moment. I said, "I have been the chairman of several corporations and been on the boards of many others. But, this is the only company with which I have been involved where I had absolutely no idea what it did!" A bit of an exaggeration, but not entirely!

CHAPTER XIII

The Years with Arnie

AS HE HAD suggested, I met Arnie after his round. We sat down in the clubhouse at PGA West and we each ordered a beer. After a few brief comments about his round, Arnie characteristically came right to the point. He said, "I want you to come in and run all my companies." I had no idea that this was on his mind, but I gave him an equally frank response. I told him that I was immensely flattered by the suggestion, but that I was not in a position to undertake a full-time job. I was already nonexecutive chairman of U.S. Shoe, and I had agreed to a similar role at Cincinnati Bell. While neither of these was a full-time job, they certainly precluded any other full-time job. We continued to discuss his interest and my availability and agreed that we would each think more about what might be doable and would talk again.

Part of the reason Arnie's offer surprised me was that I wondered— why me? I later learned the answer. In January of 1995, Joe Gibbs, the cofounder (along with Arnie) of the Golf Channel, invited me to attend and speak at the formal launch of the Golf Channel. I joined Deane Beman and Ken Schofield, then head of the European Tour, and, of course, Arnie as speakers. As fate would have it, I was seated for dinner next to Winnie Palmer, Arnie's wife. I had never met Winnie, but we hit it off immediately and totally. I'm not sure I've ever "bonded" as quickly with anyone as I did that night with Winnie. As I point out elsewhere in this book, she was a remarkable person. Arnie told me later that Winnie was concerned with what her role would be in Arnie's business affairs should he predecease her. She urged him to hire somebody who could help her with ongoing business issues. This was in no way a "slap" at Mark McCormack, founder of IMG, or IMG. Winnie simply wanted someone in the picture to be something of a "go-between."

Apparently, after the Golf Channel dinner, Winnie commented to Arnie that I was the kind of person she felt he should engage. This, then, was the catalyst for Arnie to approach me some months later when he knew that I was about to end my "tour of duty" with the LPGA.

In February or March of 1996, we did talk again, and Arnie said he had some ideas. He invited Marilyn and me to Bay Hill to have dinner with him and Winnie, as well as his closest friend, Russ Meyer, and his wife, Helen, who were visiting Bay Hill. We accepted the offer and had a very pleasant dinner. I didn't realize at the time, but my relationship with Arnie would also lead to a close friendship with Russ Meyer. Russ, who headed Cessna Aviation for many years, is widely regarded as the finest private aviation executive in the world. As an associate of Mark McCormack's in the early days of Mark's involvement with Arnie, Russ was involved in many of the early decisions and activities surrounding Arnie's career. That, plus his love of flying, has made him one of Arnie's special friends. Russ and I have worked together now for some twenty years, and I consider him a very close friend.

The next morning I went to Arnie's office, and we worked out a deal. I would act as a personal business advisor and "look over his shoulder" on items—large and small—that came across his desk. I would in no way supplant his longtime relationship with Mark McCormack and IMG but, hopefully, could bring some of my experience in both business and golf to the table. I want to be crystal clear. I could not have replaced Mark even had I wanted to. What he had started and built I'm not sure anyone could duplicate, certainly not me. Before going on, let me tell you a few things about that remarkable man.

I came to know Mark before he became a household name in the sports business. We were one year apart at Yale Law School, and, even then, it was clear this was a man to watch. It wasn't long before he and Arnie started IMG and, as they say, the rest is history. There had never been anything like IMG in the sports management business, and perhaps there never will be again. Mark's tragic and untimely death cut short a career that was far from ended. Though we had not seen one another for a number of years, our friendship was revived when I became Commissioner of the LPGA. Mark had always been a strong believer in and supporter of the LPGA, and, shortly after I became Commissioner, he called me and we got together at his office in New York City. Over the next several years, the LPGA and IMG did a number of things together. Among the most memorable was signing an agreement with the Golf Channel, which began a long and solid partnership that has given the LPGA a tremendous amount of exposure. I remember this particularly well because it was one of the first contracts that Joe Gibbs, the visionary founder of the Golf Channel, signed shortly after the Golf Channel was formed. This was also the beginning of what has become a close friendship with Joe Gibbs. When we lived in Bay Hill, I saw Joe frequently, and we remain in close touch.

One of my deals with Mark is especially memorable. We had been working on a deal together for an event that IMG was putting together for the LPGA. The deal needed to get finalized, and we decided to try to wrap it up when we were both in Augusta for the Masters. Our respective schedules and the fact that we were staying some miles apart made finding a common location for our negotiations hard to come by. I finally suggested an IHOP about midway between our houses, and we did indeed meet there and concluded the deal. I always felt that it had to be the only deal in Mark's sophisticated career that was ever concluded at an IHOP! But, it was a good deal—and the pancakes were great!

Shortly after I became Commissioner, Mark invited me to visit him at his home at Isleworth in Orlando. We wanted to get reacquainted, and I wanted to share with him some of my thoughts for the LPGA. It is important to reiterate that Mark was one of the LPGA's biggest boosters and had done an enormous amount of good for the promotion of the tour and women's golf in general. I was obviously eager to make our relationship as strong as it could be.

When I arrived, Mark was upstairs on the telephone, and his assistant showed me into a solarium-type room where I could wait until Mark could join me. It was a lovely room, and I sat down, as I recall, on a beautifully flowered couch and began to look around my surroundings. The whole house was magnificent, and this room was bright and cheerful and completely comfortable. I did note one interesting thing. There was a large rattan chair in one corner, and, because of the nature of the space, whoever sat in it would be slightly higher than anyone else sitting anywhere in the room. Now, I am not a big person—never topped five nine and a half—and Mark, of course, was over six feet tall. I thought if Mark comes in and sits down in that chair he'll be about a foot above me, and I'm not comfortable with that. So, I went over and sat in the chair. When Mark arrived in the room, he saw where I was sitting, and a smile flickered across his face as if to say Charlie understands the dynamics of this room and has picked exactly the right spot to sit! Maybe I just imagined all this, but I don't think so. I'm not suggesting that this little byplay had anything to do with our friendship or our relationship. But, I have always remembered it and considered it perhaps the most interesting instance of "positioning" for a negotiation or business discussion that I have ever been involved in.

This might be a good place to attempt to answer a question that I am often asked. That question is: What made Mark McCormack so successful? What were the traits and qualities that contributed most importantly to his achievements?

I don't profess to be an expert on this subject, and many people were closer to Mark than I, but I do have some thoughts that I think are worth sharing.

First, Mark was incredibly bright. He had great analytical skill and an ability to see the heart of the matter and not be bogged down in the trivial.

Second, he was a very hard worker. Mark knew and loved the finer things in life, but would never let them get in the way of his business focus. Focus was the key word. Nobody, in my judgment, excels in his or her field without focus.

Third, he knew how to make a deal. The simple fact is that surprisingly few people really know how to make a deal. The CEOs of big companies frequently don't know how to make a deal, but they have people around them who do. Mark, of course, had other deal makers, but the nature of his business was such that he was the principal deal maker.

Finally, he went for the best. He approached and represented the top stars in every sport, and he expanded his roster to impress others he intended to approach. And, he always surrounded himself with very good people.

Mark really had a great sense of style and panache. In my mind, it was one of the great tragedies that he died so young.

As Arnie and I worked out the details of our arrangement, Arnie said that he would like us to move to the Bay Hill Club in Orlando, where I would share an office with him in his office complex adjacent to the club. Marilyn and I were excited by this new opportunity, as the next adventure in our lives was about to begin.

In the late spring of 1996, we moved to Bay Hill, and Arnie set me up in an office that was connected to his by a door that was rarely closed.

This was the beginning of one of the happiest times in our lives.* On a typical day, I would arrive at the office around 8:00 a.m. Arnie was there already, more often than not, or he was having breakfast in the downstairs dining room. We would work until around noon and then have lunch. Typically, Arnie then either hit balls or played in the notorious Bay Hill shootout. (The shootout is legendary in golf circles. It is a special competition that takes place every day at Bay Hill. It is much too complicated to explain here. Just google "Bay Hill Club Shootout" to get the full story.) I would go back to the office and work until mid-afternoon. As I mentioned earlier, our offices were side by side, and the connecting door was almost always open. This meant that Arnie and I were sitting about eight or ten feet apart. We could talk back and forth whenever we wished, and it also meant that he could toss a letter or some other document through the door to me and say something like, "What do you think of this?"

Marilyn and I liked Orlando and were especially comfortable at Bay Hill, where we made a number of wonderful friends. I also was fortunate to get to know Arnold's family (his sisters and brother and his two delightful daughters—Amy and Peggy) and to work with his close friends and confidants: Russ Meyer, Dick Ferris, Joe Gibbs, Spider Miller, Tim Neher, Tom Ridge, and Johnny Harris, to name a few. I also continued my friendship and relationship with Mark McCormack and generated a new friendship with Alastair Johnston, Arnie's talented and longtime agent and friend at IMG. We also got to know—and became friends with—Arnie's dentist and photographer extraordinaire, Dr. Howdy Giles. Howdy and his charming wife, Carolyn, were our neighbors part of the time we lived at Bay Hill.

---

* Bay Hill has an interesting history. The course opened in 1961, and on a visit to Orlando to play in a charity event in 1965, Arnie fell in love with the golf course. In 1970 he took a lease on the course and few years later, bought it. Arnie has since redesigned and rebuilt the original golf course layout by architect Dick Wilson, and Bay Hill has become one of the great golf courses in the world, hosting one of the PGA's top events.

I want to say a word about one of Arnie's dearest friends, Dow Finsterwald, who was one of our close neighbors while we lived at Bay Hill. Dow and Arnie started on the PGA Tour at the same time and have been close friends for over fifty years. Dow was a great player in his own right and won eleven tour titles, including a PGA Championship, and played on four Ryder Cup teams. Dow and Linda, his lovely wife, live close to Arnie and Kit in the Bay Hill Marina condos. Ironically, I knew Dow even before Arnie did. Dow grew up in Athens, Ohio, just a few miles from my hometown of Nelsonville, and we actually played high school sports against one another. Small world indeed.

Finally, it is impossible to talk about Arnie without mentioning his cohort and confidant of many years—Doc Giffin. Doc was working as the press secretary at the PGA Tour when Arnold asked him to become his assistant. That was 1966, and Doc continues in that role today. He is a wonderful writer and knows more about Arnie's life and career than anyone—including Arnie! He has been a loyal and trusted friend of Arnie's, and I feel privileged to say that he and I have also become very good pals.

IF I WERE to attempt to get into detail about the next ten years, this book would make *War and Peace* look like a short story. Rather, I will relate some stories that, hopefully, will give you a feel for ten of the happiest and most exciting years of my life. Let me share a few general observations about Arnie.

First, I don't think there has ever been an athlete in any sport who interacted with a crowd the way Arnie did—and, for that matter, still does! I think the secret was that Arnie had an uncanny ability to look at thousands of people and make each person feel that Arnie was looking only at him or her. That explains why, years later, people will come up to him and reminisce about having seen him at some event and how he smiled and nodded at them. That is only one of many things that has made Arnold Palmer, without question, the most beloved figure in the history of the game.

Second, I genuinely believe that nothing of consequence goes on in the golf industry that has not first been run by Arnie for his thoughts and comments. This is true for a couple of reasons. First, his views are always helpful; moreover, no one would want to adopt an idea or pursue a project with which Arnie might disagree! Better to get his views upfront. I have seen this over and over again as the leaders of the industry call, write, or visit him personally to review some problem or new idea.

Finally, his public and private personas are identical. He is warm, friendly, and unbelievably down to earth. Though he constantly says, "I'm not very smart," he is one of the most intuitive and intelligent people I know. One of his most admirable traits, in my opinion, is that when he asks your advice he listens to it and genuinely takes it into consideration in making his decisions.

NOW A FEW of my favorite Arnie stories.

One day we were talking about the Masters Tournament. Arnie has won it four times and I was curious to get his impression of how to play the course. Holes thirteen and fifteen always present an interesting challenge. They are both par five holes and have water hazards just in front of each green—a creek on thirteen and a small lake on fifteen. More than once players have laid up on these holes, being unwilling to risk going into the hazard and recording a big score. I asked Arnie if he had ever considered laying up on thirteen or fifteen. Arnie sat quietly for a minute, and then he looked at us and said forcefully, "Do you know how many times I came in second at Augusta?" We were all a little stunned at this answer because it didn't seem to address the question we had asked. But, I (or someone) simply said, "Well, no I don't." He then said, "Neither do I!" What an answer! It was classic Arnie.

SEPTEMBER 10, 2009, was a memorable day. It was the eightieth birthday of one of the greatest sports figures in history—Arnold Palmer. Naturally, parties and events were planned, particularly in Latrobe, Pennsylvania, his home, and in Orlando, Florida, where he has spent his winters at the Bay Hill Club for many years.

I had the great privilege of attending the two-day party in Latrobe. The evening of the first day was hosted by PNC, the large banking concern headquartered in Pittsburgh, and its charismatic chairman, Jim Rohr. The function was held in the Hall of Fame Room at PNC Park, home of the Pittsburgh Pirates, and was a delightful affair. The highlight of the evening, at least for me, was when Jim Nantz, the acclaimed CBS sportscaster, interviewed Arnie. They sat on a slightly raised stage in two armchairs with a small table between them. Everyone who knows anything about Arnie knows that he enjoys his Ketel One Vodka on the rocks with a slice of lemon. Apparently, when he left his seat to go to the stage to join Nantz, he neglected to bring his drink with him. After Jim had been asking Arnie questions for fifteen minutes or so, Jim said, "King, how are you doing?" Arnie looked at the table between them, and even though it contained two glasses of water, Arnie said, "Well, I'm okay, but I feel a little like I'm in the middle of the Sahara Desert!" After a brief moment, as we all tried to figure out what he meant, it dawned on us what he was referring to, and a Ketel One on the rocks with a wedge of lemon was immediately brought to quench the Sahara Desert–like thirst.

DURING THE YEARS I was working with Arnie, he and Winnie asked me to speak at the Pro-Am dinner at the annual PGA Tour event at Bay Hill. I decided to make this a light and funny talk, and it seemed to go over well. I especially remember one part of the talk. I kidded that I had come up with an idea that I thought would revolutionize golf instruction: a full body suit made of the latest space-age materials and fitted with highly sophisticated computer clip-ons that would direct and compel your body to make the perfect golf swing. One simply put on the suit, activated the computer, and the suit would make your body execute the perfect swing. I went on to say that, as this technique developed, it could be customized so that one could imitate the swing of any particular professional. I gave two examples. There was, of course, the Tiger Woods suit, but it came with a warning that activating it might dislocate several bones or muscles and should be handled cautiously. A second suit was the Arnold Palmer suit. Although a great instructional tool, it had one characteristic that needed to be called to the attention of the prospective user. After the device finished its instruction, it automatically walked you into a crowd, where you signed autographs for the next hour and a half.

The funniest part of this story is that I gave this speech over ten years ago, and since then I have noted several stories suggesting that devices precisely like this are being developed. Oh well, just one more time when I missed making millions! Years ago, *Golf Digest* ran a picture on its cover of a man wearing every golf instructional gadget that was then on the market. It was a hilarious photo because the guy was literally covered from head to toe with gadgetry. My instructional suit would do away with all of this and would look dashing at the same time! Maybe *Golf Digest* would consider doing another cover?

IN THE SUMMER of 2009, Arnie played in a "Legends" event in Minneapolis, hosted by the delightful and successful golf promoter Hollis Cavner. I talked to Arnie on the Monday morning following the event. He was ebullient and I asked why. He said, "We [meaning he and his partner, Al Geiberger] won the tournament!" I said, "That's incredible, that's wonderful!" He said, "Yes, we eagled the last hole to win." And I said, "That's even more amazing!" And he said, "Yes, but the best part is we beat Chi Chi and Lee Trevino. Chi Chi was grumbling as we walked to the clubhouse and was saying, 'I can't believe we let those guys beat us, Lee.' To which Trevino replied, 'Why should that surprise you, Chi Chi? Arnie's been doing that to you all your life!'" Naturally, the victory pleased Arnie, but I think Trevino's comment may have pleased him even more.

Another story I love has to do with a very unusual caddy that Arnold had one day. For many years, Ed Seay ran Arnold's golf course design business. He was a big, outgoing ex-Marine and loved life. He was also a fine golf course designer and partnered well with Arnie in the course design business.

However, Ed had an unfulfilled dream. He'd always wanted to caddy for Arnie in an event. He badgered Arnie over the years and finally, during a Pro-Am, Arnie said, "Okay, Ed, you can carry the bag today."

As Ed told the story, Arnie hit a good drive down the middle of the fairway. When they got to the ball, Arnie wanted to know the distance to the hole, so he said, "How far do we have, Ed?" Ed replied, "About 150 yards, boss." Arnie stood quietly with his arms folded, and in about ten seconds repeated the question, "How far do we have, Ed?" Ed was puzzled that Arnie had asked the same question again, but gave the same answer, "We've got about 150 yards, boss." Arnie then turned to Ed and with some disgust said, "Ed, I can do 'about.'" Ed said he felt foolish because professionals of Arnie's stature don't want to know *about* how far. They want to know *exactly* how far—so, *about* just didn't do it!

NOW FOR A story with a very happy ending. One day during my years with Arnie, we got a call informing us that a couple of representatives of the USGA—including its then president, Fred Ridley—wanted to come in and visit with Arnie. We had no idea the purpose of the visit but Arnie, of course, said that he would be pleased to meet with them. He asked me to sit in. At the appointed time they arrived and, after some pleasantries, got to the point of their visit. The USGA had decided to greatly expand and modernize the museum at its headquarters, Golf House, in Far Hills, New Jersey. They had come to tell Arnie they had decided to name the museum for him. Arnie was stunned, as was I. It was the first time that the USGA had ever done anything like this, but they obviously had come to recognize that no one in the history of the game had done more to help golf and the USGA than Arnold Palmer. Arnie was visibly moved and his reply was heartfelt and, to me at least, quite moving. He said simply, "I don't know how to thank you. I feel like I just won another Open!" The museum project was undertaken and completed. It is a magnificent facility, and it has exactly the right name!

INTERESTINGLY, THIS HAPPY story brought to an end a not-so-happy story of a few years earlier. I was in the room when Ely Callaway asked Arnold Palmer if he would support Callaway's introduction of a club called the ERC II, which, because it did not conform to USGA equipment standards, could only be used for recreational play. Arnie agreed, and I fully supported his position. Arnie felt (and again I completely agreed) that this would make the game more fun and help the game grow, precisely because it was a club that would enhance one's ability to strike the ball—especially for high-handicap players and beginners.

Before going on with my story, this is an appropriate place to note that Ely Callaway was one of the most impressive and charismatic individuals I ever met. He was a master salesman and in many ways revolutionized the golf industry. I also made a wonderful lifetime friend at Callaway Golf—Steve McCracken, Callaway's senior vice president and general counsel. Steve is a superb lawyer, and he and his charming, irrepressible wife, Sue, have become warm friends of Marilyn's and mine. Steve has gone back to the active practice of law in San Diego. We remain in close touch.

Now back to the story. The uproar that followed the announcement of the ERC II was unbelievable—noisy and senseless. One would have thought that Arnie was advocating the bulldozing of Pebble Beach for use as an RV park. Even more surprising were the sources of much of the criticism. Some in the media were simply over the top in their condemnation of Arnie. One writer went so far as to title his column "Benedict Arnold." Several former heads of the USGA wrote letters to Arnie that bordered on vitriolic. All of this was directed at a man who had done more for the game and, indeed, for the USGA than any single individual before or since. Moreover, the hullabaloo seemed completely out of proportion to the significance of the development. No one was suggesting that these clubs could be used in official competition, but only in unofficial, recreational play. The critics seemed either to ignore the distinction or consider it meaningless. The word "cheater" began to be used to characterize those who ignored a rule or two when playing for fun. This struck me as ludicrous. By this definition the vast majority of those playing the game are "cheaters." Here's why.

Virtually every group I play with (again, I'm referring to nonofficial play) gives a mulligan on the first tee, ignores stroke and distance rules for balls hit out of bounds, plays winter rules for most of the summer, and gives putts under twelve inches (indeed, I find that as one grows older, the "gimme" distance grows longer!). None of this is done to "defy" the rules but, rather, to make the game more fun. Perhaps the most absurd charge of "cheating" came when I posed a hypothetical question to one of Arnie's principal critics. I said, "Suppose my wife and I are playing by ourselves on a Sunday afternoon and aren't even keeping score. She chooses to use the ERC II because she can hit it farther and straighter. By the way, she is a twenty-eight handicap. Are you telling me that under these circumstances my wife is a cheater?" After I asked the question, he hesitated only for a moment and then said, "Yes." I found this completely ridiculous—and not just ridiculous but presumptuous in the extreme—and I find it so today. As the controversy got hotter, the USGA rose up in its "righteous" anger and decreed that any score in a round in which the ERC II club was used could not be counted for handicap purposes. That, of course, ended the matter, and Callaway was forced to withdraw the club from the market.

My two major concerns from the whole shabby episode were, first, the criticism of one of the finest men I have ever known and unquestionably the player who had been the popular face of golf for over fifty years. My second concern was that the act underscored what I believed (and continue to believe) is a "blind spot" in the purist's approach to the game. In hindsight it now seems quite clear to me that Arnie was simply well ahead of his time in sensing the game's need to reexamine itself and to begin to think "outside the box" regarding its future. The simple fact is that the game is not growing and hasn't grown for over a decade. This is a matter of genuine concern to me, as I've mentioned.

In fairness it should be said that, so far as I know, no one (including the USGA) had any advance notice of the announcement Ely was about to make. It is, of course, easy to second-guess, but it is entirely possible that if some discussions had taken place with the USGA before the announcement of the new club, the whole reaction might have played out differently. I'm not at all sure this would have been the case, and it is idle speculation at this point.

IT IS WIDELY believed, and I think correctly, that Arnold Palmer has probably given more autographs than any sports figure in history—indeed, perhaps even more than any other human being in history! That's why this story is, to me, so interesting. One day during the playing of the Bay Hill Classic (now called the Arnold Palmer Invitational), I was riding around the course in a cart with Arnie. As always, there were large crowds, and Arnie tried to stay in the "shadows" so as not to disrupt anything. Nevertheless, he was approached by scores of people asking for autographs and, as usual, he obliged. That is he obliged until a young man thrust a photograph in front of him and said, "May I have your autograph?" Arnie looked directly at the young man for several seconds and then said, "I gave you an autograph earlier today and, if I'm not mistaken, you are one of those people who gets my autograph as often as possible and sells it. I think you should leave the tournament immediately." The fellow quickly turned and moved out. I said, "Arnie, I can't believe you remembered that guy with all the hundreds of autographs you have given out today." Arnold pointed out that, over the years, he had gotten very good at recognizing these professional autograph hunters and made sure that they didn't play their game with him. This incident shows something not only about Arnold's integrity but also about his incredible memory for faces!

MY FINAL ARNIE story is one that shows another dimension of this remarkable man.

Annika Sorenstam electrified the golf world and, indeed, the entire sports world when she announced in the spring of 2003 that she intended to play in the PGA Tour, Bank of America Colonial Tournament.

Her announcement brought forth the best and worst in an enormous number of people. She was both widely praised and roundly criticized. One PGA player even refused to play because she was in the field.

But, she did play, and she played amazingly well, missing the cut by only a few strokes. Indeed, if her putting had been anything close to normal, she would have made the cut with ease. However, even more impressive was the way she comported herself throughout the week— all the way from showing her extreme nervousness after her first tee shot by pretending to almost keel over to her smiles and waves to the crowd. But that is not the story I want to tell.

At the time, I was working very closely with Arnie, sharing an office with him at Bay Hill and being involved in many of his activities.

He and Annika were doing a television commercial for Callaway at the Tradition Club in La Quinta, California, and I was with them much of the day. This was after Annika made her announcement about Colonial, but before the event had taken place.

Arnie and I had talked about Annika's decision, and he was uncertain whether it was a good decision or not. During the course of shooting the TV commercial, Arnie went up to Annika, looked her straight in the eye, and said, "Why?" She looked at him a bit confused and said, "What do you mean?" And he once again simply said, "Why?" She realized that he was talking about her decision to play the Colonial. She tried to explain as best she could that she only wanted to test her abilities against the greatest players in the world, but Arnie remained skeptical.

Annika was naturally troubled by his uncertainty and asked me about it. I said, "I have an idea of how to approach him on this, and I'll try it and let you know."

A day or so later I was talking to Arnie about Annika's plans to play the Colonial. He was still having trouble understanding why she wanted to do it. I said I understood his feeling, but wanted him to think about it in a different way. I said, "Arnie, if when you were playing the PGA Tour, there had been another tour where players even better than those on the PGA Tour were playing, wouldn't you have wanted to take a crack at that group of better players?" Arnie replied, "Absolutely!" This, to me, was exactly what Annika was doing, and nothing more.

Arnie understood this instantly, and he subsequently wrote her a warm letter supporting her and wishing her all the best at the Colonial. In that letter he said, "It is certainly your privilege to do what you think is best for you and the game. Just ignore all the comments you are hearing. Do your thing, have fun, and get it done." I quoted parts of Arnie's letter when I presented Annika for induction into the World Golf Hall of Fame.* I guess the moral of this story is—the best always want to get better.

MOST OF MY ten years at Bay Hill were happy, but there were some very sad times as well. Winnie, who was one of the warmest and brightest people I have ever known, died of cancer and left a huge void in the lives of everyone who knew and loved her. Before this, Arnie had his own bout with prostate cancer, which he attacked with the same vigor that he had shown over the years on the golf course. He has been cancer-free since electing to have surgery. Arnie has since remarried and he and his charming wife, Kit, have combined their two families and live a full and happy life, alternating among homes—Orlando, Latrobe, and the Tradition Golf Club in La Quinta, California. Kit is great fun to be with. She reads widely and shares books and stories and jokes with her friends. In addition to "taking care" of Arnie, she organizes betting pools on major sporting events, and Arnie's wide circle of friends scramble to get into the action!

Interestingly, Arnie never has liked being referred to as "the King." He rarely makes an issue of it but simply feels that the game is too big and its history too deep for anyone to be considered its "King."

---

*The full text of comments I made in presenting Annika for her induction into the World Golf Hall of Fame can be found in the Appendix of this book.

Arnie and Jack

I HAVE BEEN blessed to have warm friendships with both Arnie and Jack Nicklaus. I have already told you some stories about my relationship with each of them. But, I want to say a word about the relationship between these two great players. As I have indicated earlier, I knew Jack Nicklaus long before I started working with Arnie. We first met in 1970 when he agreed to design a golf course for Taft Broadcasting at Kings Island. Working closely with Arnie from 1996 until 2006 gave me a wonderful opportunity to understand the relationship between these two legends. First of all, they genuinely like and respect one another. Their friendship is not a façade or just for public consumption. It is very real. They are, of course, fierce competitors, just as they were on the golf course. That is simply their nature. But, it is a competition without envy or pettiness, just as it was on the golf course. You had to be there when they went head to head on the golf course to appreciate and understand their relationship today. Arnold was the King, Jack the usurper. Jack was subjected to insults and jibes and taunts, but he ignored them and never felt that Arnold was sympathetic to—or encouraging of—this bad behavior. Jack once summed up their relationship in a line that I love. He said, "I had to fight Arnie's Army, but I never had to fight Arnie." Arnold, for his part, treated Jack with complete respect and warmth. And, he appreciated perhaps more than anyone Jack's immense talent. Out of this cauldron came a strong and lasting friendship that, in my opinion, grows stronger with every passing year.

They are very different people in many ways, but their core values—honesty, loyalty, and civility—are identical. They both were deeply devoted to their respective fathers and, indeed, Arnie and Charlie Nicklaus (Jack's dad) were good pals. What they each learned from their fathers—both in golf and in life—had enormous influence on their behavior on the golf course and off.

But, make no mistake, they are different, perhaps most notably in their approach to golf as they grow older. No one has ever loved the game more than Arnie, and it is a rare day when he doesn't either play or hit balls. Jack, on the other hand, played golf, I believe, for the competitive "high" it gave him and, once he no longer felt he was competitive, he began to play less and less. Today, he plays very little but seems to do quite well when he does—witness how he and Tom Watson stayed wealthy on their winnings in the old Senior Skins Game! Let me tell you my favorite story that illustrates the difference between Arnie and Jack. When I was working with Arnie, I continued to maintain a close relationship with Jack, and one day went to his office in North Palm Beach to discuss a matter. The first thing Jack asked was, "How is Arnie?" I said he was fine, and then Jack asked, "Does he really play golf *every* day?" I replied that he did. Jack just shook his head. When I got back to my Bay Hill office the next day and told Arnie I had spent some time with Jack, his first question was, "How is Jack?" I said that he seemed to be doing fine. Then Arnie, obviously alluding to the fact that Jack was not playing a lot of golf, said, "What in the world does he do all day?" Understand that neither was being critical of the other. They simply had totally different perspectives!

Winnie and Barbara

NO DISCUSSION OF Arnold Palmer and Jack Nicklaus would be complete without mentioning the two incredible women they married—Winnie and Barbara. Indeed, the depth of their friendship may have been the principal driving force that, I believe, enabled the friendship between their husbands to survive the trauma that often accompanied their intense rivalry on the golf course. If Arnold and Jack are different, Winnie and Barbara were not. Both were bright, warm, outgoing, and incredibly giving—to their husbands, their family, their friends, and their communities. Barbara has said to me more than once,

"Winnie Palmer was always my hero." Winnie in turn told me: "There is no one I admire more than Barbara Nicklaus."

Winnie was unbelievably thoughtful. If she read a book she thought you would like, she had a copy on your doorstep. If she saw an article in the *New Yorker* (her favorite), it would appear on your desk. Every birthday or anniversary would find some flowers or sweets or some remembrance. Her thoughtfulness is even more amazing when you consider the number of friends she had. Her death was a tragic loss for anyone who valued goodness and graciousness.

As I have said, Barbara had many of Winnie's qualities. But one of Barbara's strengths best sums up this remarkable woman. Every year at the Captain's Club dinner during tournament week at Muirfield Village, Barbara presents each captain with a beautiful piece of crystal, which is always accompanied by a handwritten note. This is no short, generic note that is the same for everyone, but, rather, a lengthy, personalized note of thanks with thoughts that are relevant to the particular recipient. I have seen Barbara do this with gatherings as large as thirty or forty people, and it is simply remarkable to know how she does it. Winnie used to laugh and suggest that Barbara must sleep only one or two hours a night in order to get all of her correspondence done with such warmth and her very personal touch. But perhaps the ultimate compliment to both of these ladies is how they each raised wonderful children in the midst of the turbulent life their husbands provided them! Again, I am confident that this long and deep friendship was a critical piece of the warm and close relationship that developed, and continues, between Arnie and Jack.

Moving On

IN 2005, MARILYN and I decided to leave Orlando and become 100 percent "Westerners." We already had our principal home in Jackson Hole, Wyoming, but instead of spending the winter months in Orlando, we decided to live those months in a small place we had built earlier at the Tradition Club in La Quinta, California. Tradition is another Arnold Palmer–designed golf course and one Arnie himself has said is one of the finest he has ever done. It is a charming club built around a century-old Spanish hacienda, which, in its early days, was a ranch and then became a hideaway for the Hollywood stars of the day, including Rudolph Valentino, Greta Garbo, Ginger Rogers, Joan Crawford, Marlene Dietrich, Katharine Hepburn, and Clark Gable. It also hosted some major political figures, most notably Presidents Eisenhower and Kennedy.

This was not an easy decision. We loved living at Bay Hill, and my work with Arnie was as enriching and fun as anything I had ever done. But, all three of our kids were living in the West (two in the San Francisco area and one in Boulder, Colorado), and we simply wanted to be closer to them. Any of you who are parents or grandparents will, I think, understand. So, with very mixed emotions, we moved west.

Happily, my relationship with Arnie continues, and I still review many of his personal and business issues, and the relationship continues to be a very rewarding one for me and, I hope, for him.

Mark McCormack, Arnie, Marilyn, and me. Mark pioneered sports marketing and was a great supporter of women's golf.

Another happy time with AP.

*Arnie and Annika. She explained her decision to play
in a PGA Tour event.*

Arnie and I have had a lot of fun times. This obviously was one of them!

CHAPTER XIV

The Years Since

THE YEARS SINCE working with Arnie have been busy and rewarding. Indeed, they have been much busier than I anticipated. In fact, one of my friends told me one day, "Charlie, you have totally failed at retirement." I'm afraid he's right! I serve on several corporate and foundation boards and act as a consultant/advisor to several other corporations and individuals. In addition, I remain closely connected to the LPGA and serve on the Commissioner's Advisory Council. I work with several LPGA players and former players, including Juli Inkster, Dottie Pepper, and Annika Sorenstam.

Happily, in the last ten or fifteen years, many young people have come to me for advice. I love working with them. They have led me to do all manner of things I never dreamed of—being on Facebook, having a Twitter account, learning to text, and on and on. I'm not sure I totally understand any of these things, but I do my best! I guess I am living proof that when you grow old and wrinkled and have a head of white hair, people just assume that you are wise! I certainly intend to trade on this as long as I can.

So, there you have it—the *Reader's Digest* version of eighty-two years of Charlie Mechem. I'm sure you've heard enough about me, but I truly hope that you will now have a better understanding of how I was able to interact with so many interesting people over such a long period of time and how much I learned from them. Each of my three careers was interesting, but the combination gave rise to so many exciting experiences with such a wide variety of people that I simply wanted to share them. Virtually everyone in these stories is far better known than I. These stories are about them—not me. I'm simply the "recorder." At a dinner one night a long time ago I was seated at a star-studded dais. When I was asked to make some remarks, I commented, "Looking up and down this head table, I realize that I am the only person up here that I have never heard of before!" That's very much how I feel as I relate these stories.

It is with this same humility that I have approached Part II of this book—"Lessons Learned." These are not words of wisdom from me. Rather, they are exactly what the title suggests—lessons I have learned from the people and experiences I have written about in this book. Some of these lessons are very mundane and simple. Others are a bit more philosophical and complicated. As I will point out, I have not always been able to follow the dictates of these lessons, but I have always tried. I truly hope they will be of some value to you.

Arnold Palmer teaching the proper grip to a young pupil—my grandson, Will Doering. Will knows a lot about Arnie, and he is obsessed with golf. His goals are high. He recently said to his mother, "One of these days I'll be so good that people will be drinking a 'Will Doering.'"

Part Two

LESSONS
LEARNED

LET'S BEGIN BY making it very clear that I am not an expert in identifying or defining the important lessons of a successful and rewarding life. Indeed, I have had a lifelong suspicion of "experts," and I love to illustrate my skepticism with a little story.

There was a renowned chemistry professor who was out on his annual lecture tour. He went from campus to campus discoursing on his field of expertise. To help him with the mechanics of the trip was his longtime, loyal chauffeur.

The professor always gave the same lecture at the various stops, and towards the end of the tour, both he and his chauffeur were getting a little weary of the whole exercise. As they approached the site of the last lecture, the chauffeur said, "You know, let's have a little fun tonight. I know your lecture by heart. I've heard it thirty-eight times. I'd like to deliver it."

To which the professor said, "Sounds like a wonderful idea. You do that. I'll put on your chauffeur's uniform. I'll sit in the back of the audience and pretend to be you. It will be great."

The chauffeur did a marvelous job of giving the speech and no one was the wiser. When the speech was over, there was a great round of applause. The chauffeur nodded modestly and was about to retire, when from the audience came, "Question, question." Well, of course, all lectures are followed by Q & A, so the chauffeur looked at the raised hand and said, "By all means, go ahead."

The question was from a chemistry professor at the university. He said, "What is the co-efficient of plutonium times the valence of copper as a factor of stress in the early curve of nuclear fission development when the reactor is lead based?"

Well, the chauffeur didn't miss a beat. He said, "Sir, I recognize you from photographs that I've seen in trade journals, and I know you are very renowned and respected. But I must say that I'm astounded that a man of your reputation could ask such an absolutely absurd, juvenile question. Why, my chauffer in the back of the room can answer that."

I have always loved that story because I think it tells us a lot about those who profess to be experts, but aren't, and many times they get away with it.

But I'll tell you what does help in one's quest for wisdom: it helps to be old! Yes, you heard me right. Age helps. People think that if you are over seventy and have some white hair, you must be wise. There was a great cartoon in the *New Yorker* not too long ago in which two old folks are sitting on a porch, probably at a senior citizen center. Two younger people come out and are looking over at them, when the one young person says to the other, "They don't have the secrets to anything; they're just old." Maybe that's the case. But for what it's worth, age and, I think, a little white hair do help.

I have a favorite story on the irrelevancy of age. It goes like this: An eighty-five-year-old lady was visiting her doctor because she had been feeling tired and listless. After examining her, he called her into his office and said, "Madam, I have unbelievable news—you're pregnant!" She, of course, was horrified and said, "But that's impossible. I'm eighty-five and my husband is ninety-three." The doctor nodded and said, "I certainly understand that you are shocked, but I have run all the proper tests and it is very clear—you're going to have a baby." The distraught lady raced to the phone and dialed her home phone number. When her husband answered, she practically yelled at him, "Henry, you got me pregnant!"

After a brief pause, her husband replied, "Who's this callin'?" Clearly, age is largely a state of mind.

I have to tell you, though, I have never felt as old as I did a while back when I went into Starbucks to get my morning cup of coffee. You know, I am from the era where you went into a coffee shop and said, "I want a cup of black coffee." That was it. The only option was cream or sugar. There wasn't anything else. One size, one cup, one blend, one price.

Now, of course, you have dozens of choices. While I was standing there (I'm not making this up—I could *not* make this up), a lady ordered a "decaf-iced vente sugar-free vanilla non-fat caramel macchiato." The bill was $2.56 and she paid by credit card! More recently, I was behind a man in line who ordered "a small drip in a vente cup with two extra shots." At first it sounded to me like the mob was about to eliminate a short, unpleasant person with several shots and drop him in the ocean in a weighted vente cup. But the server seemed to understand!

I know two things for certain. First, the longer you live and the more experiences you have, the more you learn what works and what doesn't. (This may be because, as Will Rogers said, "Good judgment comes from experience—and a lot of that comes from bad judgment.") Second, the more change you see, the more you realize the wisdom of the old saying "the only thing that changes is change itself."

In this era of Google and Facebook and DNA and cyberspace and WikiLeaks and reggae and rap and texting and cloud computing and on and on, there is a very natural temptation to conclude that everything has changed, that there are no absolutes, that nothing is the same as it was a hundred years ago—or fifty—or ten—or maybe even twenty minutes ago!

Yes, it would be quite natural to conclude this, but it would also be— in my judgment—quite wrong to do so.

I want to persuade you that, although change is the natural order of things, some things in fact never change. Let's talk about some of those things, those important "Lessons Learned." Some of them are quite simple, while others are more profound and complex. By sheer coincidence, there are twenty-two of them. So, pardon the pun, but let's call them "Charlie's Cache 22."

Hard Work

THE FIRST PRINCIPLE is especially interesting because it is so basic and simple. Typically, when I mention this to people, they respond with surprise and look at me with the unmistakable look of, "Gee, I never thought of *that* before!" What is this startling first suggestion? Just this—you must *Work Hard*. Every endeavor in which I have ever been involved, and every person I have known who succeeded in his or her chosen career, worked hard. There is simply no substitute. Admittedly, some successful people accomplish things with less effort than others, but all are diligent and committed to working hard. Laziness is simply not part of the makeup of such people. Neither is giving less than a complete effort to whatever task is at hand. More on that later.

Furthermore, successful people don't stop working when they become successful. Over the years I was privileged to serve on a number of boards of directors of companies, most of which were in businesses remote from the business of Taft Broadcasting Company (businesses like paper manufacturing, automobile parts suppliers, a bicycle parts maker, a life insurance company). I always suspected they thought they might get new insights from someone who was associated with a company involved in broadcasting, amusement parks, and cartoons! Service on these boards was very helpful to me in my own business activities, not in the least because it exposed me to some extraordinary people. Among the most extraordinary was a man with whom I served on the Mead Corporation board. Jack Bogle has been, by any measure, one of the greats of the investment industry since he founded the Vanguard Group in 1974. The next year he introduced the Vanguard 500 Index Fund as the first index mutual fund available to the general public. Interestingly, he has a group of followers so devoted and committed that they are known as the "Bogleheads." The thing that most impressed me about Jack is that he never "trumpeted" his intellect. He made his points clearly and simply, but the strength of his advice was always obvious. We became very good friends, and I was honored to make some remarks at his retirement dinner when he reached the mandatory age limit for board members of Mead.

Apart from his reputation in the investment and business world, there is an amazing side story. Jack's heart was giving out on him. He had been having heart problems since his thirties and had had a number of heart attacks. He naturally got the best medical advice and treatment, but his heart continued to weaken. It was obvious to all of us who saw him every few months as he became thinner and paler. He decided to have a heart transplant—and this was in 1996! He, of course, had to wait for an appropriate match, and it reached a point where his condition was so tenuous that he had to stay in the hospital in order to keep him going until a proper match was available. Incredibly, late one night a young man was killed in a motorcycle accident, and Jack received his heart. After a long and incredibly complex recovery (he once told me that he was taking over seventy pills a day!), he made a spectacular recovery. His color returned, he gained weight, and once again became the vibrant Jack Bogle we had once known. We used to tease Jack that we expected to see him on a Harley any day!

One more Bogle story. Over the years Jack always singled out a particular visual that was used in board presentations. I must confess that I don't remember what it was about, but I do remember it was some sort of graph more often than not going down instead of up where it should have been headed. At Jack's retirement party, in my remarks I alluded to Jack's continuing concern with the direction of the graph, but pointed out that I had made a surprising discovery—the graph had continually been shown the wrong way! It was always shown upside down! Therefore, by simply turning the graph in the right direction the curve was constantly going up. Jack seemed satisfied! Jack continues his prolific writing and speaking schedule. All of us would be better off if we heeded Jack's business counsel and plain, commonsense reasoning. Jack has a favorite phrase that I think sums up beautifully what Jack is all about. It is simply this—"Press on regardless."

Another example is Arnold Palmer. When I worked with Arnie, I never saw him go into a press conference or meeting without being prepared. For instance, when Arnie would go into a press conference, he would always have with him a 5 x 8 card with bullet points of the essential comments that he wanted to make. If you have ever seen an Arnold Palmer press conference, you know his presentation appears smooth and effortless. This is not an accident. He works at it. He is prepared.

A fanciful story will illustrate my point. A crow was sitting in a tree, doing nothing all day. A rabbit came along and asked him, "Can I also sit like you and do nothing all day long?" The crow answered, "Sure, why not?" So, the rabbit sat on the ground below the crow and rested. A fox jumped on the rabbit and ate it. Moral of the story: To be sitting and doing nothing, you must be sitting very high up! To put it another way: Any time the going gets easy, you'd better check and see if you are going downhill!

Let me go back to my experiences on the highway crew for a moment. One day I was directed to dig a ditch. I was stabbing away at the ground with a long-handled spade when one of the older men came along and asked me how many ditches I had dug in my life. When I admitted that the answer was none, he said, "Let me show you a thing or two" . . . and he did. Effortlessly and quickly, he accomplished the job. Then he turned to me and, with some pride, said, "Now you know how to do it properly."

The real lesson here, of course, is that no matter how mundane a job may seem, there is a right way to do it and a wrong way. A proper way and a sloppy way. Always aim to do it right.

Let me suggest an acronym that you might keep in mind if you ever question the importance of hard work. The acronym is TANSTAAFL. It stands for: "There ain't no such thing as a free lunch." One final word on this subject. It is not only important to work "hard" but to work "smart" and manage your time carefully. I think all of us have learned that sometimes you can get just as much done in much less time by simply avoiding inconsequential and non-productive things.

Broaden Your Range of Interests

I LEARNED EARLY in my law practice that the more I knew about more things, whether it was politics or sports or music or the theater or whatever, the better chance I had of getting clients and establishing relationships. They quite properly *assumed* that I knew the law. So the fact that I had gone to a great law school and was doing reasonably well as a lawyer was not that big a deal. In other words, I came to realize that the foundation of virtually all of my professional relationships was not my skill as a lawyer . . . that's what the client expected. In every case, the basis was some other interest we shared in common—sports, politics, music, art, or whatever. If you broaden your range of interests and become familiar with a wide range of ideas, I think it can help enormously in establishing worthwhile personal relationships throughout your life.

By the way, I think doing this in today's world is even tougher than it used to be. I think it is "easier" to have a narrow range of interests these days than it used to be.

Amid all of the world's complexity and opportunity, some people seek the comfort of the well defined. As I have pointed out earlier in this book, my experiences working on the county highway crew and my Army days exposed me to people and experiences that helped immeasurably in future years. One particular story stands out from my Army years. One day I pulled KP duty. For those of you too young to know what this means, it means "kitchen police," and it is one of the most dreaded jobs in the service. You spend all day working in the mess hall, and none of the work is easy or fun. On this particular day, I was assigned to the back porch of the mess hall to collect the garbage from the kitchen and be sure it was put properly in the garbage cans. Another fellow was assigned along with me. He was seventeen years old and had grown up on a farm in Illinois. Late in the day, exhausted and covered with garbage, we sat down for a brief break. My companion turned to me and said, "I wonder if a fella could get this job permanently." I laughed, thinking that he was making a joke, but he went on: "No, I mean it. You're out of doors. You do exactly the same thing every day. You know exactly what is expected of you, and you only concentrate on one thing. I really wonder if I could get this assignment permanently." Although I was stunned, I didn't want to embarrass him, so I let the matter drop, but I learned a real lesson. What might make sense for one person might not make any sense to another. What might be a useful and satisfactory life for one person would not necessarily be the same for another. I guess it's called perspective, a trait that is invaluable in life.

A good example of having a broad range of interests was my friend Mark McCormack. Mark, of course, built the preeminent sports marketing agency in the world. He was able to do this not only because he was a brilliant lawyer, but because of the breadth of his interests. He loved all sports, was an accomplished golfer, knew everything about great restaurants and great wine, and was conversant on virtually any subject. As I mentioned earlier, one of the most engaging things about Mark—I guess because it was so unusual—was that he carried a small camera with him wherever he went and would either take pictures himself or have someone else take them to "memorialize" whatever the occasion happened to be.

The term "Renaissance man" is often used loosely and, in my judgment, not always accurately. But the term has never been more appropriate than when applied to one of my dearest Cincinnati friends Dr. Charlie Barrett. Charlie was a man of many talents and he was good at all of them. A superb physician, he not only had a distinguished practice but was a towering figure in the Cincinnati medical world. His skill and his wisdom had an enormous impact on a wide range of people. As if this were not enough, for many years he also was deeply involved with Western & Southern Life Insurance Company, one of the nation's leading insurance groups, headquartered in Cincinnati.* He was also a marvelous companion, a great sportsman, and a dedicated family man. I was much younger than Charlie and sought and relied on his guidance more than once. Whatever the situation, he was always available and inevitably helpful.

One of my funniest memories of Charlie came, ironically, when he was suffering the anguish of "Montezuma's revenge" during an outing the Cincinnati Commercial Club had many years ago at a superb resort in Mexico called Tres Vidas. The club had gone there for a three-day outing and within the first twenty-four hours, at least half of the group became sick. For those of you who have not had this unpleasant experience, it is not life-threatening, nor even totally debilitating, but it is very, very unpleasant. As the number of afflicted grew, the word got out that Charlie had brought with him a supply of pills that might help reduce the discomfort. Apparently, fellows were seeking him out for a dose. When I came down with the scourge, I made my way to his room and knocked on the door. After a few minutes the door opened only a crack—just wide enough for a hand to get through—and out came Charlie's right hand with two pills in it and he dropped them in my palm. The hand quickly withdrew, and I was on my own. Charlie had already been hit by the "revenge," but was still administering to his flock!

There's another wonderful story that, although it didn't directly involve Charlie, happened on this same outing. First of all, every golf cart was equipped with several rolls of toilet paper because one could not predict when the "revenge" would strike. However, that is not the story. What happened was this. My foursome teed off on a particular hole, and the last guy who teed off hit his ball quite a long way, and it landed near the edge of the fairway. There were some workers in a service truck with a flatbed doing some cleanup work. My partner's drive took a couple of bounces and bounced right into the bed of the truck.

---

*Dr. Barrett was Chairman of Western & Southern Life Insurance Company, a firm he joined in 1942 as associate medical director. He was named president in 1973 and chairman and chief executive officer in 1984. He relinquished the title of chief executive officer in 1988.

As we raced down the fairway to retrieve the ball, the truck drove away. We stopped and made clear to the guy who had hit the ball that if the truck stopped near the green and dumped out the ball, we *absolutely* would not allow him to play the ball in that spot! He was adamant that, since it happened through no fault of his own, he should be allowed to play the ball wherever it ended up. Happily, the issue became moot because the truck drove away, and we never saw it again.

One more Charlie Barrett story. Charlie invited me to a golf outing one summer at the Kenwood Country Club in Cincinnati. We had a delightful day. As we sat down to dinner, I realized that everyone at the table was a doctor except me. The meal was the typical after-golf feast of steak and French fries topped off by apple pie a la mode. I watched as all of the doctors cleaned their plates and totally consumed the pie. I turned to Charlie and said, "Charlie, I don't get this. We are constantly being told to avoid rich meals, including virtually everything we have eaten tonight, and yet I saw every doctor eating everything in sight." Charlie smiled and said, "I understand what you're saying, but I suspect that it only makes a few 'beats of your heart' difference in your lifespan. It's all about the genes."

TO REITERATE THE main point—the more you know about a wide variety of things, the easier it will be for you to connect with others of similar interests. I have tried to make this point in the many speeches I have made over the years to students who are majoring in business. I stress to them not to allow their education to be narrow and to take courses that explore nonbusiness areas. I am convinced they will be more well-rounded and more successful if they do so.

There is a corollary here. No matter what business you are in, I think it can be helpful if you involve yourself in outside organizations and activities—typically nonprofit, charitable organizations. I found I could bring some of my skills to the nonprofit organizations with whom I worked and, equally important, I learned much from them.

Dinah Shore with Amy Alcott. Dinah looked fabulous even after jumping in the lake.

One of the great marketing slogans of all time. I was privileged to serve on the Smucker's board for over twenty years.

With my dear friend Charlie Barrett.

With one of my all-time favorites, Laura Davies.

A commemorative stamp of the unforgettable Barbara Jordan, the greatest public speaker I ever saw.

Fishing with my friend Herb Lotman in bear country.

Fred Shuttlesworth and Bobbie Sterne at the Great Living Cincinnatian dinner.

Announcement of the
Blue Chip City Economic
Development Campaign.

One of my dearest friends, Louise Suggs.

Learn to Deal with Detail but Not Be Absorbed by It

Each career that I've been involved in has required a little different approach to this challenge. Obviously, when I was practicing law, I had to be concerned with detail. But, I fought hard to avoid being trapped in it. On the other hand, when I went into the business world and was the CEO of a large company, I initially got a little more immersed in detail than I should have. So I backed off. Then I began to realize that you can't have it one way or the other. No matter how high you get in an organization, you can't ignore detail, nor should you. But, you must not allow yourself to be swallowed up by it.

Let me give you what I believe is a good example. One of the individuals on the LPGA Tour that I liked and respected most was the great British star Laura Davies. She was immensely talented and her personality was always upbeat and optimistic. By the way, Laura has played all over the world for many years and has amassed over eighty tournament victories. She is at or above any female player in history in terms of tournament wins other than possibly Kathy Whitworth at eighty-eight.

During one of my early years as Commissioner, we had an event in Florida sponsored by Oldsmobile, which also sponsored an event in Lansing, Michigan. When Laura called the LPGA office to sign up for the Florida event there was some confusion in the communication, and the office signed her up for the Lansing event but not the Florida event. When I arrived at the Florida tournament site early in the week, my officials told me that Laura was not eligible to play. This dismayed me because she was one of our top talents and a great crowd favorite. Laura was understandably upset and asked to speak with me. After speaking with her and investigating the matter further, it was plain to me that it was the LPGA office's fault that she was not properly registered. But the simple fact was that, according to the detail of the rule, she was not eligible to play.

In spite of that, I decided to allow her to enter, though this upset some tour officials. I simply felt that enforcing the precise detail of the rule would lead to the wrong result. My decision was very popular with the players because they felt it showed a certain degree of flexibility in what can be very rigid interpretations of golf's cumbersome and complicated rules. However, after the second day of play, Laura was leading the tournament, and I began to hear some grumbles from some players that she really shouldn't have been allowed into the tournament in the first place. Ultimately, Laura fell back and did not win the event. Although I would never root against her, or any other player for that matter, her not winning certainly got me off the hook. (Incidentally, this is a good example of how quickly one can go from being right to being wrong in someone's eyes as a result of happenings over which they had absolutely no control.) Most of all, I think this story illustrates how being a slave to detail can be harmful. If I had approached this problem determined to enforce the rules in detail, it would have led to the wrong result.

One of the best examples of being so focused on the trees that one overlooks the forest happened during my years as a lawyer. One of my clients, with whom I was working on an estate plan, came into my office with several large sheets of paper and a very proud look. He explained that he had spent weeks outlining in great detail an estate plan and a plan for managing his affairs until his death. He "unfurled" the papers and he had, indeed, done a careful and thorough job of planning—with one significant exception. After studying his work for a while I noted that he had made detailed calculations of all sorts of things that might happen during the rest of his life in order to have a proper assessment of the size of his estate. However, his pride and optimism quickly deflated when I pointed out to him that nowhere in his outline had he made any provisions for the cost of living during the rest of his life. Nothing for housing, nothing for clothes, nothing for food, and so forth. He looked at me blankly for a moment and then we both began to laugh. He had been so immersed in technical details, including tax rates, inflation projections, and so on that he had completely ignored the most basic thing of all—what it would cost him to live.

On the other hand, one can be too careless about detail, and I want to share with you one of my all-time favorite stories. Pat Harmon was a popular and respected sports writer for the *Cincinnati Post* for many years. We were good friends and I always enjoyed reading Pat's columns. One day when we were together with one of Pat's friends, the friend volunteered a story that ranks high on my list of great stories. Pat and his wife had eleven children. One summer night, Pat came home around dusk after enjoying a couple of beers with the boys, a common practice among sports writers since time began. When Pat got home, the yard was filled with children, and Pat's wife came out on the front porch and yelled, "Get the kids in here now for baths and bedtime." As Pat's friend tells the story, Pat went through the swirling mass of kids and in a loud voice ordered them into the house. One little boy did not immediately follow Pat's instruction, so Pat went over to the little boy and rather angrily said, "I told you to get in the house right now and I mean it!" The little boy looked at Pat and said, "But Mr. Harmon, I'm not your child." Pat always insisted the story was not true, and perhaps it wasn't. But it sure made for a great tale, and it was a good example of the need, on certain occasions, to be very sensitive to detail!

The story I related earlier about Arnold Palmer's friend and one-time caddie, Ed Seay, is a real object lesson in the need to be sensitive to detail. While the precise yardage on a golf course doesn't mean much to most of us, it means everything to a professional, especially one that performs at the highest level.

Although my final story in this section is not exactly about detail, it does underscore the importance of paying some attention to specifics. I was attending a conference in Cleveland, Ohio, during which we heard a speech from the much acclaimed business leader and visionary Dr. Simon Ramo. One of my good friends from Cincinnati was also in the audience—Don Hinckley, CEO of Emery Industries, Inc., one of Cincinnati's finest companies. It is important before going on to note that the speech was given in September. Dr. Ramo gave a superb talk and shared his vision for coming decades and even longer. It was thought provoking, to say the least. When he finished, he asked for questions. There were a number and then my friend Don raised his hand and said, "Dr. Ramo, I have truly enjoyed your vision of the future. But let me ask you this: How do you see October?" Don's question brought down the house, and Dr. Ramo shared the laughs. Just another example of the need to pay attention to detail without being absorbed by it.

It's Okay to Worry—Just Don't Agonize

THE NEXT POINT is one that I've learned the hard way, as perhaps many of you have. I believe that worry can be very therapeutic and very important in the solving of problems. However, when you cross the line from worry to agonizing, then you've got a real problem. I think worrying can be a good thing. It is agonizing that never gets you anywhere. Now, it's impossible, obviously, to precisely define the line between these two conditions. But, we all know when we've crossed that line, because we continue to go over the same ground with no new thoughts or solutions. James Thurber reportedly said, "Sixty minutes of thinking of any kind is bound to lead to confusion and unhappiness." I'm not sure I'd go that far, but, clearly, agonizing can be debilitating and is not conducive to solving a problem. It is important to take action as soon as possible if things are not going well. Don't just hope that they will magically get better.

A classic example of the point I am trying to make occurred during the moon landing of Neil Armstrong and Buzz Aldrin. For those of you too young to remember, it went something like this. The landing site programmed by NASA for the landing vehicle to put down turned out to be unsuitable when the astronauts got close enough to examine it. A crater and a collection of large boulders made a landing impossible. There was only a small amount of fuel left to land the craft and still have enough fuel remaining to leave the moon when the mission was completed. Although I have never discussed it with him, there can be no question that Neil Armstrong, as the pilot of the craft, was worried. It is equally clear that he did not agonize. Instead he found a new landing site and expertly landed the craft with just a few seconds of fuel remaining. Had he agonized—and hesitated—one of the greatest achievements in human history might have ended far differently.

Again, I firmly believe that taking time to worry is normally helpful and productive. In this regard, it is important to remember that there are very few true calamities. When we're young and we're starting on our careers, we too often say, "Oh, my God, this is a crisis. I've got to deal with this immediately. I don't dare think about it overnight. I don't have time to think it through."

There is a wonderful story about the great British statesman Benjamin Disraeli, who said, when asked to define the difference between a misfortune and a calamity, "If Mr. Gladstone [his principal adversary] fell into the Thames, that would be a misfortune. If someone pulled him out, that would be a calamity." It's a great line and it's true. There are a lot of misfortunes in all of our lives, but not very many real calamities. There is normally adequate time to indulge in some healthy worrying.*

There may be a very simple solution to the whole matter of worry/agonizing. Someone once said that the best way to forget all your troubles is to wear really tight shoes! Most of us have endured this agony, and it certainly does crowd everything else out of one's mind!

Control Your Anger

WHILE SOMETIMES VERY difficult to do, I have come to increasingly understand the importance of controlling one's anger. For one thing, anger seriously impairs one's judgment. Moreover, an outburst of anger will almost certainly further alienate the person who provoked

---

*I cannot resist at this point quoting Disraeli again with what I believe to be the greatest "put down" in history. A Member of Parliament said to Disraeli: "Sir, you will either die on the gallows or of some unspeakable disease." Disraeli replied, "That depends, Sir, on whether I embrace your policies or your mistress."

the anger. Now, controlling your anger does not necessarily mean submitting or compromising, though in certain circumstances one of those approaches may, in fact, be the right answer. The reasons for controlling your anger are, in the final analysis, basically selfish. You simply can't function rationally and effectively if anger is clouding your judgment.

As golf fans—at least older golf fans—know, one of the greatest stars and characters of the golf world in the 1940s and 1950s was Tommy Bolt. He won the 1958 U.S. Open and a number of other PGA and Senior PGA championships.

I only met Tommy once. He was retired and living at a course called Black Diamond in Florida. A friend invited me there, and we ended up having lunch with Tommy. He was delightful, telling story after story. At the time, I was living at Bay Hill and working very closely with Arnie. I mentioned this to Tommy, and he told me something Arnie had mentioned on several occasions—mainly that he and Winnie and the Bolts traveled together a lot in Arnie's early days on tour in trailers that they pulled from one event to another. He told several stories about their friendship, but the one I best remember was about throwing golf clubs. Tommy, of course, was probably the most famous club thrower in history. He had a ferocious temper and frequently launched his clubs into the air in anger or frustration. But, this story was not about his prowess. On the contrary, he told me that it was he who taught Arnie how to throw a club! As Tommy told it, they were playing one day when Arnie threw his club back over his shoulder in anger. Tommy said, "I patiently explained to him that he should never throw his club backwards because he would have to turn around and go back to retrieve it. Instead, he should throw his clubs in front of him so that he could pick them up while continuing to walk down the fairway." I must say that I am a bit dubious about the authenticity of this story because I don't think that Arnie was much of a club thrower. But, it is a great story and Tommy had fun telling it. Also, Tommy controlled his anger by making fun of it!

Remember the story I related earlier about Paul Brown taking a twelve on the first hole of our golf match at Muirfield Village? Paul could easily have gotten angry and that would have destroyed the rest of the day. Instead, he took some time to compose himself, and after a few holes he was his old self and enjoyed the rest of the round. Sometimes it may take some time to get one's anger under control, but it is very much worth taking whatever time is needed.

Similarly, the story I told earlier about Jack Nicklaus at the outing at the Camargo Club is another example of how to handle anger. Jack could not have been pleased by the "heckling" while he was explaining how to hit a sand wedge. But, rather than make an angry reply, he simply proceeded to demonstrate with his skill and finesse the point he was trying to make.

Importance of Effective Communication

THE IMPORTANCE OF the next point is clear, but needs elaboration. I refer to the importance of effective communication. In my experience, this has four different elements.

The first is just pure vocabulary. When I was chairman of the board of Taft Broadcasting Company, I would forever "beat" on my people before our board of directors meetings: "Don't come to the board meeting and start using words that the board's not going to understand. Use vocabulary that is familiar to them." The extreme of this, of course, is the tax lawyers who can carry on an entire conversation and use nothing but section numbers. But the point is equally valid, I think, with all of us. We often slip into using vocabulary we are comfortable with but that is foreign to our listeners.

The second element of effective communication is understanding the fragility of language and how a very simple word, a word understandable to everybody, can create a major problem. I love to tell this story and, I promise you, it is 100 percent true. When I first went to work at Taft Stettinius & Hollister, there were three young men who were my contemporaries as lowly associates in the firm. One of the jobs assigned to the new associates, as an extracurricular activity, was to organize and stage the annual black-tie dinner dance held every winter. This affair was a big deal because all of the senior partners attended, and it was critical that things go perfectly. Naturally, we recruited our wives to help with this, and they were having a good time with it.

But one day, some particular issue arose that needed immediate attention from the wives. I got a call at my office from one of the wives. Now, I had eight million things going on (I thought I was busy!), and I get a call from one of the wives saying, "I've got to talk to Marilyn. She's not home. Where is she?" I said, "I don't know." She said, "Have her call me tonight. I must talk to her. We've got to have a conference call and get this problem dealt with." So I took a piece of paper out of my pocket, wrote a reminder note to myself, put it back in my pocket, and completely forgot about it until that night when I got home. I went into the bedroom and unloaded my pockets on the dresser, and I came across the note. I opened it. I said, "Marilyn, come here, honey. I want to explain this note to you before I show it to you." On the note I had written, "Call girls for party." Simple words, clear meaning. But, they could have shaken my marriage if the discovery of the message had not been accompanied by an explanation. Words that ought to be so simple and so easy can often confuse. Think about double meaning.

It is so easy to say something that seems clear but carries a double meaning quite different than the one you intend. Many years ago my brother, who was a minister, sent me a number of excerpts from church bulletins that vividly—and amusingly—illustrate my point. Here are a few:

> *Irvin Benson and Jessie Carter were married on October 24 in the church. So ends a friendship that began in their school days.*

Low self-esteem group will meet Thursday at 7:00 p.m.
Please use the back door.

The sermon this morning is "Jesus Walks on the Water."
The sermon tonight is "Searching for Jesus."

Miss Charlene Mason sang "I Will Not Pass This Way Again,"
giving obvious pleasure to the congregation.

Perhaps my favorite story that illustrates the fragility of language is one that happened during my Taft Broadcasting Company days. One of Taft Broadcasting Company's themed amusement parks was Canada's Wonderland, located just north of Toronto. It was successful from the outset and, I am told, has become one of the most successful facilities of its kind in North America. Periodically, several of us would travel to the park for business meetings. The park had a great chef who would always feed us a wonderful lunch before we headed back to Cincinnati. One day, after an ample meal, he brought out a large plate of chocolate éclairs. We said we were too full to eat another bite, but the éclairs looked so good that we asked him to box them up so that we could take them back with us. Now the rest of the story.

As we were flying back in our company airplane, one of my associates raised a concern. He pointed out that we might have trouble clearing customs with food being brought on the plane from outside the country. We acknowledged that this was a real problem and decided to hide the box behind one of the seats. We always flew into a small private airport near Cincinnati, and we knew most of the customs agents. We did not expect that the agent would make a search of the airplane. We landed and taxied up to the customs location. The agent came out of his office, and we opened the door of the plane to let him in. Of course, we were not allowed to disembark until after we had been cleared. The agent mounted the steps, stuck his head into the plane, and said, "Do you have anything to declare?" The problem was that what he said sounded very much like, "Do you have anything to éclair?" We, of course, broke into a fit of laughter. He responded with, "What's so funny?" We told him that we wanted to throw ourselves on the mercy of the court and admitted that we were hiding a treasure trove of luscious chocolate éclairs. He then joined in the laughter. We all had an éclair and headed for home.

The third element of this communications piece is that, in today's world, the world of e-mails, texts, blogs, Facebook pages, and so forth, the importance of effective communication becomes even more important. I mentioned earlier the story Mark McCormack told me about two of his senior executives who had managed to get into a large argument without ever having discussed the issue face to face. Sadly, I think this is an increasing trend. I went into Starbucks one day and saw four young girls at a table all e-mailing or texting. I was rude enough to ask what they were doing, and they told me they were "talking" to one another.

Fourth, I believe it is critical that a person develop his or her speaking skills. Even in this digital world, the ability to express oneself clearly and concisely remains very important. I took several speech classes in high school and college, and I learned a lot, but, amazingly, the best advice I ever got was from my grandfather. He was a coal miner all his life, but he was also the head usher at the little church we attended in Nelsonville. During my early teenage years I attended a church camp virtually every summer. Upon return, I'd be asked to speak to the congregation during the Sunday morning service and describe our experiences at camp. My grandfather would give me certain instructions. He pointed out that his job as head usher required him to stay in the back of the church throughout the morning to seat people who arrived late. He further pointed out that he was beginning to be very hard of hearing. So, he said, "Please speak slowly and loudly so that I can hear every word. Be sure to enunciate and be sure to pause briefly between each sentence." These tips have been invaluable to me over the years, and I commend them to anyone who wants to improve their public speaking or, for that matter, their private speaking.

I have been privileged to make hundreds of speeches over the years. They have certainly not all been good ones, and they certainly have not all been memorable. But my own favorite was the speech I gave when I received the award as a Great Living Cincinnatian from the Greater Cincinnati Chamber of Commerce in 2000. Maybe the reason I remember the speech is that I decided to have fun with it. So often speeches like this become ponderous and boring, not to mention too long. I took a different approach. I noted that I had been informed in November that the award would be bestowed in the following February. So, I speculated in my speech as to what would have happened if I had died after the award had been announced but before the annual dinner at which the awards were given. My speculation ranged from the chamber finding an impersonator, or perhaps a stuffed image sitting in a chair without speaking, to perhaps simply changing the designation of the award to something like "Great Until Very Recently Living Cincinnatian," "Great Retired/Expired Cincinnatian," or "Would Have Been Great If He Was Still Around Cincinnatian."

Apart from my speech, I also have a vivid memory of that evening because I'm not sure I have ever felt more humbled than I did that night. Two other people were given the Great Living Cincinnatian award. One was my old friend and a pioneer and leader of so many causes in Cincinnati—Bobbie Sterne.

The other honoree was the Reverend Fred Shuttlesworth, who was a true legend—an icon of the civil rights movement. He, along with Martin Luther King and Ralph Abernathy, founded the Southern Christian Leadership Conference in 1957. As the pastor of Bethel Baptist Church in Birmingham, Alabama, he became a symbol of resistance in the dark days of Sheriff Bull Connor. He endured beatings, bombings, and unimaginable attacks but never lost his faith or courage. I remember as I accepted the award saying that I was humbled to receive it in his presence and that it made the night even more special for me. He was truly a GREAT Living Cincinnatian!

I have had the pleasure of hearing many superb speakers over the years. I will never forget my first meeting with William Buckley, certainly one of the most articulate conservatives of the last century. Listeners were totally swept away by his eloquence, which is why he was admired and respected by people of all political persuasions. One stunning example is when Buckley made a speech at Yale where Marilyn and I had the good fortune to be in the audience. He defended Senator Joseph McCarthy. Though 90 percent of the audience disagreed with him, he received a standing ovation at the end of his speech simply because he was so eloquent.

I also had the great privilege and pleasure of meeting and hearing the Reverend Billy Graham. He was a very good friend of our minister in Cincinnati, Emerson Colaw (also a superb speaker).

But, the most eloquent—almost hypnotic—speaker that I ever knew was Barbara Jordan. I met Barbara when we served together on the board of directors of the Mead Corporation. Barbara was a lawyer, politician, and educator who served in the United States Congress from 1970 to 1978. Indeed, she was the first African American congresswoman to come from the Deep South. She attended Texas Southern University and became one of the finest collegiate debaters in the United States. She graduated magna cum laude and went on to study at and graduate from Boston University Law School. Though Barbara had many successes in her political life, she did not become nationally known until 1974, when she was a prominent participant in the proceedings involving the impeachment of President Nixon. Perhaps her most indelible impact came when she gave the keynote address at the 1976 Democratic National Convention. It was an electric moment as she showed the crowd what an incredibly dynamic and articulate public speaker she was. Barbara and I sat next to one another at the Mead board table for years, and I got to know her quite well. With her as a Texas-Lyndon Johnson Democrat and I as an Ohio-Taft Republican, you can imagine some of the digs we exchanged. It is impossible to truly describe the way

Barbara spoke. Her voice was deep, her pace deliberate, and each word articulated precisely. Even when Barbara made some relatively unimportant comment about something going on in the board meeting, it still sounded like a great piece of oratory. Barbara was a truly remarkable human being, and she died much too young. I truly suspect there will be no one quite like her—ever.

Though Barbara Jordan ranks as the greatest public speaker I've ever heard, the most fascinating speaker I've ever observed was Howard Cosell. Although I met Howard on several occasions, there was only one time when I spent any significant amount of time with him. It was when he was the featured speaker at a large charity dinner in Cincinnati. I had arranged his appearance through my friends at ABC and felt responsible for looking out for him while he was in town. I met Howard at the airport and accompanied him to the hotel and subsequently to dinner, where I introduced him. When he got up to speak, since I was seated next to the podium, I could see that he didn't have any notes or manuscript. The podium was totally bare. He spoke eloquently, amusingly, at some length, and to the great delight of the crowd—again, without ever a glance at a note.

When the speech was over and we were headed back to the airport for Howard's return flight to New York City, I said, "Howard, you were really great tonight, and I want to really thank you for coming." Without a smile and with no attempt at false humility, Howard simply said, "Yes, I really had them in the palm of my hand, didn't I?" And, you know what—he absolutely did! I think there were several reasons for his eloquence. He was incredibly bright, had a cadence to his voice that became legendary, and, obviously, his reputation insured that the audience would listen from the first word.

Permit me to digress just a bit. One of the perils of public speaking is being the "after-dinner" speaker at the end of a very long evening. One of the funniest lines I ever heard in this regard gets my nomination for the comeback of the year award. It goes like this. A speaker drank much too much before he rose to speak. When he got up, he became so dizzy that he fell flat on the floor. The audience was aghast and didn't know quite what to do. The speaker, however, dealt with the situation in a very unique way. He said in a slurred but strong voice, "I believe I will dispense with my prepared remarks and simply take questions from the floor!"

Speaking of long dinners, another hazard of public speaking comes when you are the master of ceremonies at a dinner and need to introduce a head table made up of a large number of distinguished guests. Let me share with you one way to deal with this problem. I had the privilege and pleasure of acting as master of ceremonies on three different occasions at what may well be the biggest golf awards dinner in the country—The Francis Ouimet Award Dinner, which takes place annually in Boston. The driving force behind the dinner has been my good friend Dick Connelly of Morgan Stanley. The dinner is named for the great amateur Francis Ouimet, who won the U.S. Open in 1913, defeating two legendary British professionals, Harry Vardon and Ted Ray. His victory is widely considered to be the first major step in the growth and prominence of golf in the United States. Each year the dinner honors one of the greats of the game and always draws a crowd of over two thousand people. Among the honorees have been Arnold Palmer, Jack and Barbara Nicklaus, Nancy Lopez, and Annika Sorenstam.

The head table at this dinner is large and prestigious. One thing I learned early on is that, when you have a large head table, you need to be very careful in your introductions. Applause is the problem. If you don't control the situation, the audience will applaud every introduction of every person at the head table. This has two disadvantages. First, it takes a lot of time, and second, some people get significantly more applause than others, which is embarrassing for everyone. If, on the other hand, you ask the audience to hold their applause until everyone has been introduced, it never happens. There will inevitably be applause for certain people and not for others, which is even more embarrassing.

I finally hit on a gimmick that solves the problem and is great fun. I simply explain to the audience that there is not time to recognize each person with lengthy applause and, therefore, I want the audience to cooperate with me in a different approach. As I introduce each person at the head table, everyone will clap just once—no more, no less. At first people are curious and skeptical, but after the first few introductions, they really get into the spirit and have a lot of fun. I have done this at each of my three appearances in Boston, and it works better every time. The audience, which has many of the same people in it year after year, has come to know my gimmick and, I think, look forward to it. I am probably known by many in the audience simply as "Charlie One Clap!"

THERE ARE, OF course, different ways of communicating effectively. The best illustration I can give you involves my longtime, dear friend Herb Lotman. Herb and I became friends shortly after I became Commissioner of the LPGA. Herb had been running the McDonald's LPGA Tournament for a number of years and had raised an enormous amount of money for the Ronald McDonald House Charities. I believe that Herb's efforts led to the McDonald's event raising more money for its charity than any other golf event.

My story about Herb is one of my favorite memories. He is an amazingly generous man, and one of the many nice things he did for me was invite me on a fishing trip off Vancouver Island, British Columbia. Our base was an incredible facility named Nimmo Bay. We had wonderful cabins, a great dining room with superb food, and, most exciting of all, helicopters that took us to a different fishing location each morning and afternoon. I am not much of a fisherman, but even I caught a lot of fish! One day, we had helicoptered into an area where our guide (let's call him Joe) told us that we needed to be alert because there were bears in the area. He said, "If you see a bear, don't run or make noise. Just quietly say, 'Joe, we have a visitor.' Then I'll come to your aid. Though it has never come to this, I have a gun that I will use as a last resort." There were three of us fishing this area, and we were spaced about fifteen to twenty yards apart in the same stream. Herb was about thirty or forty yards upstream from where I was fishing and our third friend was between us. I got a big strike and the guide came running to help me land it. Apparently, although we did not hear it at the time, Herb called out softly, "Joe, we have a visitor." A bear had come out of the woods near Herb. As Joe worked with me to land my fish, Herb called out again, this time more loudly, "Joe, we have a visitor." Joe wanted to help me secure my catch and did not immediately respond to Herb's call. Finally, in a very loud voice that was not without some fear and exasperation, Herb yelled, "Joe, bring the f'ing gun!" Joe responded immediately to this call and raced to Herb's aid . . . just about the time the bear turned and reentered the woods. Maybe the bear was scared by Herb's tone, and, who knows, maybe the bear understood the word "gun"!

Herb Lotman is one of the finest men I have ever known, and our friendship has grown with the years. I am awfully glad the bear left him alone. In any case, Herb's blunt, no-nonsense method of communicating certainly did the trick!

Return Your Phone Calls and E-mails

NEXT IS A tip you rarely find in the frothy books on leadership or self-improvement. Nothing fancy here—but *really* important! Return your phone calls and respond to your e-mails as soon as you can. I cannot tell you how many times I've seen somebody create a problem for himself or herself by not returning a phone call or answering an e-mail. Admittedly, some of them probably are not that important. But how do you know? I have known some important transactions that have soured because somebody didn't have the courtesy to return a phone call or respond to an e-mail. And, that's really all it's about—simple courtesy.

To not return a phone call or answer an e-mail says to the other party that he or she is not important enough in your eyes to merit the simple courtesy of a prompt response—or that you don't have time for him or her. Neither is acceptable—or smart!

It seems to me that the tendency to ignore phone calls and/or e-mails is accelerating. Younger people simply don't seem to understand how important this point is. So, I will simply say once again—you are making a serious and foolish mistake if you don't promptly respond to your phone calls and e-mails. You may get away with it on occasion but I promise you—*I promise you*—it will create problems for you in the long run and will certainly seriously damage your reputation among people important to you.

Let me recount one episode that makes this point quite clearly. The senior partner in my old law firm (this incident occurred after I had moved from the law practice to Taft Broadcasting Company) was a very distinguished gentleman named Charles Sawyer. He had been quite active and successful in politics, and he had also served as an ambassador in the Roosevelt administration as well as Secretary of Commerce in the Truman administration. In short, not a man one should ignore. He was also the largest shareholder in the grand old Cincinnati amusement park, Coney Island. One day the *Cincinnati Enquirer* carried a story indicating that Fess Parker, the legendary Daniel Boone of television fame, intended to build a large theme park in Northern Kentucky, just across the river from Coney Island. Mr. Sawyer was understandably concerned, so he wrote a letter to Parker suggesting that, if he was serious, perhaps they should meet and consider working together. Parker never answered the letter. Mr. Sawyer was offended and was therefore quite receptive when I approached him with an offer by Taft Broadcasting Company to acquire Coney Island and build a large new theme park north of Cincinnati—Kings Island. If Parker had answered the letter, the whole scenario might well have been dramatically different. Kings Island might not exist!

One final point. If you don't have time for a full response, just a quick response will suffice and give you a little breathing room. Even something as simple as this response will cover the situation: "Got your call/e-mail. Tied up right now. Will respond as quickly as possible."

Appearance and Good Manners

IT'S ALWAYS RISKY to talk about appearance—that is, how you look. This too is seldom covered in most self-improvement books. But, I think it is extremely important. I learned this at the LPGA in a very unique way. One of the questions I was repeatedly asked as the Commissioner of the LPGA was, "What do you think about 'selling sex' as part of the LPGA's marketing plan?" I'd say, "I'm not interested in that." But, I added, "What I will sell, and what I will urge others to sell, is attractiveness." There is not a human being on the face of the earth that cannot be attractive in the way he or she dresses, his or her personal habits, cleanliness, grooming, and all the rest. I really think that in life in general it's important to be well groomed and attractive in your appearance. Anyone can do it! I don't care what the dress code of the day may be. Times have changed—no doubt about that. When I was a young lawyer at Taft Stettinius & Hollister, suit and tie were required every day. Saturday we could "relax"—only sport coat and tie were required.

Of all the celebrities I have known, two stand out in my mind when I think of appearance. The first is Dinah Shore. Many younger readers may not remember Dinah. Here's what Wikipedia says and I can't sum it up any better:

> Dinah Shore was an American singer, actress, and television personality. She reached the height of her popularity as a recording artist during the Big Band era of the 1940s and 1950s, but achieved even greater success a decade later, in television, mainly as hostess of a series of variety programs for Chevrolet.*

Though I had known Dinah before my LPGA days, it was as Commissioner of the LPGA that I got to know her well. She was the hostess and namesake of one of the LPGA's four major tournaments.

There were many attractive things about Dinah. She was friendly, approachable, and thoughtful, as well as being a marvelous entertainer. Moreover, she was quite lovely. She always looked terrific—always. Here's the best example I can give you. At the conclusion of her golf tournament she always appeared on the eighteenth green at the Mission Hills Country Club in Rancho Mirage, California, to present the winner's trophy. One year, the winner, Amy Alcott, told Dinah that following the presentation, she intended to jump into the lake adjacent to the green. Amy dared Dinah to jump in with her. Dinah agreed, but not without some careful planning. As Dinah emerged from the lake completely drenched, she was met immediately by a friend who helped her into a handsome white sport jacket and wound her head in a towel in a very professional way. So, Dinah looked attractive even under such conditions!

My second memory is quite different, but equally impressive. Gene Sarazen was one of the greatest golfers in history, but he was also—by any measure—its snappiest and most memorable dresser. Gene always appeared in plus fours (trousers that ended four inches below the knee—and thus four inches longer than traditional knickers, hence the name), a jaunty cap, a tie, and typically a sport coat or sweater. He was a delightful man, and certainly his appearance distinguished him. Incidentally, the late Payne Stewart was the only modern-day golfer to wear plus fours.

Looking good is important. So is "acting good." What I mean by this is simply remembering and practicing good manners. Increasingly in today's frenetic world I find people not saying thank you, not acknowledging your thanks with a "you're welcome," not standing when a lady enters the room, interrupting people without reason, and shouting into a cell phone to the annoyance of everyone in the vicinity. I don't think I

---

*Source: http://en.wikipedia.org/wiki/Dinah_Shore.

have to tell any readers of this book what good manners consist of, but I think we all need to be reminded from time to time that they remain very important and are the bedrock of a civil society.

Punctuality

A FETISH OF mine is punctuality. And this I attribute mainly to my mom and dad. But, it's paid off over and over again. I didn't know until after I left Taft Broadcasting, but apparently there was a saying around the office that "If you are on time for a meeting with Charlie, you're already late." Now, I'm not sure I'm proud of that, but I do believe (and I had a senior partner in our law firm tell me one time) that if you're important enough to be asked to attend a meeting, you ought to "goddamn well" be smart enough to be there on time. And it's really that simple. The interesting thing to me is that—at least in my experience—the most famous people I have known were also the most punctual people, like Neil Armstrong, Paul Brown, John Smale, Paul Smucker, Arnold Palmer, Jack Nicklaus, and Annika Sorenstam. You could set your watch by the punctuality of any one of them. Here again, this is really nothing more than common courtesy. To keep someone waiting is simply rude and gives the impression that you really don't have much respect for them. If something does come up that delays you (and this will inevitably happen upon occasion), make every effort to contact the person and explain that you are unavoidably detained and give them some idea of when you expect to show up.

In the interest of full disclosure, I must tell you about an incident that underscores what happens when one is not punctual. Fortunately, this story has a happy ending. During my years at Taft Broadcasting Company I was asked to make the principal address at the annual dinner meeting of the Cincinnati Police—the Police Appreciation Dinner. In those days I owned a yellow Porsche 911, which was an easy car to spot. The night of the Police Appreciation Dinner, I was running late, and as I raced to downtown Cincinnati to make my speech, my little yellow Porsche attracted the attention of one of Cincinnati's finest. He pulled me over and informed me that I had been speeding and asked me what I was hurrying for. I said, "Officer, you will simply never believe this, but I swear it is true. I am the principal speaker at tonight's Police Appreciation Dinner, and I'm running late." Needless to say he was stunned, but also amused. He told me that I better get going so that I could make my speech on time! Later, in making my speech, I alluded to what had just happened to me but was careful not to mention the officer's name or where I was picked up. The assembled group roared with laughter, and I still remember it as one of the happiest crowds to which I ever spoke. Ironically, if I had been on time, this incident would probably never have happened—although I must say that the yellow Porsche frequently attracted attention from guardians of the law even when not warranted!

A similar incident occurred one year when I attended The Masters. I was not able to arrange a flight out of Augusta when I was ready to leave and had to make arrangements to fly out of Aiken, South Carolina, a short drive from Augusta. Since taxi cabs are impossible to get during the week of The Masters, I arranged for a limo to pick me up and take me to Aiken. The time for the limo to arrive came and went, and I was increasingly nervous about getting to the Aiken airport in time. Then, along came an SUV and the driver stepped out and said, "Are you Mr. Mechem?" I replied that I was, and he then told me that there had been a problem at the limo company and that they had no available cars. Therefore, he had borrowed his brother-in-law's car and would use it to drive me to the airport. I said that that sounded fine and away we went. As we were driving, I told him that I didn't want to risk being pulled over for speeding, but that I had a very tight time window to make my plane. I then asked him more about the car we were in. He said that his brother-in-law was a policeman in Augusta and that he would not be using the car today. So much for that—or so I thought!

As we approached the airport, time was even tighter than we expected and the driver picked up the pace. About a mile from the airport we saw flashing red lights behind us, and we were pulled over for speeding. This was a bit of a problem, but nothing compared to what was about to happen.

The officer came over and admonished us for going too fast and then said, "Is this your car?" The driver said that it was not but that it belonged to his brother-in-law. The policeman then said, "Do you have the registration?" The driver said that he did not but that he was sure that it was somewhere in the car. At that point I opened the glove box assuming that the registration certificate would be there. When I opened the glove box my heart went completely down to my toes. Inside the glove box was a gun—I think it was a .38. The policeman said, with understandable surprise, "Is that a gun?" The driver said, "Oh, that must be my brother-in-law's gun—he's a cop in Augusta." At this point I was convinced that, not only would I miss my plane, but I was likely to miss a number of other events over the next few years while I was serving time in a South Carolina jail. At this point, a remarkable thing happened—the cop began to laugh. He said, "This is so ridiculous that it must be true. You guys better hurry so you can make your plane and then get this car back to its owner." We "gushed" our thanks and I made my flight! The cop's sense of humor saved the day—in more ways than one.

I will never again ride in any car that is owned by a police officer unless that police officer is in the car with me!

Implementation of a Decision Is Frequently as Important as the Decision Itself

YOU CAN MAKE the best decision in the world, but if you don't think through its impact on the people it's going to affect, you can blow it big time. I've seen this happen innumerable times over the years—the unexpected consequences of failing to effectively communicate a decision or, even worse, not communicating it at all. Here's a tip that has worked for me: think carefully about the people who will be affected positively or negatively by a decision you are about to make and prepare them for it before it becomes a *fait accompli*.

The way I used to do this was quite simple and basic. I made three lists—mental or written. One named those who would be favorably impacted by the decision. The second listed those who would be unaffected by it, and the third list included those who would be negatively impacted. The second group didn't need any particular attention. The first group needed to have the decision explained to them so they would understand its positive impact on them. The third group needed to be handled carefully inasmuch as the decision was not one they would welcome. Talking with this third group and explaining the reasons for my decision might persuade them that it was a decision they could live with. But, even if they continued to be troubled, they were always pleased and impressed that I had taken the time to review it with them. However you approach this issue, the important thing is to realize that the success or failure of a certain plan of action may be less impacted by the plan itself and more by how you carry it out.

Another important suggestion: as the plan and/or decision is being implemented, you must follow the implementation carefully to be sure it stays on track. Never assume that a successful venture or product will remain successful without continuous attention and improvement. Persistence is a very important behavior skill. If you strongly believe you are on the right track—stay with it!

Know Something about Everything on Your Desk

I HAD ONLY been practicing law for a few months when a client called me and said, "Mr. Mechem, what do you think about my problem?" I had to say (and you can be certain this was the last time I would ever say this), "Mrs. Jones, I haven't had a chance yet to look at your file." OMG! That was simply inexcusable!

From then on I knew something about everything on my desk, so no matter who called, I could at least say something like this, "Well, I haven't dug deeply into that yet, but I know this much about your matter . . . And I'll be getting into it in much more depth very soon. Thanks for your call. I will be in touch shortly." And, by the way, this doesn't apply only to lawyers and clients. It applies to all relationships.

Perhaps the most striking example I've seen of this point involved President Richard Nixon. For a number of years while I was serving as chairman of Taft Broadcasting, I was invited to a meeting of senior executives of broadcasting and entertainment companies. The event was held at the Wye Plantation on the Eastern Shore of Maryland, a think tank–retreat sort of place. Every year we would hear from prominent statesmen and politicians on subjects of mutual interest. After he had resigned from office, President Nixon was invited to speak to the group. This invitation caused quite a stir among the attendees. Many of the executives had never supported Nixon, and many more had turned negative as a result of Watergate. So while it may not have been a hostile audience, it certainly wasn't a friendly one. Nixon arrived, went to the stage, and stood behind a simple stand-up microphone. He had neither podium nor notes of any kind. For over an hour, he answered questions on every conceivable subject and on topics that ranged over an unbelievable array of foreign and domestic issues. He had a complete grasp of a truly amazing number of topics. At the end of his remarks, he received a standing ovation, not because he had converted anyone in the audience, but rather because of his remarkable intelligence and grasp. This is perhaps a dramatic example of the point I am trying to make, but it does demonstrate how a familiarity with everything "on your desk" can make a positive impression.

Pick Every Available Brain

I HAVE ALWAYS believed strongly in the importance of "picking" every brain available to me in reaching a decision. There really are two fundamental reasons for this. First, the old saying "There's nothing new under the sun" is really quite true. There are very few problems or issues that haven't been confronted by someone else. Second, to learn how someone else has dealt with a problem or issue can be very illuminating and helpful in choosing the right course. Let me illustrate my point by describing perhaps the most important "brain-picking" experience I ever had.

As we were seriously contemplating the building of Kings Island, I was looking for ways to justify the decision. We had done market studies and other due diligence, but I had one other thought: no one had done it better or more successfully than the Disney Corporation. It just so happened that Hanna-Barbera's lawyer, Gordon Youngman, was also on the Disney board of directors. Nicknamed "Tubby," Youngman was a delightful man who had come to Hollywood as Howard Hughes's lawyer. (Needless to say, he had some incredible stories to tell about Hughes.) I spoke to him about my thought, and he immediately responded by saying that he would arrange a meeting with Roy Disney. I was stunned. Roy Disney was, and had been for many years, the business brains of the Disney empire. His brother, Walt (the creative genius), had passed away, but Roy remained in good health.

The meeting was arranged and several of us ventured to Los Angeles to meet Mr. Disney. Frankly, I had imagined that he would be polite, but probably would only give us an hour or so. I was very mistaken. He graciously met with us for two-and-a-half to three hours. We asked scores of questions and he answered them all. Two things are most vivid in my mind about that conversation. First, I asked him if they had made any mistakes in building Disneyland. He smiled and said, "Yes, we didn't buy nearly enough land. My advice to you is to figure out how much land you need and buy five times as much." We did exactly that as we prepared to build Kings Island. And, by the way, Disney didn't make the same mistake twice. They assembled a vast amount of land for Disney World in Florida—more than twenty-seven thousand acres! Second, as we were leaving, I somewhat routinely said, "Is there anything we should have asked you that we didn't?" He said, "No, but there is one bit of advice that I want to give you. The finest small amusement park in America is located right under your nose in Cincinnati, the beautiful Coney Island on the Ohio River. It was the first park that Walt and I visited when we were contemplating Disneyland. You should go back to Cincinnati and get together with those people, and together you would be well positioned to enter the theme park business."

And, that is exactly what we did. In one of those curious twists of fate that pop up in life, it turned out that the major shareholder in Coney Island was the senior partner at Taft Stettinius & Hollister and a man with whom I had a very deep and warm friendship. Beyond that, the other major shareholder, the Wachs family, was anxious to move into the theme park business and were seeking financial backing to do so. It was truly a marriage made in business heaven. Had we not reached out to Mr. Disney, our entry into the amusement park business might have been quite different, and quite likely not as rewarding.

One of the most useful sources of guidance on how to deal with an issue is to see whether your competitors have faced a similar problem and what they did about it. Curiously, people seem reluctant to look to their competitors for guidance. I have never quite understood this, but it probably is grounded in a feeling that to learn from a competitor is a kind of surrender. The bottom line is that to be unwilling to ask advice from those who have already "been there" is a mistake. Every successful person I have ever known seeks advice from people they respect. I would recommend this approach to anyone who seeks the best and the quickest solution to a problem. In short, do not try to reinvent the wheel.

One final bit of advice: listen to the older, wiser heads—those who have been there before. One of the best examples—and certainly the funniest—that I can give on this point involved the chairman and CEO of the Kroger Company, the giant food-store chain whose headquarters are in Cincinnati. Taft's theme park in Virginia, near Richmond, was a joint venture with Kroger. The chairman was a memorable character named Jake Davis. He was a good friend of my father's, and he was wonderful to me when we came to Cincinnati and especially when I joined the ranks of the city's corporate CEOs. I remember Jake for many reasons, but I probably remember him best for something he said that I have never forgotten and that I have put into practice more than once. I was in his office, and we were discussing some sort of business proposal that we were planning to make to another company. I had some ideas, but Jake felt I was being too generous. He outlined a proposal I thought was outrageously favorable to "our side." I said, "Jake, we can't offer that kind of a deal—it's too one-sided." Jake smiled and said, "Charlie, let me tell you something. Never be ashamed to offer a guy a lousy deal." Shocking, perhaps—but words of wisdom!

My good friend Bob Wehling tells me that he always got better advice on ways to solve a problem from the women he worked with and that he learned much from people from other countries. What this suggests to me is that we probably always get better ideas from people who are different from us, whether by gender, background, or nationality, simply because they approach an issue from a very different perspective.

Respect for Others

HEAVEN KNOWS THERE have been a lot of successful people throughout history who haven't paid a lot of attention to the views or opinions of others—even associates or colleagues. But the people I most admire, those whose reputations endure, always seem to show a genuine respect for the views of other people. This makes eminent good sense. First of all, it's the polite thing to do but, equally important, it is the *smart* thing to do. The reason it's the smart thing to do is to understand that, however foolish you may think Joe's or Mary's opinion might be, there is at least a possibility—as difficult as that may be to admit—that they could be right! Watch and listen to those around you and respect their views, however much you might disagree. One of the most disturbing trends in our current society, I believe, is the loss (or at least the serious deterioration) of civility. As a matter of curiosity, I looked up the definition of civility and it includes politeness, good manners, courtesy, and "the act of showing regard for others."

I don't really know how our society has come to where it is today in this respect. I suspect that it almost certainly has something to do with the dramatic changes in our means of communication. We talk less and less *to* one another and more and more *at* one another. E-mails, texting, and blogging seem to make it more likely that courtesy and politeness are neglected. Indeed, much of the so-called blogosphere includes personal attacks. Now, this isn't as threatening to the future of the human race as nuclear war, but it does seem to me to be a very serious impediment to our nation's progress. The corollary here is to make every effort to give whoever you are dealing with your undivided attention and spend enough time with them to accommodate their needs. Most of the people who have made an impression on me over the years have this quality in common. When you are with them, they give you their complete attention and don't act as though there are a number of other things that they need to be doing. This is very hard to do. It requires patience and, sometimes, fortitude. But, it really works. I especially remember my boss at the law firm whose skill and strength with clients came from his ability to make them feel that their matter was the only thing of concern to him at the moment. He did this regardless of how busy or preoccupied he might have been. I have never been sure that I did this as well as I should, because I tend to be impatient. But, it is certainly something I always strive for.

In short, be a good listener. It is a rare talent, but extremely valuable. As someone once said, "I never learned anything while I was talking!"

Brevity in All Things

I HAVE COME to the sad conclusion that at least 80 percent (this is my number and has absolutely no scientific basis!) of all speeches, memoranda, and presentations—of all kinds, given anywhere in the world, at any given time—*are too long!* All of us should be sensitive to the length of what we are writing or saying. You will be amazed at how something can be pared down without limiting its meaning. Frequently, the meaning becomes clearer when there is less verbiage to encumber it. I ran across a great story some years ago that went like this: A teacher asked a fourth-grade student to sum up the life of Socrates in four lines. Here's what the student said:

1. Socrates lived long ago.

2. He was very intelligent.

3. Socrates gave long speeches.

4. His friends poisoned him.

Of course, it can be much more difficult to say something in a few words than to say it in many. Mark Twain reportedly once told his publisher, when he was asked to do a two-page story in two days, that he couldn't do it. He said he could do thirty pages in two days but would need thirty days to do two pages. A line that I have often used in starting a speech comes to mind. I would say to the audience, "We each have a job today. My job is to speak. Your job is to listen. If you get finished with your job before I finish with mine, please raise your hand." This always brings a laugh, but it is also a reminder of the need to keep your remarks short and to the point so that you don't lose your audience. Brevity can be dictated by many forces. This story about Louise Suggs will make the point. It is not inappropriate to call Louise "crusty." She is direct, blunt, and totally without pretense. You never have the slightest doubt where Louise stands on any given issue, and she always expresses her views in a way that eliminates any confusion. One of my favorite memories of Louise was when she received the 2007 Bob Jones Award, the highest honor the United States Golf Association can bestow, at a dinner in San Francisco. The program was arranged in the customary form, that is, the most prestigious award came as the last presentation of the evening. Often when people receive awards of this nature their acceptance speeches go on so long that one begins to question their fitness for the award! Not this time! Louise went to the microphone and said something like this, "I really appreciate this great honor. I knew Bob Jones and he was my friend. This will not be a long speech. I have not had a drink because I didn't want to do anything that would impair my ability to thank you. So thank you. I am humbled and thrilled to receive this award. That is all I need to say. This talk is over. Now I can have that drink. And so can you!"

This point has relevance in a related area—the length and style of meetings. I have a plaque hanging in my office that says, "Every great idea can be destroyed if enough meetings are held to discuss it." I have come to understand the profound wisdom of that statement. Curiously, this seems to be an even greater problem in today's world. It is possible now to have conference call meetings, meetings online, Skype meetings, meetings by e-mail, and so on. Now we not only have to worry about the length of in-person meetings, but we also have to worry about the proliferation of—and danger inherent in—the types and kinds of meetings. The great humorist and columnist Dave Barry has suggested that if you had to identify in one word the reason why the human race has never achieved its full potential, that word would be "meetings."

As I have indicated earlier when discussing the "art" of negotiating, I also think there is an "art" of conducting a meeting. Over time, I learned—sometimes the hard way—what worked best for me. I don't pretend to suggest there are not other ways, but here are a few tips I think might be useful.

1. Have a clear written agenda.

2. Have everybody in the room who is necessary to make whatever decisions are involved but don't have anyone who is not necessary. Sadly, the more people in the meeting, the tougher it is to reach decisions.

3. If there are important and difficult issues to be decided, try to meet with key people in advance of the meeting to gain their support, or at least their understanding.

4. Always ask at the appropriate time if there are any questions regarding any proposed solutions. But here is the important thing: don't wait too long for questions. Allow a reasonable time for questions to be asked but don't allow what I call a "conversational void" to go on too long. I have learned that human beings simply cannot stand a conversational void. If you wait too long, someone will feel compelled to fill the void with a question that probably is not particularly important. So, ask for questions, allow a brief time for them to be asked, and then move on.

5. Try your best never to be angry and, for goodness sake, keep a sense of humor. Many times I have been able to relieve tension and growing animosity by finding a way to get the group to laugh—or at least to smile!

But, wait a minute! If I am really going to talk about the importance of brevity, I need to stop talking about this right now!

Always Reach for Excellence

MAKE EVERY GOAL a stretch goal. One of my early experiences in the law firm is instructive. I was given a job to do by a senior partner in our firm who, by the way, was also a Yale Law School graduate. He didn't give me much time, so I felt a lot of pressure, and I did a sloppy job. I handed it in to him, and about two hours later, he called me into his office. I remember thinking, "Boy, I am going to get taken apart." Instead I learned a valuable lesson in leadership. He said, "I'm going to hand this back to you. I'm very disappointed. Not just because the work is poor, but because I know you can do so much better." Now, that was a great way of saying, "You haven't done this job right, but I know you can do it." So, I didn't leave his office with my head hanging down. I was embarrassed that I had done poorly, but I was pumped up by the fact that he knew I could do better—and I promptly went out and did. I've always told the people who work for me, "I can forgive failure, but I cannot forgive lack of effort."

The great playwright Neil Simon gave a marvelous speech (I'm not sure Neil Simon ever gave anything but a great speech) at a Williams College commencement some years back, and I want to quote you one paragraph. It's right to the point of giving it your best shot:

> *Whatever path you follow from the moment you take off those long black gowns, do it as though Gershwin had written music to underscore your every move. Romantic and idealistic? Yes. But I can't think of anything worthwhile in life that was achieved without a great deal of desire to achieve it. Don't listen to those who say it's not done that way. Maybe it's not. But maybe you will. Don't listen to those who say you're taking too big a chance. If he didn't take a big chance, Michelangelo would have painted the Sistine floor, and it would certainly have been rubbed out by today.*

The whole idea is to make every goal a stretch goal. If you get there, fabulous. If you don't get there, you're still going to get a lot farther than you would have had you not set that lofty goal as an objective in the first place. The great showman P. T. Barnum put it this way: "If I shoot at the sun, I may hit a star."

I feel so strongly about this point that I want to give you two more stories drawn from my involvement in professional sports. The first one may surprise you as it involves Pete Rose, whose image and reputation have come under considerable attack since he admitted to betting on baseball games. The point of my story is not to indict him nor excuse his behavior after he stopped playing the game. Rather, I wish to focus on the *way* he played the game. Even his harshest critics will tell you that he gave everything he had to perform at the highest level possible. He probably got more out of his talent than almost any athlete I can imagine. Sometimes he was ridiculed, such as when he ran out bases on balls. One wonderful episode is when he ran all the way from center field and fielded a ball that bounced off the left fielder's glove. Ironically, it is this side of Pete that makes the other side so difficult to evaluate and which leads to heated debate—especially in Cincinnati—as to whether Pete should be in baseball's Hall of Fame.

The other story that illustrates this point is the one I told earlier about the exchange between Arnold Palmer and Annika Sorenstam about her plan to play in a men's PGA Tour event. As I said, Arnie was at first puzzled but when he understood that all she was really doing was reaching for excellence and testing her own skills to the ultimate level, then he understood.

I guess one of the morals of this story is—the best always want to get better. But perhaps more importantly, it underscores the importance of reaching for excellence and setting your goals high.

There is a corollary to this point—and an important one. It is simply this: try never to settle on something if the little voice deep in your brain keeps whispering, "You can do better than this." Let me give you an example. During the year I served as president of the Greater Cincinnati Chamber of Commerce, we were working to start an economic development campaign for the region. We had things pretty well organized, but we still didn't have a name for the campaign that we felt was both descriptive and catchy. We had several meetings and a number of names were suggested, but none really seemed to be just right. We decided to have one more meeting to discuss the matter, and I remember thinking before that meeting that if no better name emerged we would simply have to go with one of the earlier suggestions. I was not happy about this because that little voice in my brain kept telling me that we should keep working until we were satisfied. Happily, at the next meeting, a suggestion came forth that rang like a church bell on a cold January morning—clear and loud. The name that was suggested and that was immediately endorsed was the "Blue Chip City Campaign." So far as I know, that name is still being used in some fashion in the work of the Cincinnati Chamber.

One of the most touching examples of reaching for excellence happened some years ago when I took three of my friends to Muirfield Village for a round of golf. When we were getting ready to play, the caddy master, whom I knew quite well, pulled me aside and told me of a dilemma that he was facing. He explained that play that day was unusually heavy, and although he could assign one experienced caddy to our group, he simply did not have a second. He went on to say that he had a favor to ask. The favor was whether I would agree to allow a young man (I think he was around fourteen or fifteen) to be my caddy that day. The young man had never caddied before, but the caddy master assured me that he was a fine young man who would work hard. I said I would be delighted to have him join our group.

He was a little fellow, and even though we lightened the bag considerably, it still almost dragged the ground. But he kept up with the group, and you could tell that he was watching the experienced caddy's every move in an effort to learn. One of the things he noticed was the experienced caddy looking at yardage markers on the sprinkler heads so he could advise his players of the distance to the green. What happened next was classic! As I was lining up my shot to the green, the young man looked at the nearest sprinkler head for the yardage number. Now, I must explain that sprinkler heads also have manufacturers' serial numbers on them, and that was the number the young man saw. So, he came over to me, and as authoritatively as he could possibly be said, "Sir, you have 894 yards to the pin." I started to laugh and then realized that was absolutely the wrong thing to do because it would embarrass him. Instead, I pulled him aside, put my arm around him, and told him how much I appreciated how hard he was trying and explained to him the serial/yardage number distinction. Naturally, he tried to apologize, but I refused. I told him how much I was impressed with everything he was doing and how important it is in life to try to learn from others and strive to be the very best that you can be. We had a delightful day, and I had a memory that I cherish.

The point is: whenever possible, don't settle for less than the best. Let me illustrate this point with one of my favorite stories. I think it illustrates the danger of trying to sell an idea or a product that is something less than it should be. The CEO of a large company that manufactured and sold dog food was speaking at the company's annual gathering of its sales force. He was being sharply critical because sales were really not good. He said something like this: "I just don't understand it. We have a great marketing plan, we have superb advertising, our packaging is outstanding, and we pay all of you guys a lot of money. Why aren't we selling more dog food?" There was momentary silence, and then a man in the back of the room raised his hand. The boss said, "Well, what is it? What's our problem?" The man in the back of the room said somewhat hesitantly, "Sir, the dogs don't like it." Enough said.

Be Wary of Things You Don't Understand

I THINK WE are all guilty of accepting things from time to time that we really don't understand. This can occur in a business context or a personal one. It usually stems from our embarrassment about admitting that we simply don't "get" something. The good news is that as you grow older, you tend to be more honest and open and more willing to probe a point of view or opinion that you don't understand. The simple fact is that there is no possible way that you can understand something unless you ask questions and insist that the answers are comprehensible. Here's the really important thing: You will find that some things are not understandable simply because "there is no there there," as Gertrude Stein famously said. They are gibberish or at least poorly reasoned.

I could cite you several major business failures over the last thirty or forty years that occurred simply because the underlying business concept was a fantasy and, therefore, unperformable. But no one had the courage to say, "That doesn't make any sense." I'll tell you about a situation in Cincinnati some years ago where a good friend of mine ran a very big company. He was mystified because another mutual friend of ours (we'll call him Joe) was running a company that was making all these deals that were incredibly complex and murky. So my friend said to me one day, "I got the prospectus for Joe's latest deal, and I got all my financial guys in our conference room, and we started with the first page of the prospectus, and we diagrammed it all the way through to the last page. It took up the whole blackboard. Charlie, there's nothing there. Damn it! It simply doesn't work." And I said, "That is not surprising. I've always been suspicious." Within six months, this particular company that he had analyzed fell through because there was, in fact, nothing there. So, don't be ashamed or afraid to probe and question. There is no downside.

Speaking of being wary of things we don't understand, we sometimes fall for something we don't truly comprehend for fear of being left out of something we are sure everybody else understands. A classic example of this is the full-page ad that supposedly ran in a major metropolitan newspaper some years ago that said simply, "Last Day to Send in Your Dollar" and then listed a P.O. box to which the money should be sent. Apparently, thousands of dollars came flooding in from people who obviously had no idea what they were doing but didn't want to be left out.

Avoid Hubris

IN MY OPINION, an inflated, unfettered ego is perhaps the most dangerous trait that can infect a person. A sense of self-worth and a comfortable ego are important qualities, but you must always strive to avoid exaggerated pride or inflated self-confidence. If your head gets too big, your brain rattles around a lot! One of my favorite expressions (and one that I need to remind myself of from time to time) is "The cemeteries are filled with indispensable people!"

Interestingly enough, it seems that those who are entitled to the biggest egos are usually those with the smallest. Let me give you a good example.

On any list of great baseball managers, Walter E. Alston would doubtlessly be near the top. As the manager of the Brooklyn and Los Angeles Dodgers for twenty-three years, his record was incredible. Smokey, as he was known, was a graduate of Miami University and we met one night at a college function. We instantly became friends because we both liked to play pool, and that's a marvelous way to bond. As we talked that evening over the pool table, I put to him a question that had always intrigued me: namely, how important is a manager to a baseball team? So, I asked him the question and have never forgotten the answer. He smiled and in his quiet, unassuming way, said, "I don't think a manager is responsible for more than five or six games a year." I was amazed and he could tell it. He explained that managers are either the beneficiary or the victim of the talent on their teams, and if the talent is great, the manager simply lets them go. If the talent is mediocre or poor, even the most able of managers can do very little.

There is certainly some logic in Alston's comment, but just consider this: Alston won seven National League pennants and four World Series in his twenty-three-year tenure as Dodgers manager. He was named Manager of the Year six times. Perhaps what is more interesting is, at his request, he never had more than a one-year contract—for twenty-three years! This sounds to me very much like someone of enormous ability who has his ego very much under control, and I suspect he was being excessively modest in his view on the value of managers.

Let me tell a little joke—one of my favorites—that will also illustrate this point. A "big deal" rancher from Texas was traveling through the countryside of Vermont when he spotted an old farmer plowing his field near the road. He stopped his car, walked over, and introduced himself. He then said to the old farmer, "How big of a spread have you got here, old man?" The farmer, in a classic clipped Vermont twang, said, "'bout seventy acres." The rancher replied, "That sure don't amount to much. Do you know that at my ranch I can get up in the morning, get in my car, and drive all day, and still not be at the other end of my land? Whaddaya think of that?" The Vermont farmer thought a minute, smiled, and said, "That so? I had a car like that once!"

The great UCLA basketball coach John Wooden had an interesting take on this whole issue. He said, simply, "It's what you learn after you think you know it all that really matters."

Don't Be Afraid of Change and Innovation

THE MESSAGE IS simple: Embrace change, encourage innovation, and look to those who have this ability for leadership. There is a great quote in the best-seller *The Lovely Bones* by Alice Sebold, where she says, "In my junior high yearbook, I had a quote from a Spanish poet my sister had turned me on to, Juan Ramon Jimenez. It went like this: 'If they give you ruled paper, write the other way.'" I love that line. Write across the lines. Don't feel compelled to write within them.

I always remember an incident that occurred early in my life as a lawyer when I met with the Superintendent of Insurance of the State of Ohio. I was attempting to persuade him to make a fairly significant change to one of the department's more confusing regulations. After I had made my pitch, he looked at me with a rather stern eye and said,

"Mr. Mechem, do you realize that you are asking me to set a precedent?" This was said as though I was suggesting that he jump out of his office window. I thought for a moment and replied, "Yes, sir. That's exactly what I'm asking you to do, because it is the right thing to do in this circumstance." This gentleman was, I'm sure, a very nice man, but he was a political appointee and was not about to "create a precedent" then or in the future. I have never forgotten the meeting and his look of shock and disbelief that I was asking him to do something different and new.

Paul Brown was one of the great innovators in the history of sports. As I got to know him better, it became quite clear that his success was based not only on being a great coach in a technical sense but also on his ability to innovate—to think outside the box. For example, Paul's won-lost records are well recognized. But less well known are these facts: He invented the facemask, was the first to use a written playbook, and popularized the practice of substituting a player on virtually every play (originally, guards) to bring the next play in to the quarterback—and many other game changers.

Another great innovator that I was privileged to know was Paul Smucker, the longtime CEO of the J. M. Smucker Company. Of the many things that Paul did to grow the Smucker Company, I think one of the most important was when he agreed with the company's advertising agency to adopt the now famous slogan "With a name like Smucker's, it has to be good." Believe me, a lot of people in Paul's position would have rejected the idea of making fun of the family name. Paul saw it quite differently—and was he ever right! It has become one of the great tag lines in the history of American business. And, it is a classic example of a willingness to think differently. There is an interesting backstory to Paul's decision. His son Richard told me that before making the final decision, Paul called a small meeting of major family members and explained to them the slogan that had been proposed. He pointed out that he didn't want to go ahead with this (inasmuch as it made fun of the family name) without the group's agreement. As Richard tells the story, one of the older members of the family asked Paul whether he felt the slogan might help business and lead to higher dividends. When he said he thought it might she said, "Count me in!"

In my own experience, I would cite Taft's entrance into the theme park business as an example of innovation. It was a totally new venture for us—and one that raised a lot of eyebrows. But we thought it through, did our homework, and my associates who were responsible for building and operating the park led by Dudley Taft and Gary Wachs did a superb job. There were a couple of interesting examples of innovation within the Kings Island experience. First, we located the park some twenty miles north of Cincinnati, and we opted for a so-called pay-one-price policy. (The old amusement parks had a small entrance fee, and you purchased tickets for each ride or attraction.) During the building of the park, these two changes were strongly questioned. Many people were skeptical that patrons would drive "all that distance," and another group was convinced that the six-dollar admission price was too high (it is now $53.99!).

The next story I want to tell in this connection is not exactly an example of innovation, but rather an instance of being willing to accept something different and finding it works just fine. Here's the story: We had some great trips during the late 1980s before my LPGA days began. After the sale of Taft Broadcasting Company, Marilyn and I traveled with our good friends Roger and Joyce Howe to New Zealand. Originally another couple had intended to go with us but at the last moment needed to cancel. When I thought there would be six of us in the party with a lot of luggage (we intended to stay several weeks), I called Avis and told them I wanted to reserve a van that would carry six to eight people with a lot of luggage. They assured me there would be one available. When we arrived in Christchurch, I went to the Avis counter to check in and advised them that there had been a last-minute change, and there were only four of us. Therefore, I said, we wouldn't need as large a van. They said they were sorry but they only had the van they had originally reserved for us, but, if I would drive it for a couple of days, there would undoubtedly be a replacement available. We agreed. We went out to the parking area—what we saw made us stop dead in our tracks. There sat a big white van with the word AVIS written in large red letters on the side. I wasn't too happy with this development but really had no choice. So, away we went. Amazingly, over the next couple of days, I fell in love with the van because it had no hood (the engine was in the back), and the driver sat up rather high. This combination made it much easier to navigate while driving on the "wrong" side of the road, as is the practice in New Zealand. So, after a couple of days I called Avis and told them that we were happy with the larger van and would keep it. This all worked wonderfully well except for one thing—a most amusing thing! Throughout our three weeks in New Zealand, every time we pulled into a new hotel, several people would think we were the airport van and would try to board for their trip to the airport!

Among the most wonderful trips that we ever took was to the Isle of Islay, off the east coast of Scotland. We were planning a golf trip, and I called a friend of mine whose business was planning golf vacations and told him that I wanted to go to a course that was as close to the early links courses as he could possibly find. One of these courses is Machrie. It was everything that he promised—remote, wild, windy, and absolutely breathtaking in its simplicity. But, the story I want to tell is about not the golf course but, rather, the small hotel at the golf course. It only had seven or eight rooms and there was a cozy pub and restaurant in the main building. The first night we were there, we went into the pub for dinner. When the bartender asked what we would like to drink, I said, "Whenever I go to a pub in Scotland I always like to try the local scotch." He smiled and, in that marvelous Scottish brogue, said, "There'd be eight of them, sir!" In other words, there were eight distilleries on this little island, each of which turned out a superb single malt scotch. (By the way, I think there are still at least seven or eight distilleries on Islay.) So, I said, "Well, then I guess I'll have your favorite."

The bartender replied, "That would be the Lagavulin, sir." That's what we had, and it was a good choice!

Think of being comfortable with change as your ability to be flexible and adaptable in the face of new and unexpected circumstances. One of my all-time favorite jokes makes this point very well. It seems that a young man had just started working in a grocery store. On his very first day on the job, a man came in and said, "Son, I'd like to buy a half a head of lettuce." The young boy thought this was very strange, but, following the old theory that the customer is always right, he took a knife and sliced the head in half, wrapped the half, and gave it to the gentleman. Thinking that the man had left the store, he turned to one of the other clerks and said, "Boy, what a crazy start to my new career. That nutty guy wanted half a head of lettuce." He then realized to his dismay that the man had not actually left the store but was standing right behind him. So, he quickly said to the other clerk, "Fortunately, this fine gentleman wanted to buy the other half."

The manager had heard this exchange and came up to the young man and said, "That was an amazing display of flexibility and adaptability. You might have a real future in this store. Tell me about yourself." The young man replied, "Well, there really isn't much to tell. I'm only seventeen years old, and I just came from Lost Moose up in Canada, but I just had to get out of Lost Moose because there is nothing there but hockey players and hookers." The manager suddenly frowned and said, "Just a minute, young man, my wife is from Lost Moose." Without missing a beat, the young man said, "Is that so? What position did she play?" Flexibility at its finest!

Qualities of Success Can Bring Failure

THE NEXT POINT that I want to mention is a bit solemn, but I think it's extremely important. Many years ago I came upon a newspaper article that impressed me because I had never seen this idea expressed before. The essence of the article was that it is critical as one's career advances to not assume that the qualities that got you from point A to point B are the same qualities that will get you from point B to point C—or beyond. In other words, as you move up the ladder, you need constantly to reassess your strengths and weaknesses and recognize the need to adapt. You must develop flexibility and bring to bear whatever strengths and qualities may be demanded for the new job.

I had never thought about this point until I read the article. But having read it, I can certainly attest to its wisdom and importance. I know personally of several instances where an individual has been elevated to a higher job in a sizable enterprise only to cling ferociously to old habits and tactics. Every step of the ladder should be accompanied by appropriate changes in one's approach to the new role. In the cases to which I refer, none of the individuals was able to bring the necessary flexibility to the challenge, and each lost his job quickly.

This is perhaps a good point for me to touch upon the matter of styles of leadership. As people progress through the hierarchy of any organization, they are increasingly required to exhibit leadership. Obviously, the higher you go, the greater your leadership responsibilities. But, however large or small these responsibilities may be, I think there are several things that you need to keep in mind. Over the years I have observed many people in leadership roles. I have concluded that there are basically three types of leadership styles: two are to be avoided, but the third is to be sought after.

First, there is leadership by fear or intimidation. The leader so frightens and intimidates his associates that they will do anything he asks them to do without question or debate for fear of retribution.

The second style of leadership is what I might call leadership by bribery. This type of leader lavishes upon his associates salaries and perks that are beyond reason, but which bind his associates to him out of fear of losing these excessive benefits.

The third style of leadership is what might be called leadership through loyalty. Under this style, employees follow their leader because they respect him, like him, and simply can't bear to let him down.

Sometimes the first two styles of leadership seem to work. The problem is that, when the going gets tough or hard times descend, these kinds of leaders are likely to look over their shoulder and find there are no followers. Those who rule by intimidation or bribery simply cannot survive adversity. On the contrary, leadership from loyalty has the opposite effect. The tougher things get, the better your people perform and the harder they work to support you. The rewards are obvious.

There may be other styles of leadership, and there are certainly subsets of the ones I have identified, but I'm sure you get the point. Adopt a leadership style that motivates and encourages the people upon whom you must rely for your own success.

Have a Defined Value System

YOU HAVE TO know what you stand for. Likewise, those around you have to know what you stand for. In other words, you have to have a set of basic values. I'm old-fashioned enough to believe that there are such things. Things like courage, kindness, honesty, integrity, respect for one's fellow man, loyalty, and humility. Someone has called these the "eternal verities." Truisms? Of course, but truisms are called truisms because they are true!! It's truly amazing to me and, frankly, quite depressing, to have watched, especially in recent years, the abandonment (or at least the weakening) of those basic values by so many individuals, corporations, and institutions. What I find fascinating is not just the disregard for basic values, but the incredible assumption (at least I think it's incredible) that you can somehow get away with it. Don't believe it! Remember—there are *always* consequences.

At the heart of this, I think, are arrogance and greed. Arrogance in believing that one is above the "law" or can somehow circumvent it. Greed, in that many people abandon what they know is right because of a lust for material gain light-years beyond even the most liberal definition of "enough."

There is a wonderful story I like to quote in discussing this whole subject of arrogance. It's the story of a ship's captain as told by Frank Koch in *Proceedings*, the magazine of the Naval Institute. One night at sea he saw what looked like the light of another ship heading toward him. He had his signalman blink to the other ship. He said, "Change your course ten degrees south." The reply came back, "Change your course ten degrees north." Well, the captain answered, "I am a captain. Change your course south." To which the reply was, "Well, I'm a seaman, change your course north!" This, of course, infuriated the captain so he signaled back, "DAMN IT! I say change your course south. I'm on a battleship!" To which the reply came back, "I say change your course north. I'm in a lighthouse!"

Arrogance clouds your judgment—your internal compass. The fundamental values exist, and they're going to come back and get you every time! They are lighthouses, and we'd better learn how to navigate with them and by them. Bernard Baruch, the great philanthropist and counselor to presidents, once observed that in his eighty-seven years, though he had seen a whole succession of technological revolutions, none of them had eliminated the need for character or the ability to think.

No one had a stronger or more well-defined set of values than my dad. He was scrupulously honest, and he carried this quality into his service in the Ohio State Senate, where he served for more than twenty-five years and became the majority leader of that body. He loved to tell this story. In his first year in the Senate, he said he kept hearing stories about some legislators being given money by some people attempting to influence their vote, and that the money was sometimes passed from one hand to another at social functions. One day my dad mentioned this to one of his colleagues and said, "I don't understand this. No one ever tried to give me money." His friend said, "Stan, do you have flaps on the pockets of the suit coats you wear?" Dad replied, "Yes, but so what?" His friend then explained: "If you have flaps on your pockets, then it is impossible to slide money into the pockets. Either wear suits without flaps or tuck the flaps in!" So, I guess the moral (or should I say immoral) of this story is that, if you're going to cheat, you need to dress properly!

Relating this story reminds me of a similar story. When we lived in Cincinnati I had a terrific tailor, a little Italian guy. (It seems that all tailors are little Italian guys!) He was a delightful character, and I loved to visit with him whenever I went into his shop. He never quite got my name right and would always greet me with open arms and a shout— "Hello, Mr. Mechee!" He really was a fine tailor, but his organizational skills left a lot to be desired. He simply had no system and could never find your clothes when you went to pick them up. His most famous gaffe was when he mixed up our son's navy blue graduation suit with another blue suit belonging to a different customer. The suit he gave my son fit him fine, but there was a problem—it was a wool suit, and our son was allergic to wool! Dan didn't put the suit on until just before leaving for graduation, so the problem didn't become serious until the graduation commenced—on one of those insufferably hot and humid summer nights for which Cincinnati is famous. Suffice it to say that it was an unforgettable night for Dan.

What I remember best about my tailor, however, is that when I took out my wallet to pay him (always in cash), he would smile and say, "Pay me the Italian way," as he indicated where and how I should slide the bills into his pocket!

Perhaps the best way I can illustrate the importance of a system of values is to quote something I read some time ago. It is an anonymous homage to wine called "The Philosophy of Wine." I love this story and only wish that I knew who first came up with it.

> *A philosophy professor stood before his class with some items in front of him. When the class began, without a word, he picked up a very large empty jar and proceeded to fill it with rocks, each about two inches in diameter. He then asked the class if the jar was full. They all agreed that it was. So the professor*

*then picked up a box of pebbles and poured them into the jar. He
shook the jar lightly. The pebbles, of course, rolled into the open
areas between the rocks.*

*He then asked the class again if the jar was full. They all
agreed it was. The professor picked up a bag of sand and poured
it into the jar. The sand filled in between the pebbles. He then
asked once more if the jar was full. The students responded with
a unanimous yes.*

*The professor then produced a bottle of red wine from under
the table and proceeded to pour the entire contents into the jar
effectively filling the empty space between the sand.*

*"Now," said the professor, "I want you to recognize that
this jar represents your life. The rocks being the important
things—your family, your health, and your children—things
that if everything else were lost and only they remained, your
life would still be full.*

*"The pebbles are the other things that matter, like your job,
your house, your car. The sand is everything else . . . the small
stuff.*

*"If you put the sand into the jar first there would be no room
for the pebbles or the rocks. The same goes for your life. If you
spend all your time and energy on the small stuff, you will never
have room for the things that really matter. Set your priorities.
The rest is just sand." One of the students raised her hand and
inquired what the wine represented.*

*The professor smiled, "I'm glad you asked. It just goes to
show you that no matter how full your life may seem, there's
always room for a good bottle of wine."*

There are two more "Lessons Learned." But before I explain them, let
me tell you about a little parlor game that I think I may have invented.
It's fun and I urge you to try it sometime when you have a small group
of friends together. It goes like this. Just before you arrive on earth, God
has a conversation with you, and he says something like this: "Over on
the wall on the other side of this room is a list of all of the qualities and

characteristics that make up a happy and successful person. I will allow you to choose two that you would like to take with you as you join the human race. I wish I could allow you to take more, but there is such heavy demand that I can only allow you two. You will have to develop the others for yourself. Oh, and by the way, I will assure you of reasonable intelligence and health. Don't worry about those." Now you say to your friends, "Before we part today think about the two qualities that you would most like to have in your life from the moment you are born." You will be surprised and fascinated at what people choose. It's really a fun game, and maybe I should copyright it!

Obviously, at this point you will want to know what my choices are. Quite simply, they are patience and a sense of humor. Not surprisingly then, these are my final two "Lessons Learned."

Patience

ALTHOUGH THERE ARE exceptions, most of the successful people I have known—and certainly most of the people mentioned in this book—have been patient people. *Webster* defines patience as "bearing trials calmly or without complaint" or "manifesting forbearance of provocation or strain." Another definition is "not being hasty or impetuous." I think all of these definitions are accurate. Clearly it is sometimes extremely difficult to be patient, but it is *always* the right thing to do. You compromise nothing by doing so, and patience almost always leads to a more calm and reasoned solution to whatever the problem may be. Now, don't confuse patience with procrastination. The two are quite different. Patience promotes a solid conclusion. Procrastination prohibits it.

One of the best—and funniest—stories of patience that I know came from one of my very best friends on the LPGA Tour—the striking Swedish star Helen Alfredsson. Helen is not only a great player; she is extremely intelligent, very outspoken, and has a wonderful sense of humor. She has played well, over a number of years, and never better than during the last couple of years. Moreover, she has been an important part of the LPGA's Player Board of Directors.

I have many wonderful memories of fun times with Helen, but one that stands out in my memory took place in Japan during a Pro-Am. Helen and I were playing with the chairman of the sponsoring company, a delightful man who enjoyed golf tremendously, as virtually all Japanese do. We were on the first tee, and I was standing next to Helen as the chairman addressed the ball. He was not a tall man, but in spite of that, he took an unbelievably wide stance. This, of course, made his swing very awkward, and as he took a big swipe, the heel of the club face hit the ball and sent the ball directly backwards between his legs. I had never seen such a shot before and have never seen one since. It is virtually impossible to hit the ball so far back on the heel that it, indeed, comes right back through your legs. In any event, we tried to keep our composure, but I did steal a glance at Helen. She didn't move a muscle—except she rolled her eyes . . . which said it all. Her unspoken comment was, "My God, Charlie, we've got eighteen holes of this to endure." But we did, had a great time, and had that unforgettable memory as a result. Helen could have been unpleasant, upset, and all the rest. But, she was patient, which allowed everyone in the group to have an enjoyable day.

I recently played with Helen in the Pro-Am at the Kraft-Nabisco Championship. She hasn't changed a bit—funny, irreverent, warm, and a hell of a golfer. Her husband went around with us that day. Kent Nilsson is a great guy and a former star in the National Hockey League. Indeed, a couple of friends of mine who were former NHL players have told me that Kent was great back in the days when hockey was a really rough sport! Hard for me to imagine that it was rougher than it is presently!

Sense of Humor

A SENSE OF humor will make your life immensely more pleasant and fulfilling over the years. Especially the ability and willingness to laugh at oneself and the human condition. Research shows that leaders who achieve the best results get people to laugh three times more often than mediocre leaders. Now, frankly, I have no idea where that statistic came from—probably from thin air. As the comedian Steven Wright says, "42.7 percent of all statistics are made up on the spot." (This, by the way, is the same guy who said, "Half the people you know are below average.")

Whatever the stats, I can tell you without equivocation that the ability to laugh and cause others to laugh is one of the most powerful qualities of most great leaders. Winston Churchill, Franklin Roosevelt, Abraham Lincoln, John Kennedy, and Ronald Reagan are just a few who come to mind. I can't tell you how many times I've seen tension and anger defused by a lighthearted comment or a reminder of how unimportant, or minor, the issue that was generating all the heat really was. Most people (sadly, not everybody) like to laugh. Most people like to let steam out when it's been built up to an explosive level. They need an opportunity to do that. That's why a sense of humor is so important. One critical caveat: Your sense of humor should never be at the expense of someone else—unless, of course, you are doing a "roast."

I have long been a believer in using anecdotes in speeches or presentations to make a point. I have found this works because people tend to remember stories and jokes longer than they remember some relatively dry commentary on a particular point you are trying to make. The best example of this is what I call "the oil well fire" joke. I have used it scores of times, and it never has failed me. I particularly remember telling it at a meeting of the United States Golf Association Executive Committee when Judy Bell, a member of the committee who later became the first woman president of the USGA, loved the joke. Whenever I would appear before an audience of which she was a part, she would always say, "Charlie, tell 'the oil well fire' joke." So Judy—just for you—here it is.

The point of the story is to show that what may appear to be an act of courage is sometimes not quite what it seems. There was an oil well fire burning in Texas that was out of control. It had raged for days, and all efforts by the owners to extinguish it had failed. They had brought in all of the great oil well firefighters from all over the world, including those whose performance was so outstanding during the Iraq War. All of these efforts failed. The fire continued to burn. The owners met to try to figure out what on earth they might do as they watched, literally, their fortune go up in smoke. Finally, one of the owners said, "There is one thing we haven't tried. Let's run a full-page ad in a number of newspapers offering a $2 million reward for anyone who can put out the fire. The ad appeared and a number of people came in to try, but failed. One day the owners were standing on a high hill overlooking the valley in which the fire continued to burn. Suddenly, they heard a loud noise as an old dump truck raced by them heading right down the hill towards the fire. The driver appeared to be an old fellow in bib overalls and a straw hat, and the bed of the truck was filled with a truly motley crew. To everyone's amazement, the truck drove right into the middle of the fire, and everyone in the truck began beating at the fire with blankets, seat covers, old burlap bags, and anything else they could get their hands on. Miraculously, in about five minutes the fire went out! The owners were, of course, overjoyed, and they ran down the hill to congratulate and thank the firefighters. When they got there the old fellow in the bib overalls was dusting off his clothes and straightening his hat when one of the owners said, "This is unbelievable. You have put out the fire. You are heroes. But even more important, you have won the $2 million reward. What do you intend to do with all that money?" The old fellow thought a minute and then said, "I don't know what I'll do with all of it, but the first thing I'm gonna do is buy brakes for that goddamn truck!"

So, just remember: what might first look like courage is often nothing but a lack of brakes!

I could detail scores of amusing situations that have occurred in my relationships with the "rich and famous." Time and space prohibit me from listing them all, but here are a few of my favorites.

We spent the summers in Jackson Hole, Wyoming, for over twenty-five years and lived at an Arnold Palmer–designed golf course located outside Jackson, called Teton Pines.*

About an hour north of Jackson in Yellowstone National Park is the Jackson Lake Lodge. Every year, for many years, the Federal Reserve Governors and the leading financial ministers from all over the world gathered at Jackson Lake Lodge to enjoy a little peace and quiet, fresh air, and, of course, to plan, strategize, and share their successes and failures. During the years he was chairman, Alan Greenspan was one of the most prominent attendees at this conference. One year during the conference, I received a phone call from the general manager of Teton Pines, telling me that he was playing golf the following morning with Mr. Greenspan and Jim Wolfensohn, the legendary financier and, at that time, the head of the World Bank. The manager asked me if I would like to be the fourth. Of course, I was thrilled and accepted. The next morning we gathered on the first tee and prepared to hit our first shots. When Mr. Greenspan stepped to the tee, he explained to us that he rarely played golf, but that he enjoyed it very much and was looking forward to the day. His drive, unfortunately, was a line drive left that struck the limb of a dead tree, causing that limb to fall to the ground. Greenspan turned to us and with a slight smile said, "Well, I guess the Fed has a new 'branch' in Wyoming!" The rest of the golf game was memorable, but nothing quite as memorable as that first shot and the accompanying comment.

---

*It was the second golf course built in Jackson Hole and was designed by Arnold in 1987. We were first introduced to Jackson Hole and the magnificent Teton Mountain range in the late 1960s. We fell in love with the area and kept going back every few years. When we learned that Teton Pines had been developed, we made a visit, immediately fell in love with the place, bought a lot, and built a house. There is one very curious aspect to the Teton Pines Golf Course. Remember, it is located virtually in the shadow of the majestic Teton Mountain range, and yet, as Arnie once told me, it has the smallest elevation change of any golf course he ever built anywhere in the world. The reason is simple—it literally sits in Jackson Hole, an area that is completely flat. The area was originally called "Jackson's Hole" and is thought to have been named after a beaver trapper, Davey Jackson, who worked the area in the early 1800s. Jackson Hole and Teton Pines were a big and very happy part of our family's life.

Every few years at Taft Broadcasting Company we had a photograph taken of our board of directors to include in the annual report to shareholders. We had a terrific board with a number of people of national reputation, but by far, the best known among them was Neil Armstrong. We had a wonderful photographer who was not only good at his craft but was a delightful guy with a great sense of humor. One year, when we were taking the photograph, he had us all lined up exactly the way he wanted us. He had fussed and worked to get it just right. He then retreated under the black cloth of the old box camera and got ready to snap the picture. But then, abruptly, he stepped out and stood up and said to Neil, "Pardon me, Mr. Armstrong, but would you please take one small step forward." I don't think we stopped laughing for twenty minutes. Every time I'm involved in any kind of a group photograph, this delightful story comes to my mind.*

I would also like to remind you of the story I told earlier of how my colleague in our harrowing airplane flight simply made the observation that he didn't want to perish on "somebody else's number." This is not only funny, but it is a wonderful example of how humor can relieve tension.

ANOTHER EXAMPLE OF how a sense of humor can smooth out what otherwise might be a "sticky" situation came during a negotiation I had with one of Cincinnati's toughest and smartest business leaders. Jack Schiff was one of Cincinnati's most outstanding businessmen. He built a superb financial institution, and he was extraordinarily shrewd. Jack was in my office one day to talk about some business arrangement our two companies were discussing. As we exchanged thoughts, I made a proposal to Jack. Perhaps because of the influence of Jake Davis's

---

*Interesting historical footnote: Neil has pointed out that his actual statement from the moon was slightly garbled in transmission. What he actually said was, "One small step for a man. One giant leap for mankind." The word "a" never came through.

admonition, it was definitely slanted to my company's advantage. Jack looked at me for a minute and then smiled and said, "Charlie, if I were to accept that proposal, you would be entitled to at least a full chapter in the New Testament!" I don't remember for sure, but my guess is that I blushed and quickly changed the subject.

Of course, sometimes an attempt at humor can backfire. One of my most memorable examples of this involved a man named Sy Fischer, who ran some of Taft's operations on the West Coast. Each year when we were preparing the company's annual report, we asked all of our group heads to send a photograph of themselves that could be used in the report. Sy, who had a great sense of humor and mischief, sent in a photograph that showed him sitting behind his desk with his coat, shirt, and tie in disarray and a half-empty bottle of scotch sitting on the desk. When I got this, I had an equally mischievous idea. I asked our public relations people to speak to the printer of the annual report and see if we could get four or five copies printed with Sy's bogus photograph. They said that it would be no problem, and within a few days I had several copies.

I called Sy and said, "Sy, we've got a serious problem. There has been a terrible error. The bogus photograph you sent has actually been included in the annual report, and it has gone out to all of our thousands of stockholders. I am sending you several copies. I don't know what to do about this. This is embarrassing and big trouble." Sy was, of course, horrified, and I let him twist in the wind for four or five minutes before my laughter overwhelmed me, and I explained that the joke was on him. Needless to say, Sy was relieved. I suspect he never used a phony photograph again.

I HAVE COME to believe that one of the most effective forms of humor is self-deprecation. Making fun of yourself is almost always good for a laugh. Let me give you an example. One of the most talented, brightest, and most civil men I have known is Nick Clooney. Nick has been a television personality and a first-rate news anchor for many years. My closest times with Nick were when he anchored the number-one newscast in Cincinnati for the Taft station WKRC. I have many happy memories of my friendship with Nick, but the funniest occurred some years after Taft Broadcasting was sold, and I was walking through the Cincinnati airport and ran into Nick. I was very happy to see him and I said, "How are you?" His answer was vintage Nick. He said, "I'm fine, but I have to live with the fact that I spent the first half of my life as Rosie's brother and am spending the last half as George's father." Everyone with a pulse knows who George Clooney is, but the younger generation may not realize that Nick's sister Rosemary was one of the country's top pop singers for four decades beginning in the 1950s and was in the holiday movie classic *White Christmas*.

Of all the characteristics that I have noted in people that I have admired, their sense of humor ranked high up there with integrity and openness. I simply cannot overstress the necessity of keeping things light whenever possible and never failing to smile at the human condition—and at yourself!

So, I will leave you with a rhyme. Sadly, I don't know who the author was. But, I think if you live your life by these few lines, the odds are you will be successful and, even more important, happy. It goes like this:

> *He was a very cautious lad.*
> *He never romped or played.*
> *He never smoked, he never drank,*
> *Nor even kissed a maid,*
> *And when he upped and passed away,*
> *Insurance was denied,*
> *For since he hadn't ever lived,*
> *They claimed he never died.*

Something to keep in mind! And never forget that he who laughs, lasts!

Epilogue

So, there you have it—the abridged version of my first eighty-two years, along with many of my experiences throughout these years and profiles of many of the scores of people with whom I shared these times. I have also tried to share some of the lessons I have learned along the way. They have proven invaluable to me and I hope they will be of some help to you as well.

I was once labeled a "terminal optimist" by a golf writer. I *think* this was said as a compliment, and I certainly always at least *try* to see the bright side of things. I think this is partly because I have always loved being around young people and have tried to never "think old." The great writer A. J. Liebling, in one of his classic pieces on boxing—"Ahab and Nemesis"—put it this way:

> *The world is not going backward if you can just stay young enough to remember what it was really like when you were really young.*

Nick Clooney once wrote a column in the *Cincinnati Post* with a theme that, like so many of Nick's ideas, was wonderfully creative. He asked a number of his friends and colleagues in and around Cincinnati to write what they would want their own epitaph to be. He was nice enough to include mine. It goes like this:

> *Dear God,*
> *Thanks for letting me visit. I had a wonderful time.*

I have, indeed, had a wonderful life, and that's really what this book is all about.

Let me bring this to a close with the following reminiscence. Some years ago I was reflecting not just on my career but on the typical career of someone who had been fortunate enough to have a reasonably full and active life. I thought about it and concluded that there were seven stages in a career. They are as follows:

Stage One: Overwhelming naiveté mixed with puppy-like eagerness

Stage Two: Mindless panic and nervous stomach as reality dawns and crushing workloads descend

Stage Three: Thrilling discovery that there are few truly successful people and most of *them* are lucky rather than smart

Stage Four: Success without recognition or reward

Stage Five: Recognition and reward without success

Stage Six: Undeserved honors from those who forgive and forget

Stage Seven: Oblivion

I remain clinging tenaciously to the end of Stage Six but, whenever Stage Seven overtakes me, I will definitely have had a "wonderful time."

Some Thank You's

To MY DEAR FRIEND Neil Armstrong, whose Foreword to this book left me speechless and reminded me once again that there has never been a hero of this magnitude with such humility.

To another dear friend, Arnold Palmer, whom I believe to be the most admired and respected figure in the history of the game of golf. My ten years of working closely with him on a daily basis, and our continuing friendship in the years since, are highlights in my life. As you know, many of the stories in this book involve this amazing man.

To my indefatigable and very talented assistant, Gretlyn Thomas. Without her this book would simply never have happened. Working twenty-five hundred miles away, she took my dictation, helped it make sense, and handled expertly all the tedious details.

I owe much to Jaime Diaz, one of the finest writers in golf or in any other world, not only for his flattering Introduction but also for sitting down with me in the early stages of this effort and getting me on the right track.

To my wonderful Cincinnati friends Roger Howe and Bob Wehling, who provided sound advice and thoughts on organization and content.

It just occurred to me that I really need to thank my mother and dad. They were truly great people, but, let's be clear, if they hadn't fallen in love and married, not only I would never have written this book, I wouldn't be doing much of anything. Thanks, Mom and Dad!

And, finally, to my family—my extraordinary wife and my three wonderful children and their spouses. The twin pillars of our family have been—and always will be—love and laugher. My family has formed and inspired my life more than they will ever know.

CSM, Jr.

Appendix

Eulogy for Neil Armstrong
Given by Charles S. Mechem, Jr.
Friday, August 31, 2012
The Camargo Club

I AM DEEPLY honored and very humbled to be here today. Frankly, I am even more humbled than I expected to be. The reason is that I have been seated in a row with two U. S. senators and a number of hall of fame astronauts. So, as I looked up and down the row, I came to realize that I was the only one in the row that I had never heard of before.

This will not be a sad or maudlin eulogy, although it would be easy to make it such. Because our hearts are filled with shock and sadness at the loss of this extraordinary man and our dear friend. But, to make this day and this hour sad is not the way to honor Neil Armstrong. Rather, let's celebrate one of the great heroes of our age, who also just happened to be our pal.

I'm not going to talk much about the headlines Neil made. I can add little or nothing to the millions of words that have and will be written about his great adventure. Rather, I want to talk briefly about the human qualities that made Neil such a truly unique and wonderful person.

Interestingly, it was one of these qualities—his insatiable curiosity about everything—that first brought us together.

When Neil left the space program, he and his family returned to Ohio, and he bought a farm near where Taft Broadcasting Company was building Kings Island. I learned that he had expressed his interest in seeing what was going on at the construction site, and so I called him and offered a "guided" tour with me as the guide. We had a great tour and he was obviously very interested in the project. Following our meeting I began to wonder if he would consider joining the Taft board. So, I approached him and to my great delight he said yes. Not surprisingly, he was a superb board member for a number of years.

Next, his humility and understated manner. Winston Churchill once said of his adversary Clement Attlee, "Mr. Attlee is a modest man—and no one has more reason to be so." Let me paraphrase Sir Winston, "Neil Armstrong was a very modest man—and no one had less reason to be so."

I never once—ever—heard Neil say anything that could be even remotely construed as self-congratulatory. *Never*.

When I was at the LPGA, Neil often came out to tournaments and we played in a number of Pro-Ams together. One day I introduced him to one of the young players on the putting green. I said, "Betty, I'd like you to meet Neil Armstrong." She smiled and extended her hand, and as they shook hands she said, "I'm so pleased to meet you. You know you have the same name as the man who went to the moon!" Now, I don't have to tell you that most worldwide celebrities would not have been particularly pleased with this remark. Not Neil. He laughed and shook her hand while I explained, "Betty, this *is* the man who went to the moon."

I'm sure many of you may have been with Neil when someone would approach him and say, "Aren't you Neil Armstrong?" And he would reply, "Well, I'm one of them." I'll never forget one day when a young woman approached us and said to Neil, "Aren't you someone I should know." And he replied, "Probably not."

I remember another golf outing when we were paired with a loud, boisterous guy who insisted on badgering Neil with questions. On one hole—a sandy, rocky spot—this guy said, "Look at this Neil; it looks just like the moon. What was it like on the moon?" Neil quietly turned to the guy and said, "Great view, lousy service." He then walked away and proceeded to hit his next shot.

Another great story that was told to me by Dudley Taft and Roger Howe took place when they were going tarpon fishing in Florida with Neil. It seems that the captain of the fishing boat had been a pilot and was overwhelmed that Neil would be one of his passengers on the fishing trip. He said to Neil how incredible he thought the moon shot was and how he was completely mystified as to how the navigation had been handled. He said, "I simply can't imagine how you managed to navigate to the moon. Neil's response was another classic. He said simply, "It wasn't a big problem. We could see it all the way."

The next quality—which will surprise no one in this room—is to note that Neil was a truly brilliant man. Since he was so quiet and humble we only got brief glimpses of this from time to time. But, he just plain knew everything about everything. Once on a trip to Tuscany, we went to the Leonardo da Vinci Museum in the little town of Vinci. There was a striking exhibit of many of Leonardo's inventions done in miniature and in wood. We had little idea what any of these were about, nor for that matter did the curator, but Neil did and he proceeded to explain not only what they were but how they worked. As he talked, a small crowd gathered and listened attentively. I always suspected that many in the crowd simply thought Neil was a tour guide! He loved the museum and we couldn't get him to leave! It was a touching moment—almost mystical— of one great mind admiring the genius of another.

Another time we were driving through the vast windmill farm just north of Palm Springs, California, and we commented that we never had understood how these windmills worked to generate electricity. You will not be surprised to learn that Neil explained the whole process in detail.

Neil served on the Taft Broadcasting Company board for many years. I was thrilled when he accepted my invitation to join the board. He was an incredible board member. He always asked the questions that nobody else thought of, and he always pressed management to justify its actions. A couple of times when he was pressing me hard I remember thinking, "Who asked this guy to be on the board?" Not really.

Neil was deeply patriotic. He served his country as a combat pilot in Korea and as one of the world's great test pilots. After retiring from the space program, he was constantly doing things to support the troops and made visits to both Iraq and Afghanistan to be with the troops. Naturally, he never talked about any of these things.

Flying was his first love. I asked one of his very good friends, Russ Meyer, who headed Cessna aviation for many years and is a fine pilot himself how a pilot viewed Neil. Here's what Russ said. "Amazingly, Neil accomplished every pilot's dreams. He earned his wings. He engaged in combat. He had a distinguished career as an experimental test pilot, made emergency procedures seem routine, and he landed on the moon. Unbelievable. When I think of aviation, I think of four people: the Wright Brothers, Charles Lindbergh, and Neil Armstrong."

I think that, after flying, his greatest passion was golf. Just like many of you in this audience today, I had many wonderful experiences with Neil on the golf course. We were both high handicappers and referred to ourselves as "brothers in mediocrity." We were truly bumblers of the ancient art. But, oh, how he loved the game. I can still hear him say after hitting a good shot, "Well, that's one in a row!" He played the game the way he lived his life. He never "picked up." He played every hole to its conclusion and gave it his total effort. He never surrendered to the mysteries and frustrations of that maddening game.

And, Neil, if you are listening, do me a favor. You are up there with the big guys—Bobby Jones, Ben Hogan, Sam Snead, Byron Nelson— even old Tom Morris! Get some tips! Find out how to do it! And then get word back to me. I know you can do it!

The final quality that I would mention is wit and his love of laughter. Neil smiled and laughed a lot. The day after his death I watched again his interview with *60 Minutes* in 2005. Take another look at it. He was smiling practically every minute of the interview.

If anyone doubts that Neil enjoyed warmth and laughter, just ask the guys that he played poker with at the C & C Club outings. Just ask any of the guys at Taft Broadcasting Company who would sing with him at night after dinner at our annual management meetings. Ask any of his fellow conquistadores.

Neil loved good jokes. I'll bet most of you have seen him when he laughed because it was as though his whole body was animated. He would almost jump up and down. He didn't tell a lot of jokes because he loved to hear jokes from others. But he told me what I think is maybe the funniest joke I've ever heard, and Neil, I hope you won't mind if I share this. Folks, this is a thinking man's joke. Whenever I have told this story I am not sure that I always gave you credit. But I want to make it very clear—this is your joke!

Two guys were walking down the street on a very hot and humid day. They each had their dog with them and were enjoying their stroll except for one thing. They were both hot and dry, and the one fellow said to the other, "I'm dying for a beer." The other fellow replied, "So am I and—look—we're in luck, there's a bar." They started to enter the bar when one of the guys noticed a sign in the window that read—in bold black letters—no dogs allowed! At first they were devastated, but then one of the guys said, "I've got an idea. I'll go inside and if the bartender challenges me, I'll simply say this is my seeing-eye dog. If I'm not back out here on the street in five minutes, then you will know it's safe for you to come in." The other guy said, "Sounds like a great idea. Go do it."

So, the first guy goes in the bar, and the bartender immediately says, "Hey buddy, you can't come in here with that dog. Dogs are not allowed." The guy responds, "Oh, I'm so sorry sir. But I'm blind and this is my seeing-eye dog." Well, the bartender is embarrassed and says, "I'm so sorry. I didn't realize. Let me help you here over to the bar, and the beer's on the house." Meanwhile, about five minutes have gone by, and the guy who stayed outside decides that the coast is clear, and he walks into the bar with his dog. The bartender says, "What's going on here?

Can't you read? No dogs allowed!" The fellow says, "I'm very sorry, sir. I didn't know about the no-dog rule because I am blind, and this is my seeing-eye dog." The bartender says, "Wait just a minute, buddy; that's a Chihuahua." And the guy says, "What, they gave me a Chihuahua?!"

Let me close with this. Neil's historic statement from the surface of the moon said that it was one small step for a man—one giant leap for mankind. Well, it may have been a small step, but it was taken by a giant of a man. He was that rarest of men—one who simply did what he believed was right. Nothing more—nothing less. Every time.

Rest well, commander. Your nation, the world, and all your buddies salute you. You had—and have—our unconditional admiration, our deepest respect, and our undying love.

New York Times Article
October 22, 1992
No Green Jackets, but Maybe Gold

AUGUSTA, GA., OCT. 21—There would be a mini-Olympic Village for the athletes, and men and women on the course of Augusta National under a plan proposed today by the Atlanta Committee for the 1996 Summer Olympic Games, which formally announced its intention to push for the inclusion of golf.

"We wouldn't be here if we didn't think our chances were good," said Billy Payne, president and chief executive officer of the Atlanta Committee for the Olympic Games.

Today's news conference was called by the committee and was attended by Payne, the United States Olympic Committee president, LeRoy Walker, and the heads of the Professional Golfers Association and the Ladies Professional Golfers Association. Its purpose was to set out the proposed conditions under which golf would return to the Olympics for the first time since 1904.

EQUAL ACCESS

Each country would be allowed its own selection process. The only provision is that selection couldn't be strictly off a money list or any other professional rating system, because amateurs must have equal access. That provision probably means that some sort of Olympic points system will be devised in the United States for amateurs and professionals.

The plan needs approval from the International Olympic Committee, which is expected to begin considering it in December. The World Amateur Golf Council, which would organize the competition, recently voted to permit competition between pros and amateurs in Olympic golf.

"This course is known by every IOC member and known the world over," Walker said of Augusta Nation. "I'm sure that is going to carry some weight with them."

An Olympic tournament would be the first women's tournament at Augusta National. "We consider this a very positive step for women's golf," said Charles Mechem, Jr., commissioner of the L.P.G.A.

The plan calls for 72-hole tournaments for men and women to be played at different times during the Olympics. Although both Deane Beman, Commissioner of the PGA Tour, and Mechem expressed their support, not all golfers were immediately so enamored of the idea.

"I'm not juiced about it," the United States Open champion, Tom Kite, told The Associated Press. "I don't know of anyone who really is. We have a lot of international events that serve the same purpose."

Summary of Statement from
LPGA Commissioner Charles S. Mechem, Jr.
Du Pont Country Club, Wilmington, Delaware
Saturday, May 13, 1995

I have known Ben Wright for a long time, and I have never had reason to doubt either his integrity or his commitment to women's golf.

Quite obviously, if he made the remarks attributed to him, it is inappropriate for him to broadcast an LPGA event. If he did not make the alleged remarks, as he maintains, it would be terribly unfair and prematurely judgmental for us to insist that he be replaced. When the true facts are established, I feel sure that we will have no trouble in reaching an understanding with CBS as to the appropriate course of action.

My involvement with the LPGA goes back far beyond my term as Commissioner. For twelve years (1978–1989) the company of which I was chairman, Taft Broadcasting Company, was the sponsor of the LPGA Championship when it was held in Cincinnati, Ohio, and I'd like my comments this morning to be viewed against this backdrop.

The tragedy of this situation is dramatized, in my judgment, by what is happening right here, right now. As we sit here, just a few yards away from some of the greatest golfers in the world—and the best in women's golf—are playing the game with consummate skill. But we aren't out there watching. We aren't out there learning and laughing and cheering. We are in here dealing with this absurd and ugly charge that lesbianism is stunting the growth of the LPGA Tour. What is wrong with this picture? What in the name of everything that is decent and civil in this world are we doing? There are great stories right outside on that golf course and we're in here.

You can obviously tell that I am angry. The absurdity of this charge both saddens and angers me. I am sad because it is an unfair attack—a cheap shot—on a group of talented professional women that I truly love and genuinely respect.

Let me share with you some thoughts that I have on the matter.

We, of course, have read the comments about lifestyle and we occasionally read, or hear, that we are oblivious to our—quote—"real"—end quote—image.

Frankly, after four-and-one-half years in this job, I find that I am increasingly annoyed and impatient with those kinds of comments—for several reasons.

First of all, such comments often take the form of what I might call "locker room gossip"—usually from men, but sometimes from women. And, they are often said with a smirk and in a spirit that suggests that they really hope there is a problem.

And, you know, I have come to understand that to a degree these comments are leveled at all women's sports and, for that matter, at virtually any successful unmarried professional women. It is a way of demeaning or trivializing their performance and their accomplishments. I suppose we may get more of it because we are one of the more visible of the women's groups.

Secondly, I believe very strongly that personal lifestyle is just that—personal—and it ought to be a totally private matter. It should be a public matter only if it manifests itself in some public way.

Third, I look upon every single one of these young women of the LPGA in the same fundamental way—as talented, hard-working women who have made it to the top of their profession and who should be judged only by that standard. The only relevant measure is talent and performance.

Fourth, we did a tremendous amount of research last year to find out what our image is in the minds of the public. We went to a number of LPGA events and conducted thousands of interviews and a number of focus groups—and the answer was loud and clear—and quite encouraging, by the way. They said that our players are warm, friendly, enjoyable, and approachable. Not once, not once did this issue come up. It clearly wasn't an issue that concerns people.

And finally—and most importantly—to say that this lifestyle issue is a major problem for the LPGA is simply at odds with all of my experience over the last five years, and is totally inconsistent with the facts concerning our growth.

In my five years, I can honestly say to you that this has never been an issue—for me or the organization. I have not had one phone call or one letter from a sponsor or a fan to suggest that it is a problem.

I'd like to read you something from a letter I received today from the President of the LPGA Tournament Sponsors Association, and I'll extract since this was a personal letter. I quote:

> *Never have the sponsors, the LPGA, and the players enjoyed a more harmonious relationship than they do now.*

And this is what baffles and frustrates me. In the last five years, we have experienced tremendous growth. Here are the facts:

Prize money is up over 40 percent, to almost $25 million.

We have five events over $1 million.

We have only one event without a title sponsor.

18 of our sponsors increased their prize money just this year.

And just this week on Wednesday, before all of this even happened, we came to an agreement with organizers of this event and McDonald's for an evergreen contract for the McDonald's LPGA Championship, a rolling agreement that lasts long into the future.

That means we now have a rolling agreement with every one of our four major championships. All of our majors are strong and secure, and with strong prestigious organizations.

Is this what happens to an organization that has a problem? I cannot make sense of that.

For the life of me, I cannot equate these facts with the charge that we have a serious problem with the lifestyle issue.

The LPGA's major problem and its biggest challenge by far is not the personal lifestyle of its players. It is much less complex than that. Any problem we have is in being a women's organization. This is a systemic, societal problem.

I am enough of a historian to know that things have changed light-years since the days of someone like the great Louise Suggs, who is in this audience today. That gives me hope for the future.

Let me close by saying that what has happened here in the last couple of days is just plain wrong. There are no other words for it—no other way to put it. It is just plain wrong. Talented young women have been crudely and needlessly harmed—and for what? What does this have to do with golf? What does it have to do with raising millions of dollars for charity? Indeed, what does it have to do with anything that is relevant to this event, or to the Tour in general? To say it another way, what good has come from this? What purpose has been served? What cause advanced? This answer is none—nothing! Then why do it? Why do it? I'm afraid I will never understand.

My wife, Marilyn, and I were in San Francisco to see our new grand-daughter when all this broke, and our daughter Melissa, who is herself a pediatrician, was holding the baby and she said: "I hope that May [that's the baby's name] will grow up in a world where she will be judged only on merit and by accomplishment." I devoutly hope so, too.

Annika Sorenstam Presentation
Charles S. Mechem, Jr.
World Golf Hall of Fame
October 20, 2003

Annika Sorenstam's journey to the Hall of Fame began officially when she recorded her very first victory as a professional at the Broadmoor in 1995, her second year on the LPGA tour. Now, this was no ordinary win. It just so happens that it was the United States Women's Open—an event that

Annika had dreamed of winning since golf became her passion at age twelve. She, like countless other aspiring young golfers before and since, practiced putting pretending that "this putt is to win the U.S. Open."

And, now, she had realized her dream with a victory, which she still regards—eight years later—as the high point of her career. But, there was a troubling aspect to this happy time.

Her dreams had been so totally fulfilled by this victory, that physically and emotionally overwhelmed, she said to herself, "Oh my goodness, what am I going to do now! What's left for me to do?"

Well, how about forty-six more victories, six majors, five Vare trophies, five player of the year awards, a fifty-nine, and one dive into a lake wearing red shoes. I think you'll agree that she has effectively answered her own question of what do I do now. By the way, Annika, your sister, Charlotta, had a great answer to what you do from now on. She said simply, "Just do it all over again!"

In truth, Annika's journey to the Hall of Fame started long before that treasured win at the Broadmoor.

It began when she and her sister, Charlotta, went with their parents—both good players—to the golf course where the girls would go to the putting green where their golf education began. Later, Annika became a part of a group of juniors in a so-called training week. Her father tells me that her handicap fell from fifty-four to thirty-five in one week!

He says she was a good little girl—nice and quiet and shy—good in all sports including badminton! But always from the beginning—very competitive—even at cards.

She continued to surprise her parents with her accomplishments not because they didn't expect them, but because they always came more quickly then they anticipated. As her dad said, "Maybe we were a little slow, but she was always a little ahead of us!"

The one thing that gave her parents some concern was that for a period of time she told them she would rather be the runner-up than the winner because the winner had to give a speech!! She has quite obviously gotten over that! In short, a close, warm, loving family—then and now. And, by the way, her girlhood idols were Bjorn Borg and Liselotte Neumann—not just for their greatness on the field of play but also for their dignity and poise as champions—traits that she obviously learned well from them.

I cited some statistics earlier regarding Annika's career and the LPGA Media Guide has three pages in very small type recounting her achievements. But, here are a couple of new ones:

Youngest player in the World Golf Hall of Fame, and

First player in the LPGA Hall of Fame from a foreign country.

But, these figures and stats only tell *what* she has done, not *how* or *why*. And, it occurred to me that the "how and the why" could only come from those who have been there—from those greats of the game who can appreciate more than anyone the magnitude of this remarkable young woman's accomplishments. So, I asked some of them.

Mickey Wright, with whom Annika is most often compared, told me: "Annika has 'IT.' You can't define 'IT' precisely but you know it when you see it—emotional control, style, focus, and obviously great ability."

The great Louise Suggs—or "Little Miss Sluggs," as Bob Hope called her—was characteristically direct: "I've never seen a player with such focus and concentration. She's a real whiz-bang."

Two players who frequently go head to head with Annika (and do quite nicely, thank you) are Juli Inkster and Beth Daniel. They had much the same view—Annika is driven and dedicated in the very best sense. She is truly committed to being the best. She takes nothing for granted.

And, Nancy Lopez told me that she truly admires Annika, both as a person and as a golfer, and feels that any goal that she sets for herself she will reach.

Now, I'll bet you thought I wasn't going to quote any men. Well, as an old German law professor I once had used to say, "You couldn't be wronger."

Jack Nicklaus told me, "She has handled herself extremely well." Then, as he is wont to do, Jack put a little different twist on the reasons for her success. "I'm not sure it's all concentration and focus," he said. "She simply has that air of—not cockiness—but of knowing you can do it and then just going out and doing it."

Tiger had this to say: "There has never been anyone more deserving of induction into the Hall of Fame, and particularly at such a young age. She has dominated the world of women's golf. It is not often that you can say you have seen the best, but in Annika I think perhaps we have." And, Arnie said it simply: "She's the best. She is the epitome of integrity and class. She is truly great."

It is not widely known but Arnie wrote Annika a letter shortly before her appearance at The Colonial—a letter she treasures. In part he said, "It is certainly your privilege to do what you think is best for you and the game. Just ignore all the comments you are hearing. Do your thing, have fun, and get it done."

And, that tireless supporter and longtime champion of women's golf, Dan Jenkins, had this to say in his most recent column in *Golf Digest:* "Fact is, the Shot of the Year still belongs to Annika—her opening tee shot at Colonial. It had more pressure on it and far greater build up to it than anything else in 2003."

"Stir in the Colonial gig with her performance in the Majors and you also have Player of the Year: Annika, even over any guy."

Ah, Colonial.

When Annika first told me of her decision to play, an old line regarding women's upward mobility came to my mind. "There is no glass ceiling—only a thick layer of men." But, you know, it didn't turn out that way. Her playing partners, fans of both sexes and all ages, and the media all cheered her on. I think I know why. And I think you do too. It's because Colonial wasn't about golf—it was all about respect, humility, dignity, pride, sportsmanship, and class. It was about respect and the quest for excellence, about reaching as high as you can reach. And anyone who knows Annika well was not surprised—for those closest to her know her as honest, humble, not judgmental, compassionate, and dedicated—just the sort of person to act precisely as she did.

Reaching for the stars. Striving for excellence. The great playwright Neil Simon put it this way:

> *Live your life as though Gershwin had written music to underscore your every move. I can't think of anything worthwhile in life that was achieved without a great deal of desire to achieve it. Don't listen to those who say it's not done that way. Maybe it's not. But maybe you will. Don't listen to those who say you're taking too big a chance. If he didn't take a big chance, Michelangelo would have painted the floor of the Sistine Chapel, and it certainly would have been rubbed out by today.*

I mentioned respect. This to me is the bottom line. Annika, you have earned the single most important reward that anyone striving for excellence can obtain—the unqualified respect of your peers and of all who know you or have watched you play. Respect—in the end nothing matters more.

I am deeply honored to present Annika Sorenstam for induction into the World Golf Hall of Fame.

Charles S. Mechem, Jr.
Comments presenting Nancy Lopez
as the Memorial 2011 Honoree
May 31, 2011

I was greatly flattered when Nancy asked me to introduce her as today's Honoree. Nancy and I have been good friends for a long time—before I became Commissioner of the LPGA Tour. She is a remarkable person and is certainly a worthy Honoree.

In presenting her for this award I don't want to spend any time on statistics, as remarkable as they are. Rather I thought it would be more meaningful to simply share some stories, both my own and those of several of Nancy's friends that will give you a better appreciation of this warm and lovely lady than any batch of statistics could do.

Nancy—Story Number 1   Nancy is a wonderfully warm person—an emotional person. She laughs a lot and she cries a lot—often at the same time! I've often said that if crying were an Olympic sport, Nancy would have more gold medals than Michael Phelps. There is a wonderful story about her loving father and teacher, Domingo, telling her that she must not cry while competing in events because if she cried she wouldn't be able to see the flag sticks. Well, she must have figured it out because she sure saw a lot of flag sticks quite clearly.

The Juli Inkster Story   I asked the Hall of Famer Juli Inkster to tell me about Nancy's style in captaining the victorious U.S. Solheim Cup team in the 2005 matches. Here is what Juli said: "She was like our mother— and I mean that in the best sense. And, that was especially important because there were so many young players on the team. She was firm, but fair. She worked hard and only made one demand—that we give our maximum effort and simply do our best. If you won, fine. If you lost, you had nothing to be ashamed of."

JoAnne Carner Story about Nancy Lopez   Here's a story from JoAnne Carner—LPGA Hall of Famer and 2009 Memorial Tournament Honoree.

When Nancy joined the Tour in 1977 the dominant player was "Big Momma" JoAnne Carner. She had won the U.S. Open the year before and had earlier been named Player of the Year and leading money winner.

As JoAnne tells the story, when Nancy burst on the scene (and she did indeed burst—winning nine tournaments in her rookie year) the media, not surprisingly, tried to stir up a rivalry between the reigning queen and the new sensation. Neither would cooperate, but the reporters kept on trying. Finally, at one event, where JoAnne was leading going into the final day, the question came up again—well, what about Nancy? JoAnne said she was sick and tired of the question and simply wanted to end the discussion. So she said, "Tomorrow I'm going to dust her, I'm going to lap her." Now let me quote JoAnne: "So, I went out the next day and shot 68. Know what, I lost! To guess who!"

The Autograph Story   The tour was playing an event, I think, Rochester. Rochester has always been one of the best stops on the LPGA Tour. A terrific sponsor, a fine golf course, and unbelievable crowds. And, not surprisingly, Nancy Lopez was hugely popular and drew large crowds wherever she went and however well she was playing. She was unfailingly polite and friendly, but I never saw anything quite like what happened one day when I was standing behind the ninth green as Nancy holed out and headed for the tenth tee.

As I said, the crowds were large but very respectful—except for one person. As Nancy walked to the next tee, someone thrust a piece of paper toward her and said, "Sign this for Tammy." Nancy was a bit startled but instead of ignoring the outstretched hand, she quietly said, "Do you spell that with a 'y' or an 'ie'?" That kind of says it all!

Shooting 62   One of my favorite Nancy Lopez memories is of an incident which occurred during an LPGA Championship. Nancy shot a brilliant 62 but was penalized two strokes for slow play. She was not happy about this, to put it mildly! She expressed her frustration at the press conference following her round and she did so with a few sharp words and, of course, a few tears. When she left the press conference I pulled her aside and told her that she should not be so upset because, after all, she was still leading the tournament with a score of 64. She looked at me with a twinkle in her eye and said, "I know I am leading the tournament but what makes me so angry is that I don't see how I could have been playing slowly. After all, I only swung sixty-two times." We had a good laugh, and I told her that even the USGA would have trouble refuting that argument!

Annika's Nancy Remarks   "Nancy has been a role model to a lot of young girls because of her smile, charisma, and her talents. She really put women's golf on the map. I've had the pleasure of playing with Nancy many times throughout my career and one thing that stands out to me is how extremely competitive she was on the course but when she was off the course, you really didn't see the tough competitor. You saw her sweet personality, all the smiles, and the warm and friendly personality. I admire her as a player and as a friend."

Charles S. Mechem, Jr.
Remarks, "Dinner with Dinah"
Tuesday, March 22, 1994

First, let me take this opportunity to thank you and all the folks at Nabisco for your magnificent—and very visible—support of the LPGA. It is very important to us, and we are very grateful.

The highest honor the LPGA can bestow is election to its Hall of Fame. Widely acknowledged as the most difficult Hall of Fame in sports to achieve, it has admitted only thirteen women in forty-plus years—all of them superlative players of the game:

> *Patty Berg, Betty Jameson, Louise Suggs, Babe Didrikson*
> *Zaharias, Betsy Rawls, Mickey Wright, Kathy Whitworth,*
> *Sandra Haynie, Carol Mann, JoAnne Carner, Nancy Lopez,*
> *Pat Bradley, Patty Sheehan*

Tonight, the LPGA breaks with tradition, and does so with enthusiasm and joy. On behalf of all of our Hall of Fame members and all of our players—past and present—I am happy to announce that Dinah Shore has been named as an honorary member of the LPGA Hall of Fame, the first time such an honor has been accorded.

By any standard, Dinah belongs in the Hall of Fame, and the Hall will be richer for her presence, but for those, if any, who need statistics for such a step, I would only remind you that Dinah was the winner of every Nabisco Dinah Shore ever played, and that's twenty-two majors right there. Beyond that, she was, through her incomparable support of women's golf, importantly responsible for scores of young women winning tournaments all over the world. In short, this is not an honor being bestowed—this is an honor earned.

There is one additional thing we would like to do. For us, it is not enough just to honor Dinah; we want to remember her. In that spirit, I am very pleased to announce tonight the institution of the Dinah Shore Scholarships, to be administered by the LPGA Foundation to develop funds and grant scholarships to deserving young women based on a set of criteria including both academics and golf. The LPGA is beginning the Dinah Shore Scholarship Fund.

And so it is with respect, admiration, and love that the players of the LPGA—past, present, and, perhaps most of all, future—say thank you, Dinah.

Fiftieth Birthday Party Song by Sammy Cahn "All the Way"

Well, I guess that did it
And we really tried to kid it
All the way

Tried to rhyme it nicely
And to tell it most precisely
All the way!

Honors no one just inherits
Honors must all be won
That's why Charlie Mechem merits
All of this for all he has done

He is more than nifty
And looks real young for fifty
All the way!

His family is glowing
Their love and pride is showing
May I say
It's been a most wond'rous evening

Following a perfect day
And one thing's more than certain
We were blessed by having Burton
Who sure can play,
All the way!

Fin'ly with your glass in hand
Kindly stand and toast this day
Toast Charlie Mechem proudly

And sing happy birthday loudly
All the way!!! All the way!!!

Happy birthday!!!!